BILLY BATSON
AND THE MAGIC OF
SHAZAM!
MR. MIND OVER MATTER

ART BALTAZAR & FRANCO
Writers

BYRON VAUGHNS
Artist & Covers

DAVID TANGUAY
Colors

STEVE WANDS
TRAVIS LANHAM
Letterers

BILLY BATSON AND THE MAGIC OF SHAZAM!

MR. MIND OVER MATTER

Dan DiDio Editor-original series
Simona Martore Assistant Editor-original series
Bob Harras Group Editor-Collected Editions
Robbin Brosterman Design Director-Books

DC COMICS

Diane Nelson President
Dan DiDio and **Jim Lee** Co-Publishers
Geoff Johns Chief Creative Officer
Patrick Caldon EVP-Finance and Administration
John Rood EVP-Sales, Marketing and Business Development
Amy Genkins SVP-Business and Legal Affairs
Steve Rotterdam SVP-Sales and Marketing
John Cunningham VP-Marketing
Terri Cunningham VP-Managing Editor
Alison Gill VP-Manufacturing
David Hyde VP-Publicity
Sue Pohja VP-Book Trade Sales
Alysse Soll VP-Advertising and Custom Publishing
Bob Wayne VP-Sales
Mark Chiarello Art Director

BILLY BATSON AND THE MAGIC OF SHAZAM!: MR. MIND OVER MATTER

Published by DC Comics. Cover and compilation Copyright © 2011 DC Comics. All Rights Reserved.

Originally published in single magazine form in BILLY BATSON AND THE MAGIC OF SHAZAM! #7-12. Copyright © 2009, 2010 DC Comics. All Rights Reserved. All characters, their distinctive likenesses and related elements featured in this publication are trademarks of DC Comics. The stories, characters and incidents featured in this publication are entirely fictional. DC Comics does not read or accept unsolicited submissions of ideas, stories or artwork.

DC Comics, 1700 Broadway, New York, NY 10019
A Warner Bros. Entertainment Company
Printed by Quad/Graphics, Dubuque, IA, USA. 1/28/11. First printing.
ISBN: 978-1-4012-2993-1

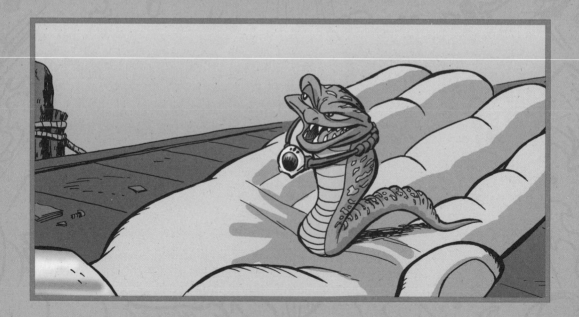

DECEPTION RECEPTION

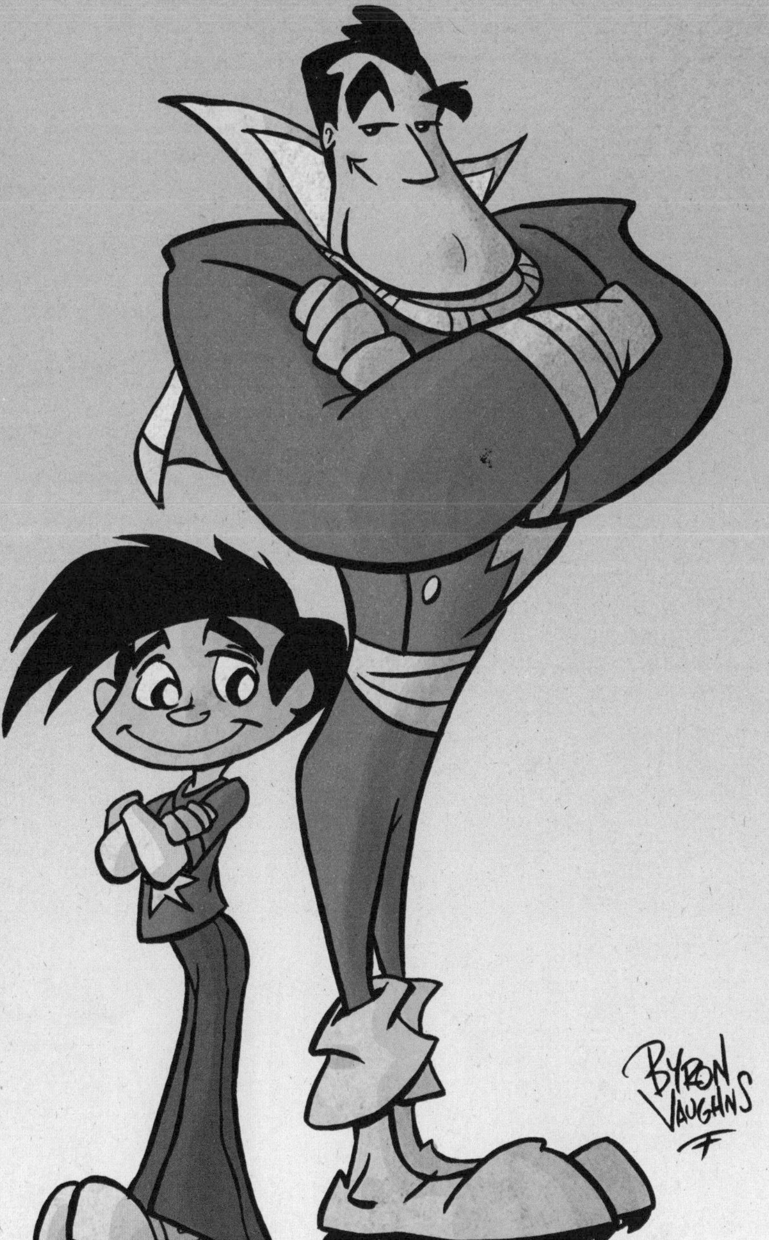
BYRON VAUGHNS

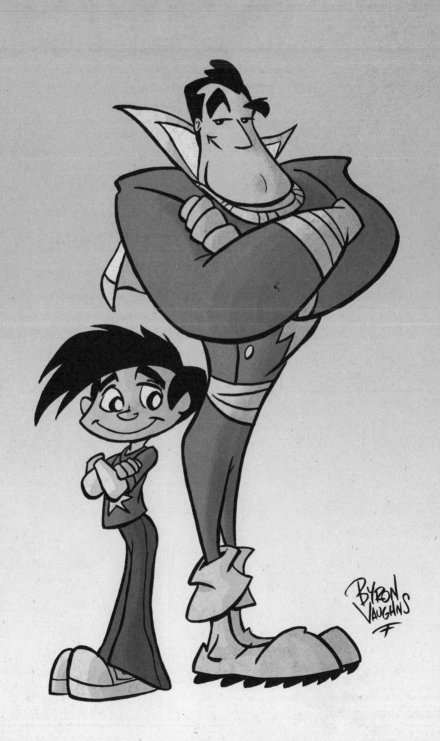

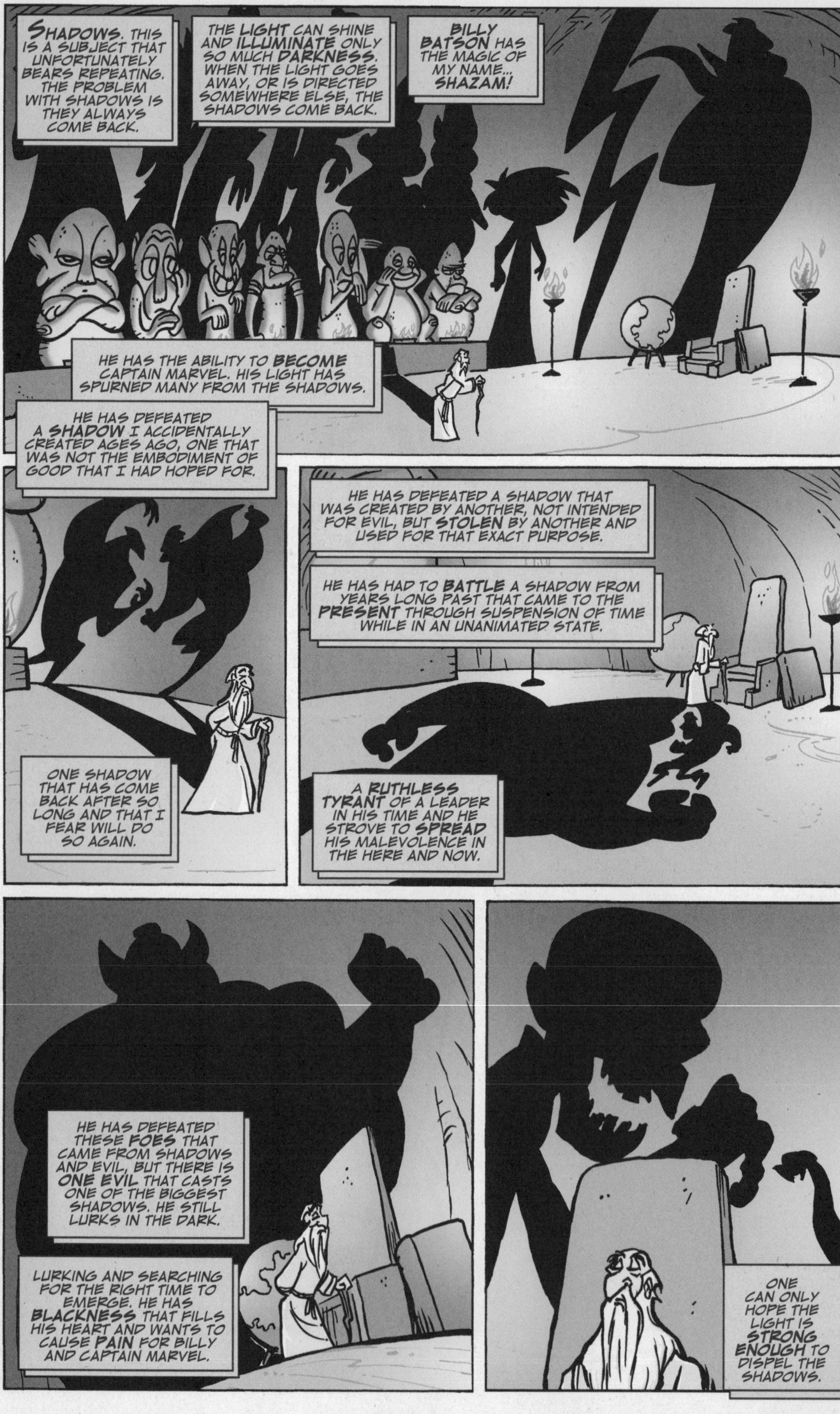
SHADOWS. THIS IS A SUBJECT THAT UNFORTUNATELY BEARS REPEATING. THE PROBLEM WITH SHADOWS IS THEY ALWAYS COME BACK.
THE LIGHT CAN SHINE AND ILLUMINATE ONLY SO MUCH DARKNESS. WHEN THE LIGHT GOES AWAY, OR IS DIRECTED SOMEWHERE ELSE, THE SHADOWS COME BACK.
BILLY BATSON HAS THE MAGIC OF MY NAME... SHAZAM!
HE HAS THE ABILITY TO BECOME CAPTAIN MARVEL. HIS LIGHT HAS SPURNED MANY FROM THE SHADOWS.
HE HAS DEFEATED A SHADOW I ACCIDENTALLY CREATED AGES AGO, ONE THAT WAS NOT THE EMBODIMENT OF GOOD THAT I HAD HOPED FOR.
ONE SHADOW THAT HAS COME BACK AFTER SO LONG AND THAT I FEAR WILL DO SO AGAIN.
HE HAS DEFEATED A SHADOW THAT WAS CREATED BY ANOTHER, NOT INTENDED FOR EVIL, BUT STOLEN BY ANOTHER AND USED FOR THAT EXACT PURPOSE.
HE HAS HAD TO BATTLE A SHADOW FROM YEARS LONG PAST THAT CAME TO THE PRESENT THROUGH SUSPENSION OF TIME WHILE IN AN UNANIMATED STATE.
A RUTHLESS TYRANT OF A LEADER IN HIS TIME AND HE STROVE TO SPREAD HIS MALEVOLENCE IN THE HERE AND NOW.
HE HAS DEFEATED THESE FOES THAT CAME FROM SHADOWS AND EVIL, BUT THERE IS ONE EVIL THAT CASTS ONE OF THE BIGGEST SHADOWS. HE STILL LURKS IN THE DARK.
LURKING AND SEARCHING FOR THE RIGHT TIME TO EMERGE. HE HAS BLACKNESS THAT FILLS HIS HEART AND WANTS TO CAUSE PAIN FOR BILLY AND CAPTAIN MARVEL.
ONE CAN ONLY HOPE THE LIGHT IS STRONG ENOUGH TO DISPEL THE SHADOWS.

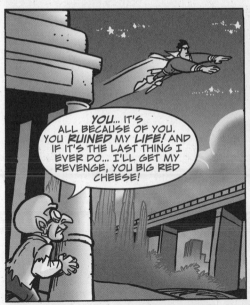

YOU... IT'S ALL BECAUSE OF YOU. YOU *RUINED* MY LIFE! AND IF IT'S THE LAST THING I EVER DO... I'LL GET MY REVENGE, YOU BIG RED CHEESE!

HEY *DOC*! HOW COME WE GOTTA SLEEP OUT HERE WHEN WE GOT A PERFECTLY GOOD WARM PLACE TO SLEEP?

NOT TO MENTION THE *OTHER* PLACE WE HAVE TOO.

YEAH! WE GOT *TWO PLACES* WE CAN STAY, YET WE'RE OUT HERE IN THE *COLD*!

I'VE *EXPLAINED* THIS TO YOU BEFORE. YOU--

EVENING JOE, BILL, DOC... HOW YOU BOYS BEEN? HAVEN'T SEEN YOU IN A WHILE. THOUGHT MAYBE SOMETHING HAD *HAPPENED* TO YOU.

ME AND A COUPLE OF THE OTHER GUYS WERE GOING TO COME LOOK FOR YOU TOMORROW.

OH! HEH HEH...NO NEED FOR THAT. YOU KNOW HOW THE *VAGRANT LIFE* CAN BE, WANDERING AIMLESSLY FROM PLACE TO PLACE...

HEH HEH. NO, NO TROUBLE HERE, JUST LIVING THE LIFESTYLE OF THE *BROKE* AND *HOMELESS*...

YES... WELL... GLAD TO SEE YOU BOYS ARE OK.

HAVE A *GOOD NIGHT*!

HOW MANY TIMES DO I HAVE TO *EXPLAIN* THIS? THAT IS *EXACTLY* WHY WE HAVE TO SLEEP OUT HERE. BECAUSE PEOPLE WILL WONDER WHERE WE'VE BEEN.

WE DO NOT WANT TO *ATTRACT* ANY *ATTENTION* TO THE WAREHOUSE OR THE BUILDING WHERE WE BROUGHT THAT *KULL STATUE*. EVERY ONCE IN A WHILE, FOR THE FORESEEABLE FUTURE, WE NEED TO PRETEND LIKE WE ARE STILL *HOMELESS*, SO SHUT UP AND GO TO SLEEP NOW!

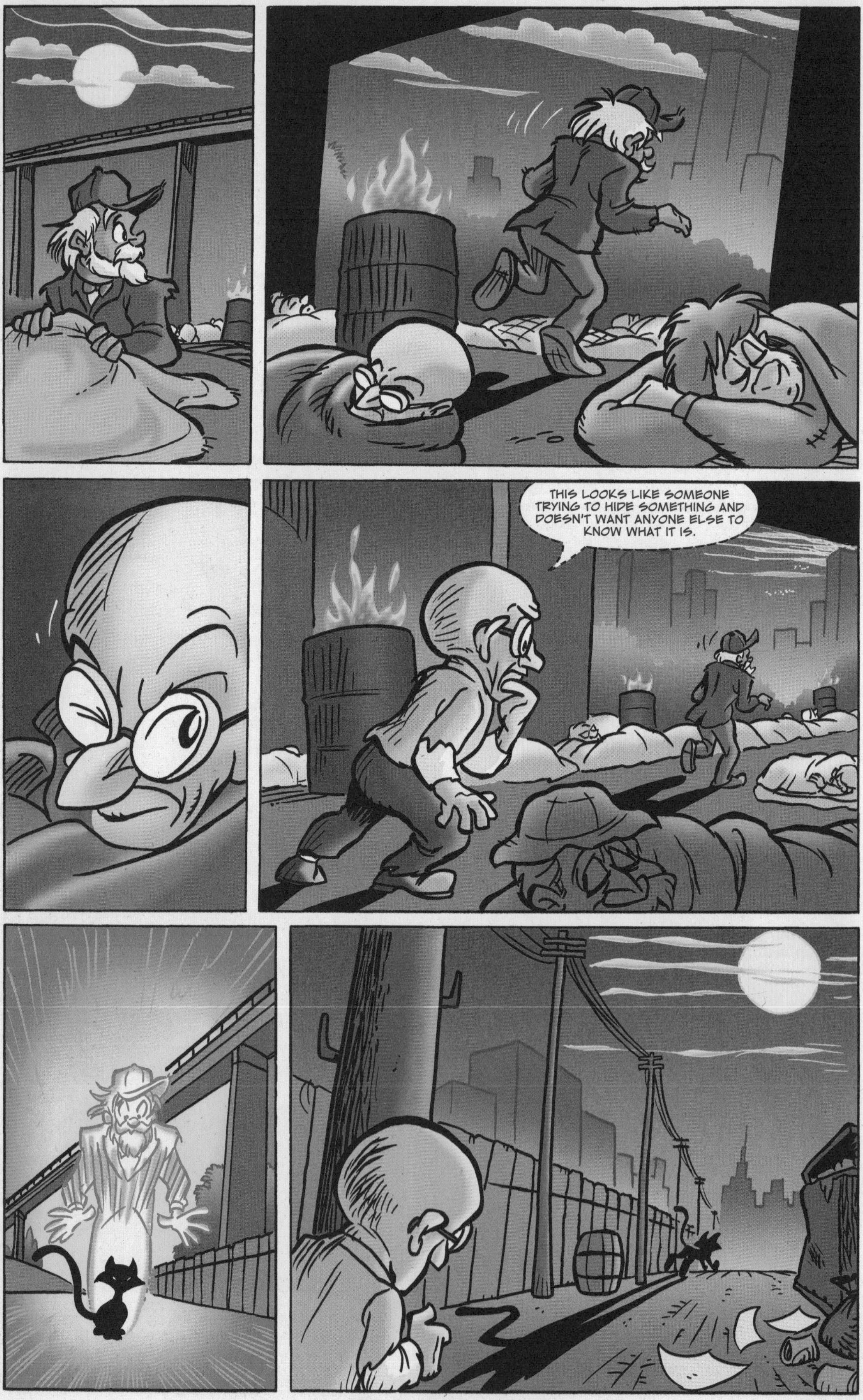
THIS LOOKS LIKE SOMEONE TRYING TO HIDE SOMETHING AND DOESN'T WANT ANYONE ELSE TO KNOW WHAT IT IS.

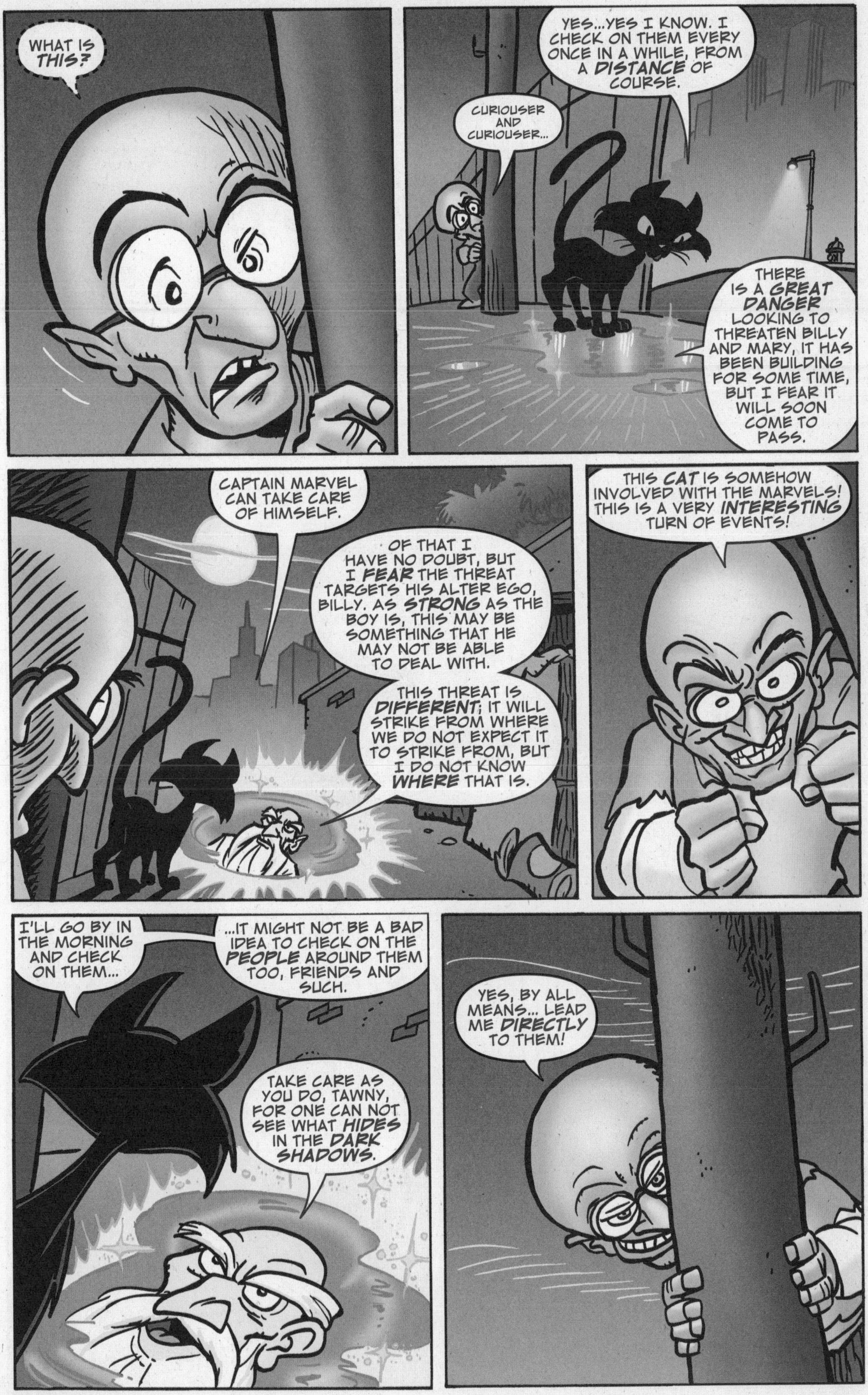
WHAT IS THIS?
YES...YES I KNOW. I CHECK ON THEM EVERY ONCE IN A WHILE, FROM A DISTANCE OF COURSE.
CURIOUSER AND CURIOUSER...
THERE IS A GREAT DANGER LOOKING TO THREATEN BILLY AND MARY, IT HAS BEEN BUILDING FOR SOME TIME, BUT I FEAR IT WILL SOON COME TO PASS.
CAPTAIN MARVEL CAN TAKE CARE OF HIMSELF.
OF THAT I HAVE NO DOUBT, BUT I FEAR THE THREAT TARGETS HIS ALTER EGO, BILLY. AS STRONG AS THE BOY IS, THIS MAY BE SOMETHING THAT HE MAY NOT BE ABLE TO DEAL WITH.
THIS THREAT IS DIFFERENT; IT WILL STRIKE FROM WHERE WE DO NOT EXPECT IT TO STRIKE FROM, BUT I DO NOT KNOW WHERE THAT IS.
THIS CAT IS SOMEHOW INVOLVED WITH THE MARVELS! THIS IS A VERY INTERESTING TURN OF EVENTS!
I'LL GO BY IN THE MORNING AND CHECK ON THEM...
...IT MIGHT NOT BE A BAD IDEA TO CHECK ON THE PEOPLE AROUND THEM TOO, FRIENDS AND SUCH.
TAKE CARE AS YOU DO, TAWNY, FOR ONE CAN NOT SEE WHAT HIDES IN THE DARK SHADOWS.
YES, BY ALL MEANS... LEAD ME DIRECTLY TO THEM!

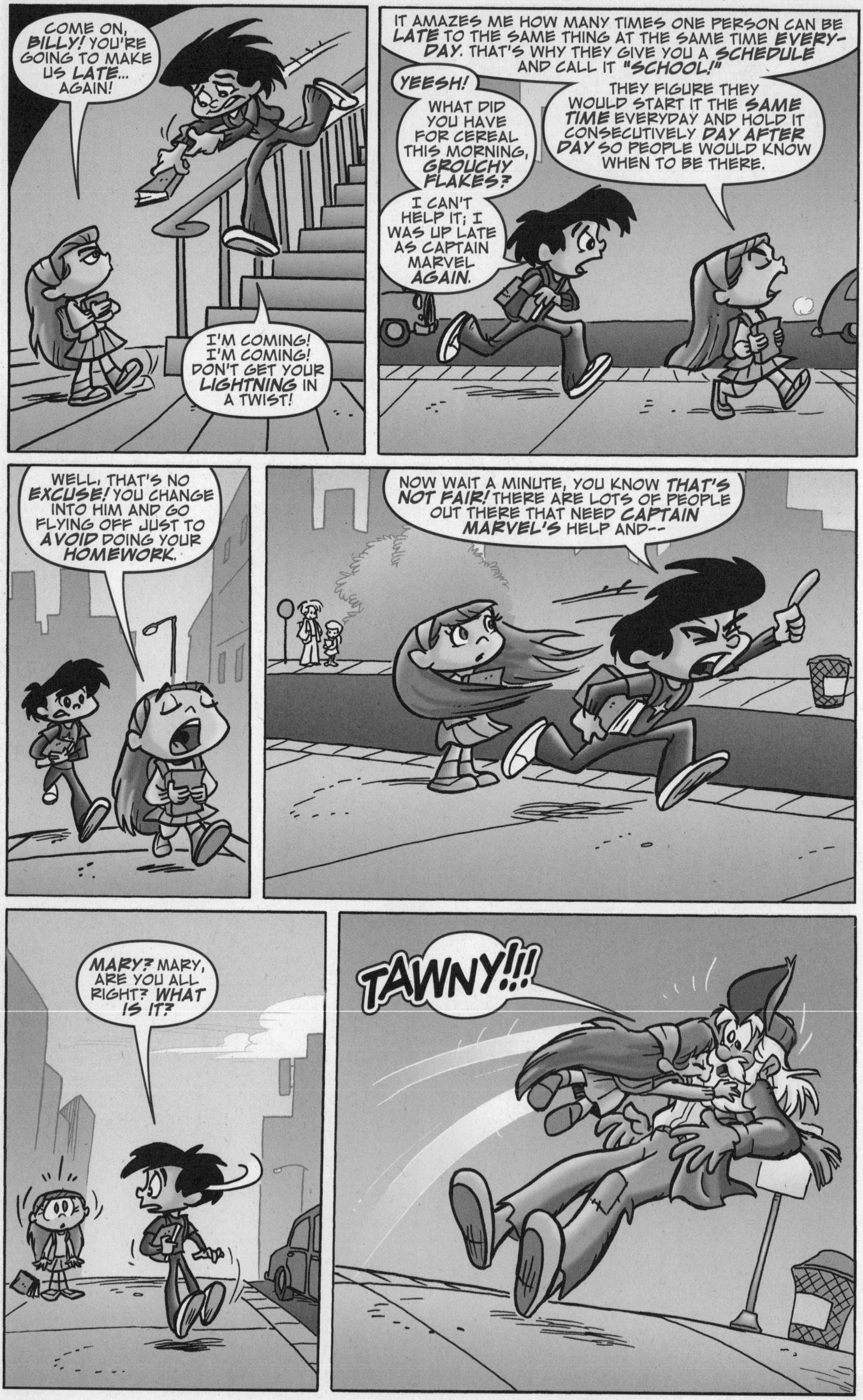
COME ON, BILLY! YOU'RE GOING TO MAKE US LATE... AGAIN!
I'M COMING! I'M COMING! DON'T GET YOUR LIGHTNING IN A TWIST!
IT AMAZES ME HOW MANY TIMES ONE PERSON CAN BE LATE TO THE SAME THING AT THE SAME TIME EVERY-DAY. THAT'S WHY THEY GIVE YOU A SCHEDULE AND CALL IT "SCHOOL!"
THEY FIGURE THEY WOULD START IT THE SAME TIME EVERYDAY AND HOLD IT CONSECUTIVELY DAY AFTER DAY SO PEOPLE WOULD KNOW WHEN TO BE THERE.
YEESH! WHAT DID YOU HAVE FOR CEREAL THIS MORNING, GROUCHY FLAKES?
I CAN'T HELP IT; I WAS UP LATE AS CAPTAIN MARVEL AGAIN.
WELL, THAT'S NO EXCUSE! YOU CHANGE INTO HIM AND GO FLYING OFF JUST TO AVOID DOING YOUR HOMEWORK.
NOW WAIT A MINUTE, YOU KNOW THAT'S NOT FAIR! THERE ARE LOTS OF PEOPLE OUT THERE THAT NEED CAPTAIN MARVEL'S HELP AND--
MARY? MARY, ARE YOU ALL RIGHT? WHAT IS IT?
TAWNY!!!

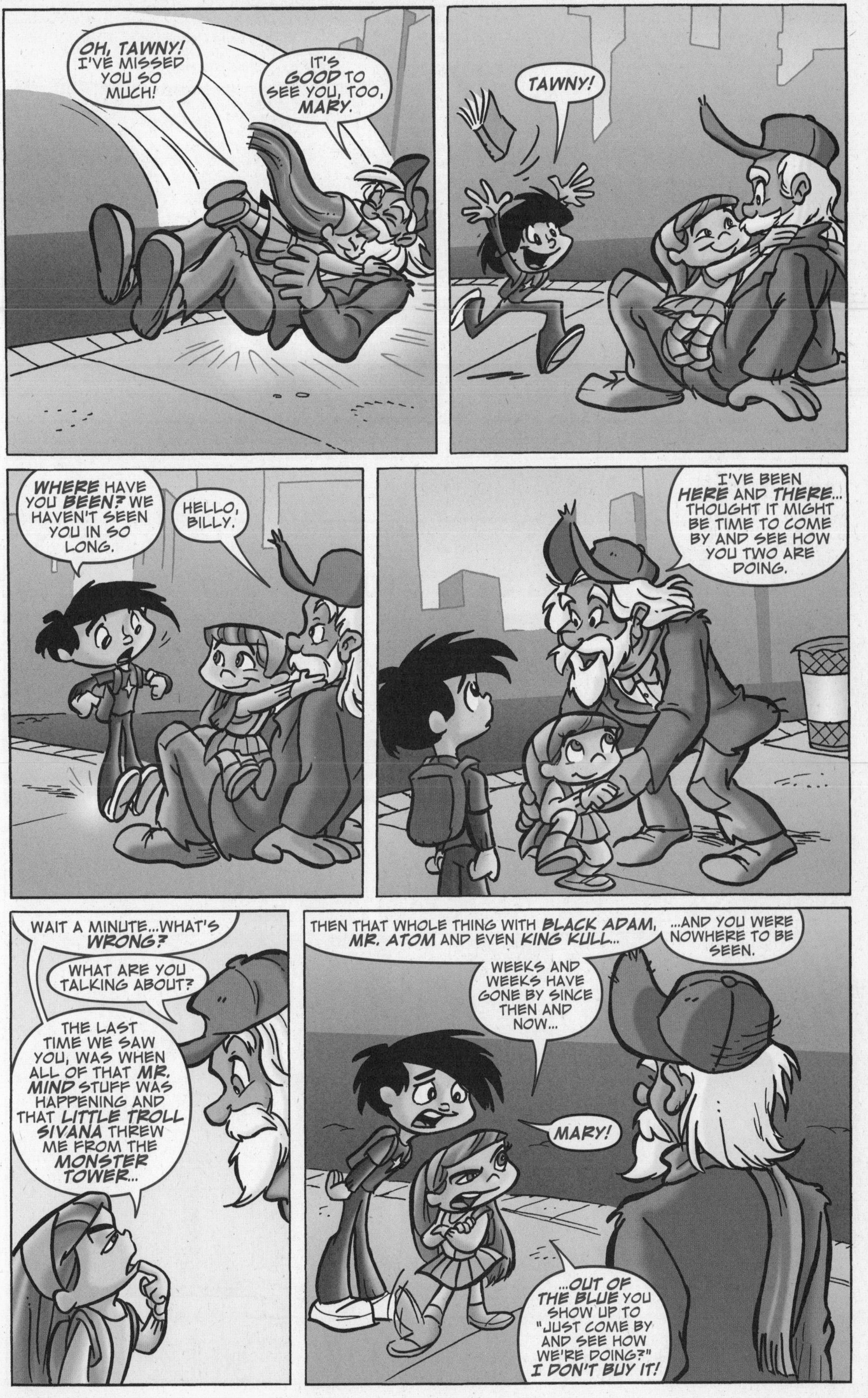
OH, TAWNY! I'VE MISSED YOU SO MUCH!
IT'S GOOD TO SEE YOU, TOO, MARY.
TAWNY!
WHERE HAVE YOU BEEN? WE HAVEN'T SEEN YOU IN SO LONG.
HELLO, BILLY.
I'VE BEEN HERE AND THERE... THOUGHT IT MIGHT BE TIME TO COME BY AND SEE HOW YOU TWO ARE DOING.
WAIT A MINUTE...WHAT'S WRONG?
WHAT ARE YOU TALKING ABOUT?
THE LAST TIME WE SAW YOU, WAS WHEN ALL OF THAT MR. MIND STUFF WAS HAPPENING AND THAT LITTLE TROLL SIVANA THREW ME FROM THE MONSTER TOWER...
THEN THAT WHOLE THING WITH BLACK ADAM, MR. ATOM AND EVEN KING KULL...
...AND YOU WERE NOWHERE TO BE SEEN.
WEEKS AND WEEKS HAVE GONE BY SINCE THEN AND NOW...
MARY!
...OUT OF THE BLUE YOU SHOW UP TO "JUST COME BY AND SEE HOW WE'RE DOING?" I DON'T BUY IT!

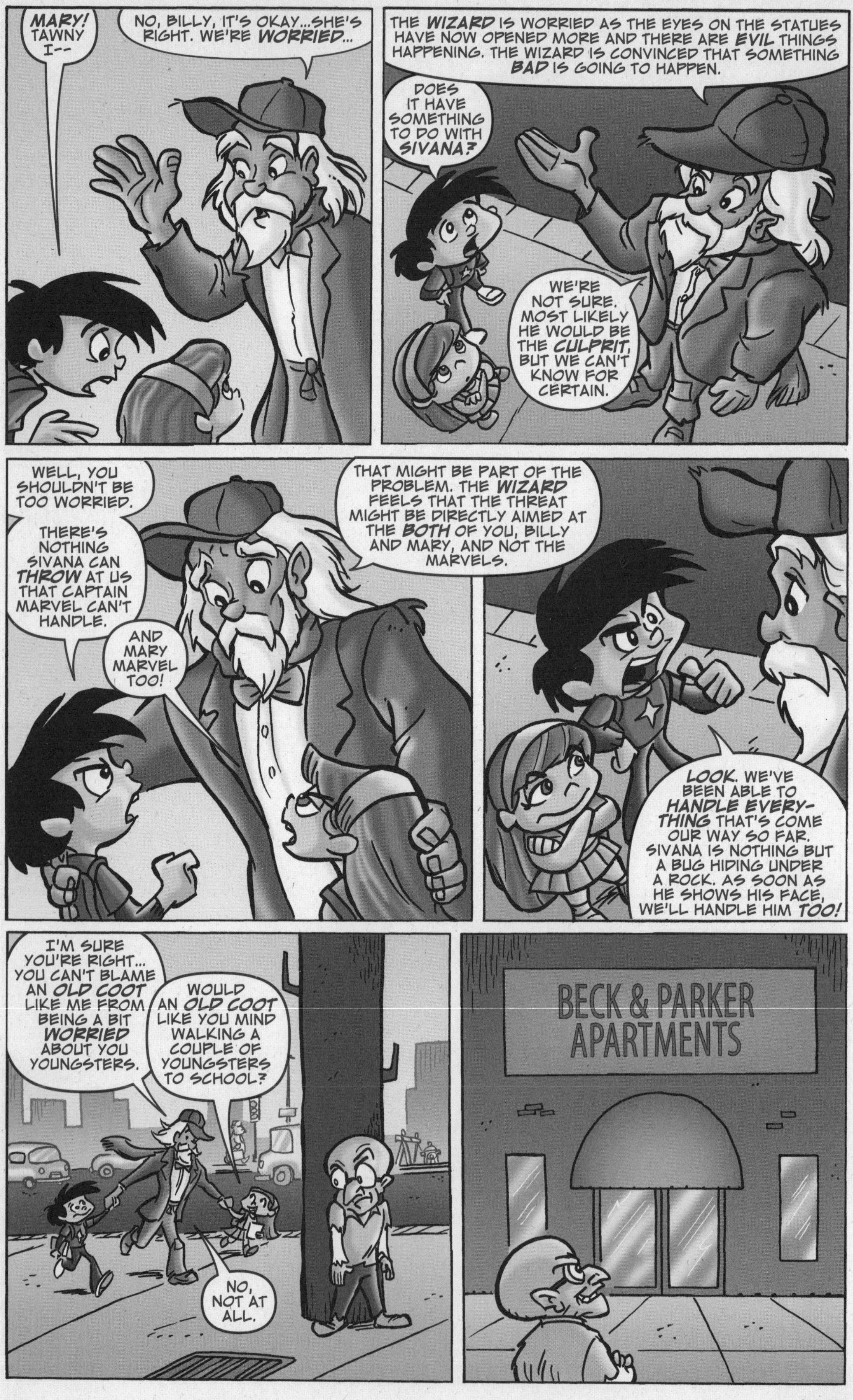
MARY! TAWNY I--
NO, BILLY, IT'S OKAY...SHE'S RIGHT. WE'RE WORRIED...
THE WIZARD IS WORRIED AS THE EYES ON THE STATUES HAVE NOW OPENED MORE AND THERE ARE EVIL THINGS HAPPENING. THE WIZARD IS CONVINCED THAT SOMETHING BAD IS GOING TO HAPPEN.
DOES IT HAVE SOMETHING TO DO WITH SIVANA?
WE'RE NOT SURE. MOST LIKELY HE WOULD BE THE CULPRIT, BUT WE CAN'T KNOW FOR CERTAIN.
WELL, YOU SHOULDN'T BE TOO WORRIED.
THERE'S NOTHING SIVANA CAN THROW AT US THAT CAPTAIN MARVEL CAN'T HANDLE.
AND MARY MARVEL TOO!
THAT MIGHT BE PART OF THE PROBLEM. THE WIZARD FEELS THAT THE THREAT MIGHT BE DIRECTLY AIMED AT THE BOTH OF YOU, BILLY AND MARY, AND NOT THE MARVELS.
LOOK. WE'VE BEEN ABLE TO HANDLE EVERY-THING THAT'S COME OUR WAY SO FAR. SIVANA IS NOTHING BUT A BUG HIDING UNDER A ROCK. AS SOON AS HE SHOWS HIS FACE, WE'LL HANDLE HIM TOO!
I'M SURE YOU'RE RIGHT... YOU CAN'T BLAME AN OLD COOT LIKE ME FROM BEING A BIT WORRIED ABOUT YOU YOUNGSTERS.
WOULD AN OLD COOT LIKE YOU MIND WALKING A COUPLE OF YOUNGSTERS TO SCHOOL?
NO, NOT AT ALL.
BECK & PARKER APARTMENTS

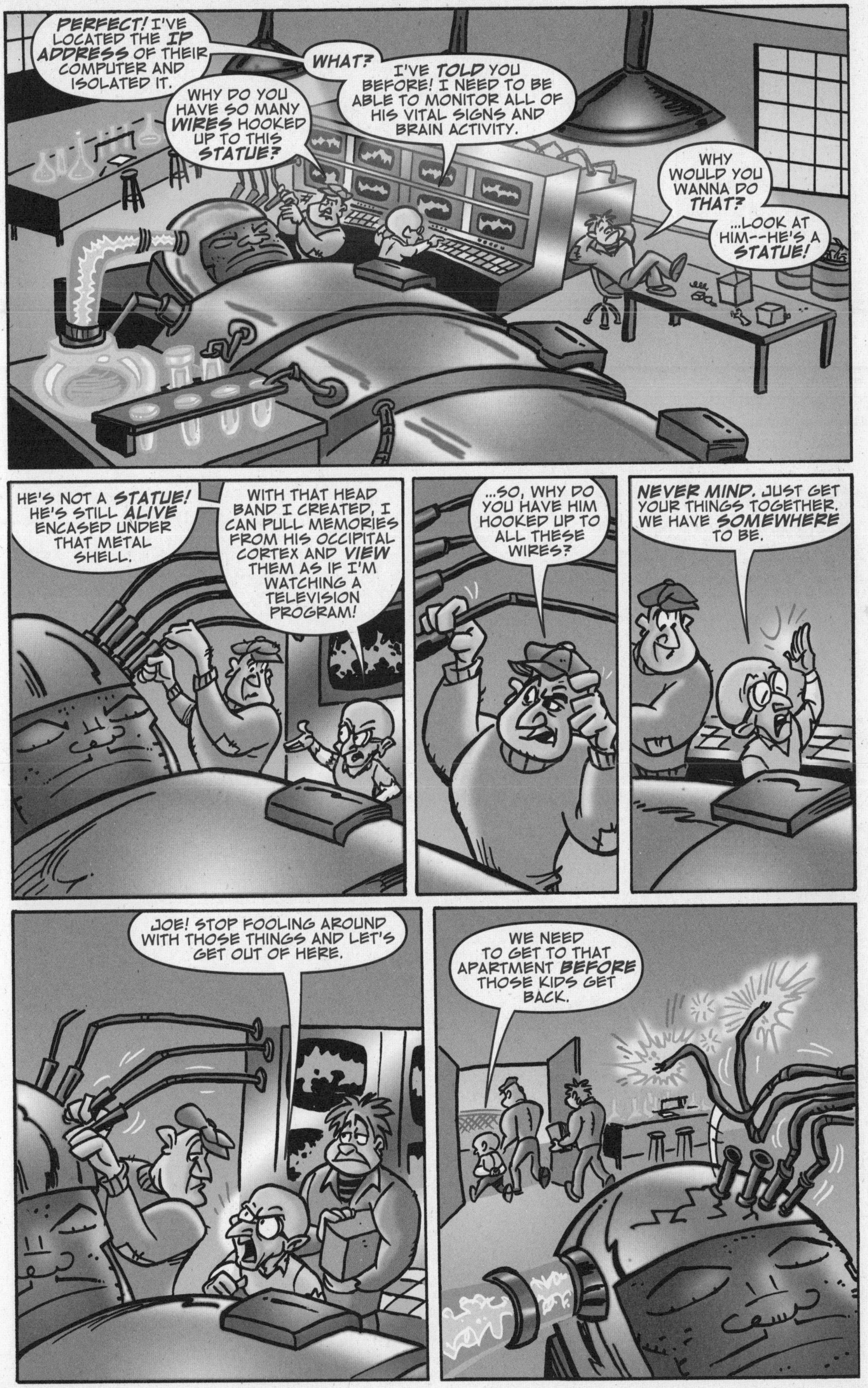
PERFECT! I'VE LOCATED THE IP ADDRESS OF THEIR COMPUTER AND ISOLATED IT.
WHAT?
WHY DO YOU HAVE SO MANY WIRES HOOKED UP TO THIS STATUE?
I'VE TOLD YOU BEFORE! I NEED TO BE ABLE TO MONITOR ALL OF HIS VITAL SIGNS AND BRAIN ACTIVITY.
WHY WOULD YOU WANNA DO THAT?
...LOOK AT HIM--HE'S A STATUE!
HE'S NOT A STATUE! HE'S STILL ALIVE ENCASED UNDER THAT METAL SHELL.
WITH THAT HEAD BAND I CREATED, I CAN PULL MEMORIES FROM HIS OCCIPITAL CORTEX AND VIEW THEM AS IF I'M WATCHING A TELEVISION PROGRAM!
...SO, WHY DO YOU HAVE HIM HOOKED UP TO ALL THESE WIRES?
NEVER MIND. JUST GET YOUR THINGS TOGETHER. WE HAVE SOMEWHERE TO BE.
JOE! STOP FOOLING AROUND WITH THOSE THINGS AND LET'S GET OUT OF HERE.
WE NEED TO GET TO THAT APARTMENT BEFORE THOSE KIDS GET BACK.

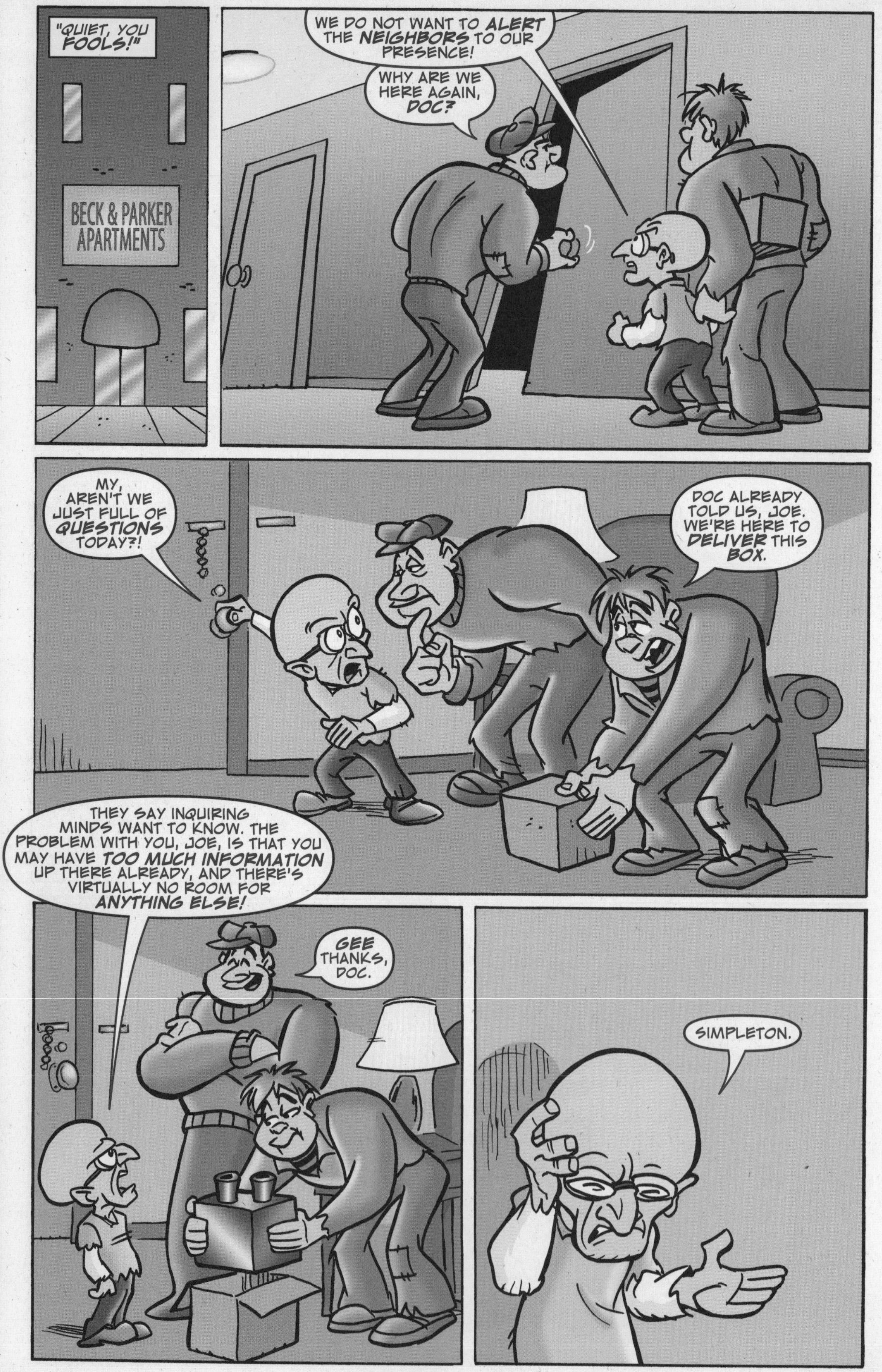
"QUIET, YOU FOOLS!"
BECK & PARKER APARTMENTS
WE DO NOT WANT TO ALERT THE NEIGHBORS TO OUR PRESENCE!
WHY ARE WE HERE AGAIN, DOC?
MY, AREN'T WE JUST FULL OF QUESTIONS TODAY?!
DOC ALREADY TOLD US, JOE. WE'RE HERE TO DELIVER THIS BOX.
THEY SAY INQUIRING MINDS WANT TO KNOW. THE PROBLEM WITH YOU, JOE, IS THAT YOU MAY HAVE TOO MUCH INFORMATION UP THERE ALREADY, AND THERE'S VIRTUALLY NO ROOM FOR ANYTHING ELSE!
GEE THANKS, DOC.
SIMPLETON.

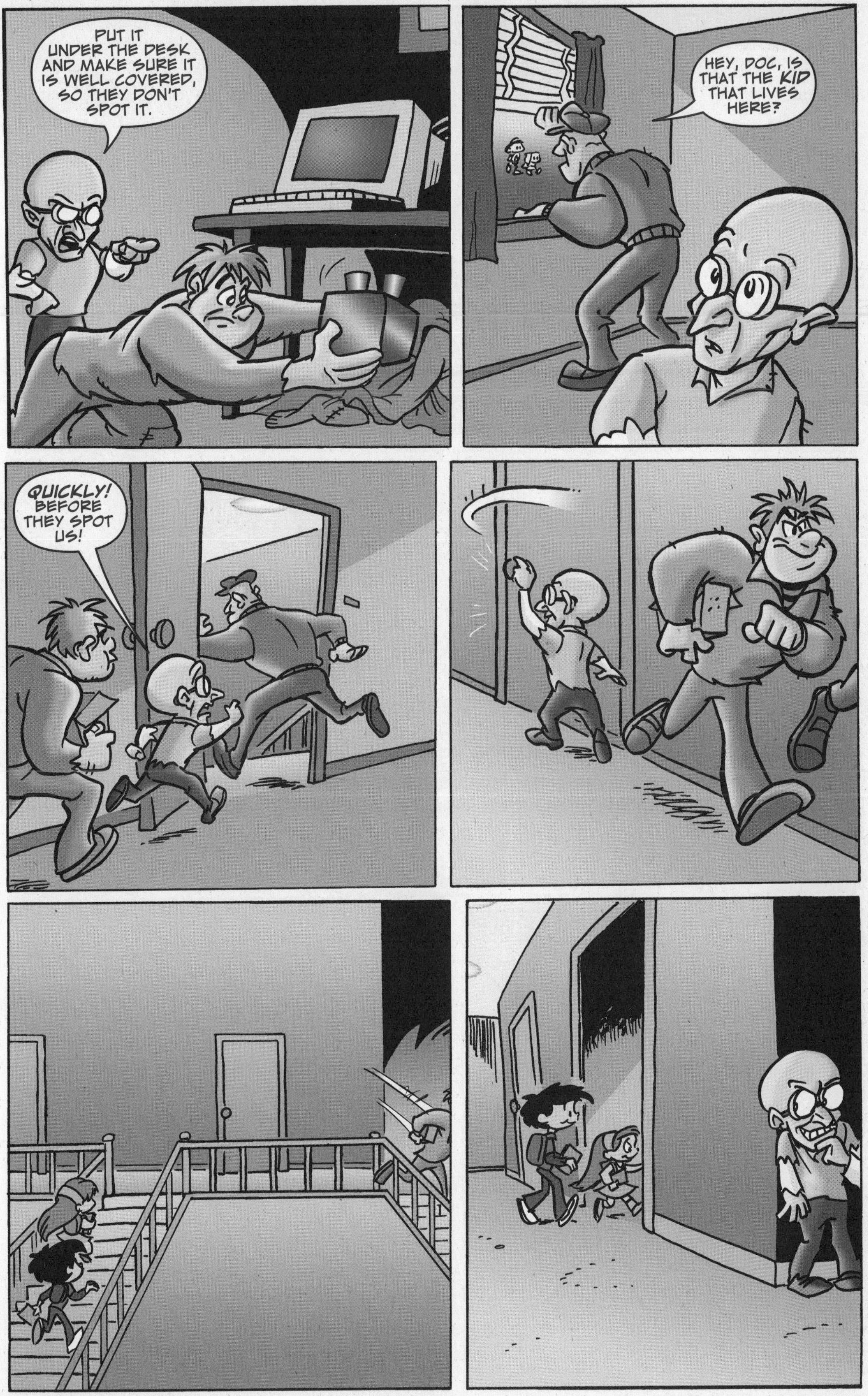
PUT IT UNDER THE DESK AND MAKE SURE IT IS WELL COVERED, SO THEY DON'T SPOT IT.
HEY, DOC, IS THAT THE KID THAT LIVES HERE?
QUICKLY! BEFORE THEY SPOT US!

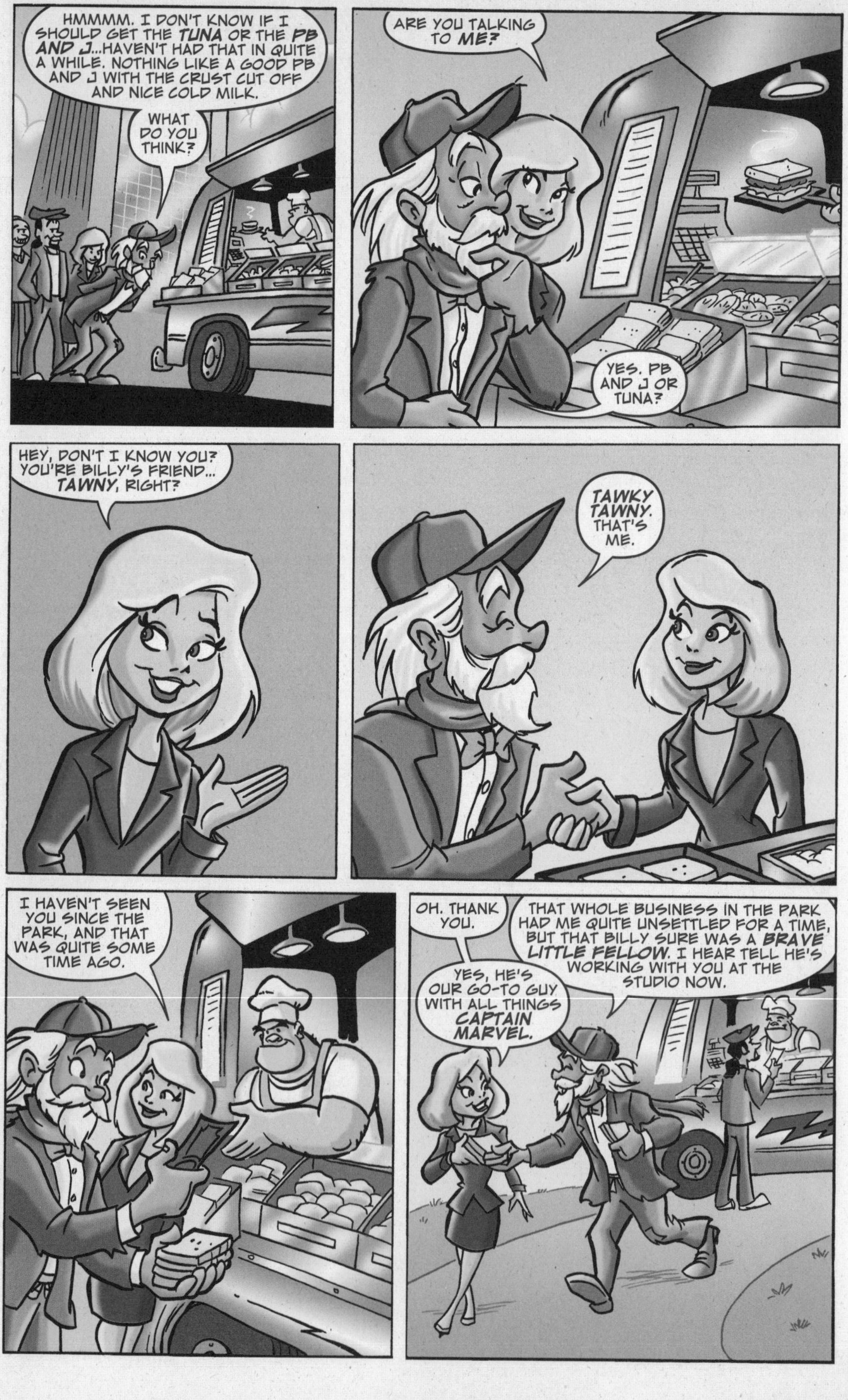
HMMMM. I DON'T KNOW IF I SHOULD GET THE TUNA OR THE PB AND J...HAVEN'T HAD THAT IN QUITE A WHILE. NOTHING LIKE A GOOD PB AND J WITH THE CRUST CUT OFF AND NICE COLD MILK.
WHAT DO YOU THINK?
ARE YOU TALKING TO ME?
YES. PB AND J OR TUNA?
HEY, DON'T I KNOW YOU? YOU'RE BILLY'S FRIEND... TAWNY, RIGHT?
TAWKY TAWNY. THAT'S ME.
I HAVEN'T SEEN YOU SINCE THE PARK, AND THAT WAS QUITE SOME TIME AGO.
OH. THANK YOU.
THAT WHOLE BUSINESS IN THE PARK HAD ME QUITE UNSETTLED FOR A TIME, BUT THAT BILLY SURE WAS A BRAVE LITTLE FELLOW. I HEAR TELL HE'S WORKING WITH YOU AT THE STUDIO NOW.
YES, HE'S OUR GO-TO GUY WITH ALL THINGS CAPTAIN MARVEL.

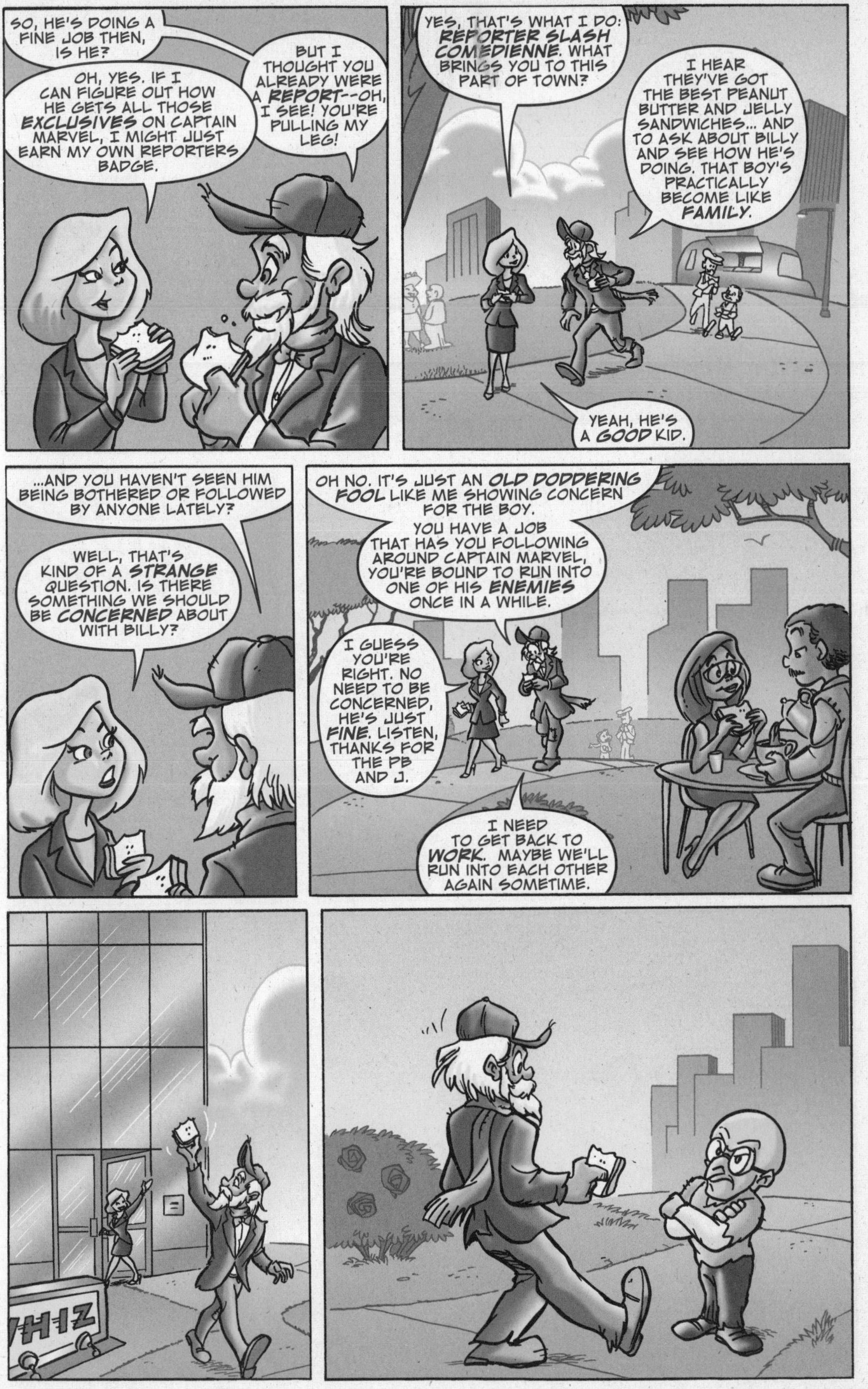
SO, HE'S DOING A FINE JOB THEN, IS HE?
OH, YES. IF I CAN FIGURE OUT HOW HE GETS ALL THOSE EXCLUSIVES ON CAPTAIN MARVEL, I MIGHT JUST EARN MY OWN REPORTERS BADGE.
BUT I THOUGHT YOU ALREADY WERE A REPORT--OH, I SEE! YOU'RE PULLING MY LEG!
YES, THAT'S WHAT I DO: REPORTER SLASH COMEDIENNE. WHAT BRINGS YOU TO THIS PART OF TOWN?
I HEAR THEY'VE GOT THE BEST PEANUT BUTTER AND JELLY SANDWICHES... AND TO ASK ABOUT BILLY AND SEE HOW HE'S DOING. THAT BOY'S PRACTICALLY BECOME LIKE FAMILY.
YEAH, HE'S A GOOD KID.
...AND YOU HAVEN'T SEEN HIM BEING BOTHERED OR FOLLOWED BY ANYONE LATELY?
WELL, THAT'S KIND OF A STRANGE QUESTION. IS THERE SOMETHING WE SHOULD BE CONCERNED ABOUT WITH BILLY?
OH NO. IT'S JUST AN OLD DODDERING FOOL LIKE ME SHOWING CONCERN FOR THE BOY.
YOU HAVE A JOB THAT HAS YOU FOLLOWING AROUND CAPTAIN MARVEL, YOU'RE BOUND TO RUN INTO ONE OF HIS ENEMIES ONCE IN A WHILE.
I GUESS YOU'RE RIGHT. NO NEED TO BE CONCERNED, HE'S JUST FINE. LISTEN, THANKS FOR THE PB AND J.
I NEED TO GET BACK TO WORK. MAYBE WE'LL RUN INTO EACH OTHER AGAIN SOMETIME.
WHIZ

OH HEY *DOC*! WHAT ARE YOU DOING *HERE*?

OH, I'VE COME FOR *YOU*... TAWNY.

ME? WHAT CAN I DO FOR YOU?

YOU CAN HELP ME GET *REVENGE* ON THE BIG RED CHEESE!

WHAT ARE YOU TALKING ABOUT, DOC?

OH, STOP *PRETENDING*! YOU ARE AFFILIATED WITH THAT SO-CALLED "SUPER-HERO" CAPTAIN MARVEL AND YOU ARE GOING TO HELP ME TEACH HIM A *LESSON* AND *END* HIS *CAREER*!

GRAB HIM, BOYS!

ROAR!

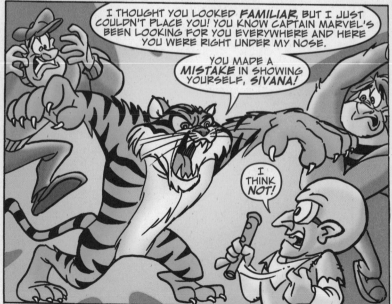

I THOUGHT YOU LOOKED *FAMILIAR*, BUT I JUST COULDN'T PLACE YOU! YOU KNOW CAPTAIN MARVEL'S BEEN LOOKING FOR YOU EVERYWHERE AND HERE YOU WERE RIGHT UNDER MY NOSE.

YOU MADE A *MISTAKE* IN SHOWING YOURSELF, *SIVANA*!

I THINK *NOT*!

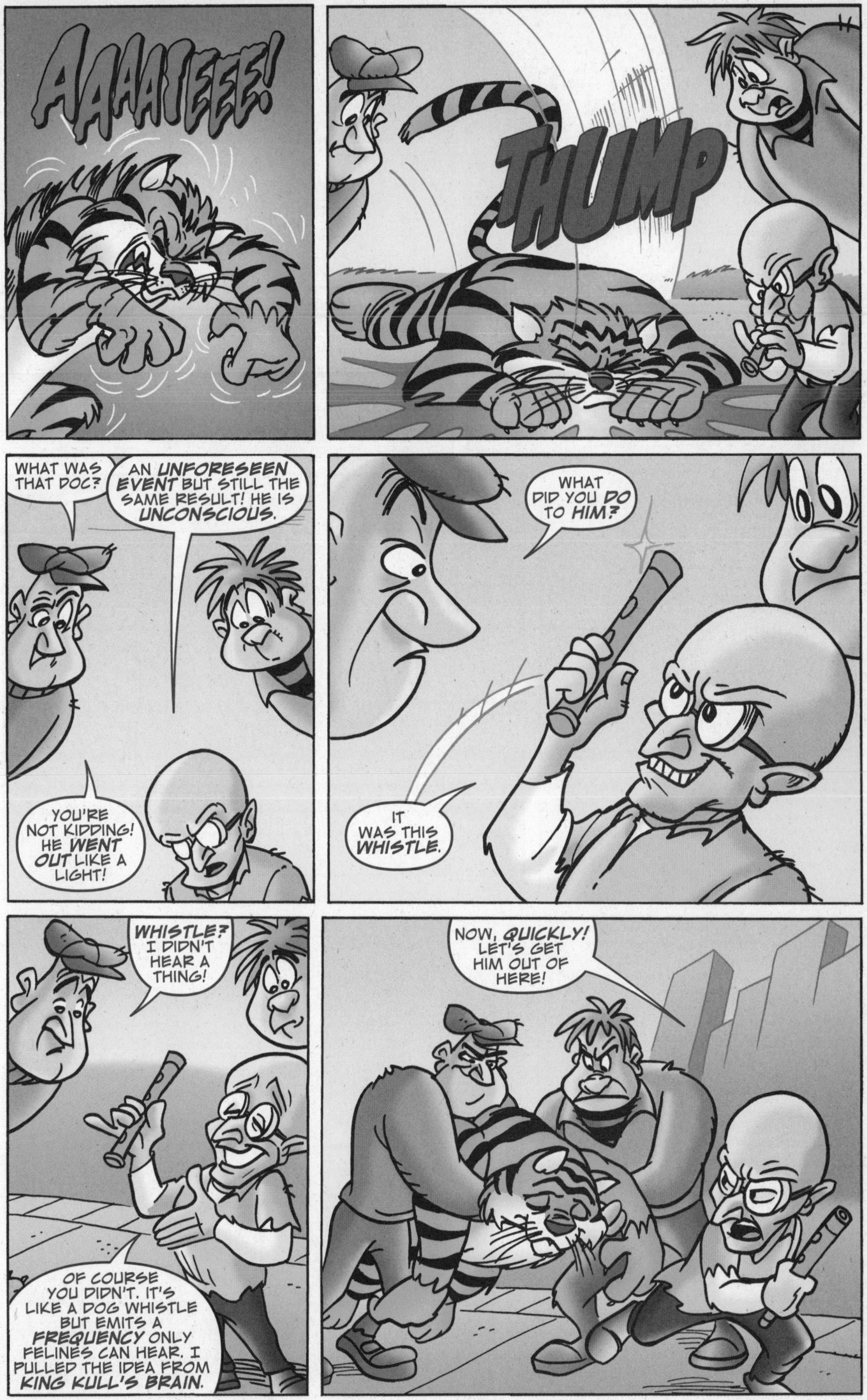
AAAAIEEE!
THUMP
WHAT WAS THAT DOC?
AN UNFORESEEN EVENT BUT STILL THE SAME RESULT! HE IS UNCONSCIOUS.
YOU'RE NOT KIDDING! HE WENT OUT LIKE A LIGHT!
WHAT DID YOU DO TO HIM?
IT WAS THIS WHISTLE.
WHISTLE? I DIDN'T HEAR A THING!
OF COURSE YOU DIDN'T. IT'S LIKE A DOG WHISTLE BUT EMITS A FREQUENCY ONLY FELINES CAN HEAR. I PULLED THE IDEA FROM KING KULL'S BRAIN.
NOW, QUICKLY! LET'S GET HIM OUT OF HERE!

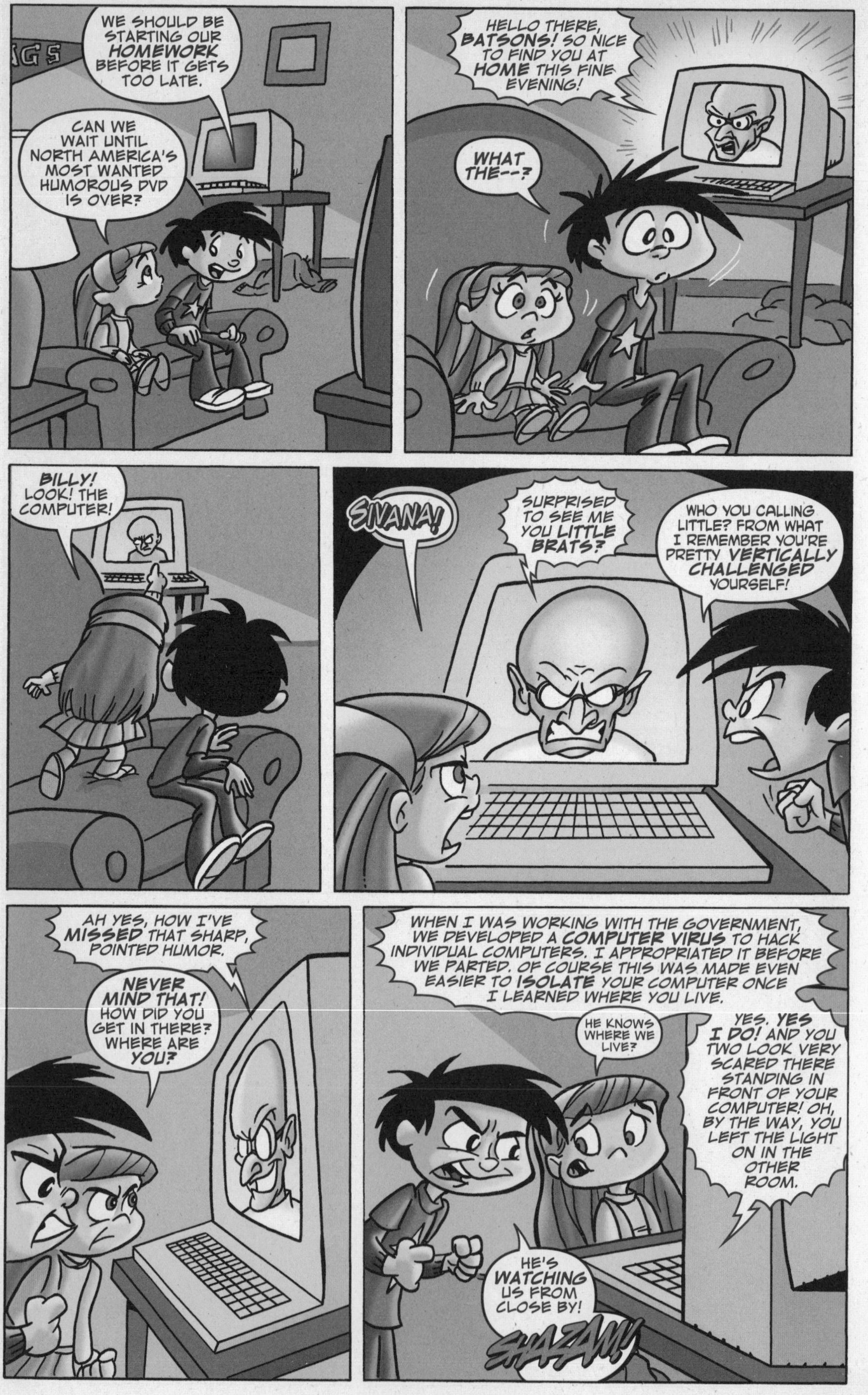
WE SHOULD BE STARTING OUR HOMEWORK BEFORE IT GETS TOO LATE.
CAN WE WAIT UNTIL NORTH AMERICA'S MOST WANTED HUMOROUS DVD IS OVER?
HELLO THERE, BATSONS! SO NICE TO FIND YOU AT HOME THIS FINE EVENING!
WHAT THE--?
BILLY! LOOK! THE COMPUTER!
SIVANA!
SURPRISED TO SEE ME YOU LITTLE BRATS?
WHO YOU CALLING LITTLE? FROM WHAT I REMEMBER YOU'RE PRETTY VERTICALLY CHALLENGED YOURSELF!
AH YES, HOW I'VE MISSED THAT SHARP, POINTED HUMOR.
NEVER MIND THAT! HOW DID YOU GET IN THERE? WHERE ARE YOU?
WHEN I WAS WORKING WITH THE GOVERNMENT, WE DEVELOPED A COMPUTER VIRUS TO HACK INDIVIDUAL COMPUTERS. I APPROPRIATED IT BEFORE WE PARTED. OF COURSE THIS WAS MADE EVEN EASIER TO ISOLATE YOUR COMPUTER ONCE I LEARNED WHERE YOU LIVE.
HE KNOWS WHERE WE LIVE?
YES. YES I DO! AND YOU TWO LOOK VERY SCARED THERE STANDING IN FRONT OF YOUR COMPUTER! OH, BY THE WAY, YOU LEFT THE LIGHT ON IN THE OTHER ROOM.
HE'S WATCHING US FROM CLOSE BY!
SHAZAM!

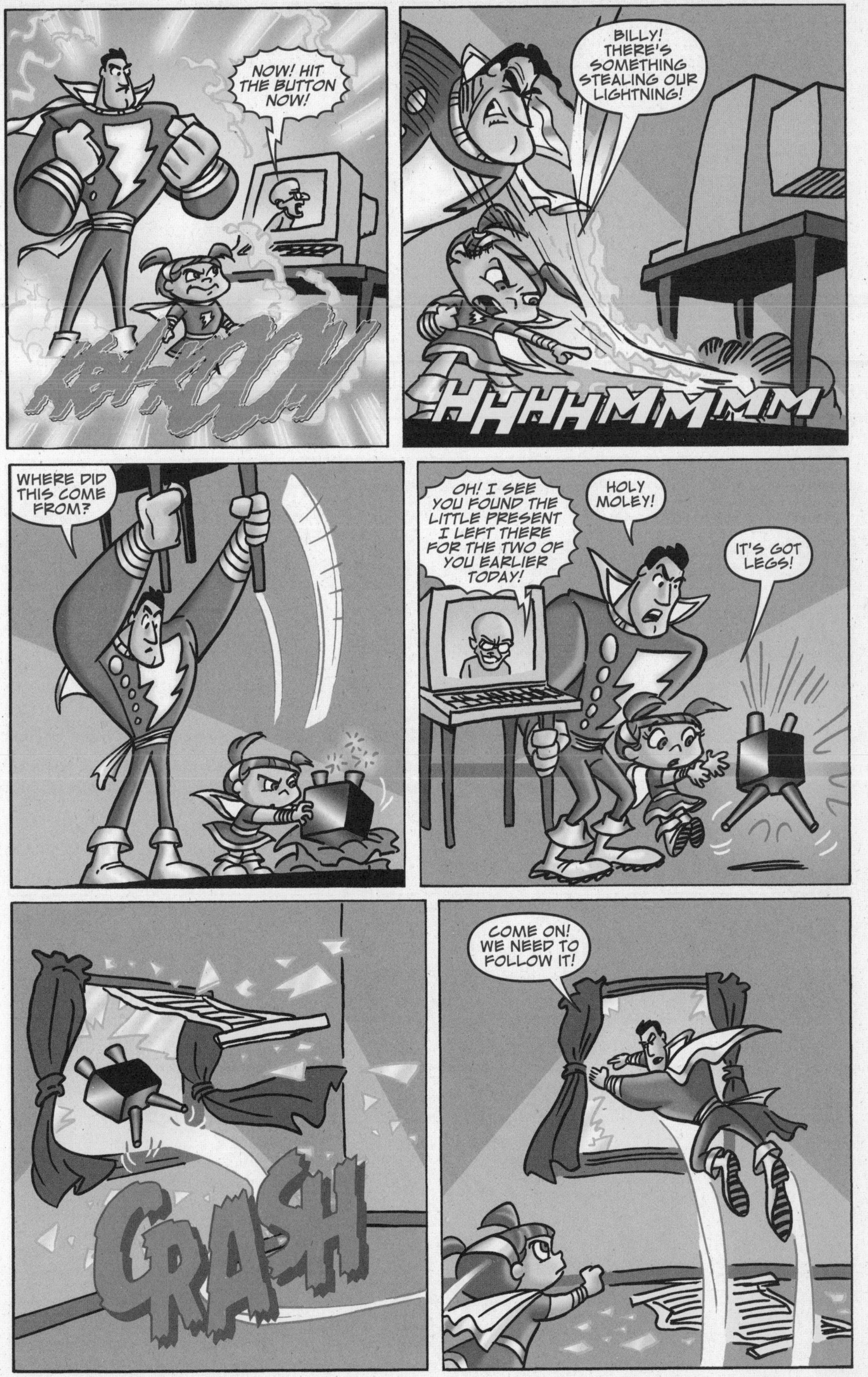
NOW! HIT THE BUTTON NOW!
BILLY! THERE'S SOMETHING STEALING OUR LIGHTNING!
HHHHMMMMM
WHERE DID THIS COME FROM?
OH! I SEE YOU FOUND THE LITTLE PRESENT I LEFT THERE FOR THE TWO OF YOU EARLIER TODAY!
HOLY MOLEY!
IT'S GOT LEGS!
CRASH
COME ON! WE NEED TO FOLLOW IT!

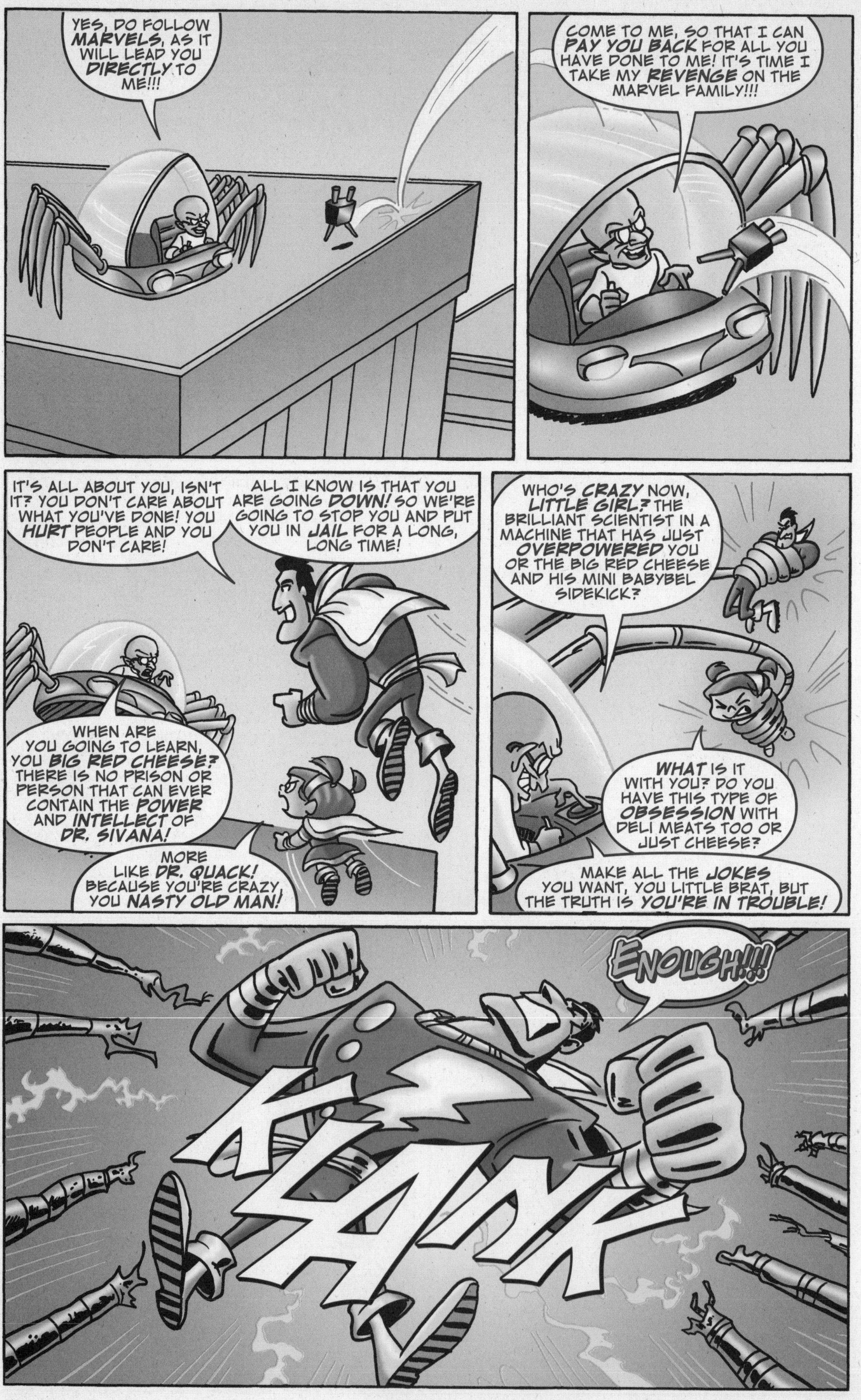
YES, DO FOLLOW MARVELS, AS IT WILL LEAD YOU DIRECTLY TO ME!!!
COME TO ME, SO THAT I CAN PAY YOU BACK FOR ALL YOU HAVE DONE TO ME! IT'S TIME I TAKE MY REVENGE ON THE MARVEL FAMILY!!!
IT'S ALL ABOUT YOU, ISN'T IT? YOU DON'T CARE ABOUT WHAT YOU'VE DONE! YOU HURT PEOPLE AND YOU DON'T CARE!
ALL I KNOW IS THAT YOU ARE GOING DOWN! SO WE'RE GOING TO STOP YOU AND PUT YOU IN JAIL FOR A LONG, LONG TIME!
WHEN ARE YOU GOING TO LEARN, YOU BIG RED CHEESE? THERE IS NO PRISON OR PERSON THAT CAN EVER CONTAIN THE POWER AND INTELLECT OF DR. SIVANA!
MORE LIKE DR. QUACK! BECAUSE YOU'RE CRAZY, YOU NASTY OLD MAN!
WHO'S CRAZY NOW, LITTLE GIRL? THE BRILLIANT SCIENTIST IN A MACHINE THAT HAS JUST OVERPOWERED YOU OR THE BIG RED CHEESE AND HIS MINI BABYBEL SIDEKICK?
WHAT IS IT WITH YOU? DO YOU HAVE THIS TYPE OF OBSESSION WITH DELI MEATS TOO OR JUST CHEESE?
MAKE ALL THE JOKES YOU WANT, YOU LITTLE BRAT, BUT THE TRUTH IS YOU'RE IN TROUBLE!
ENOUGH!!!
KLANK

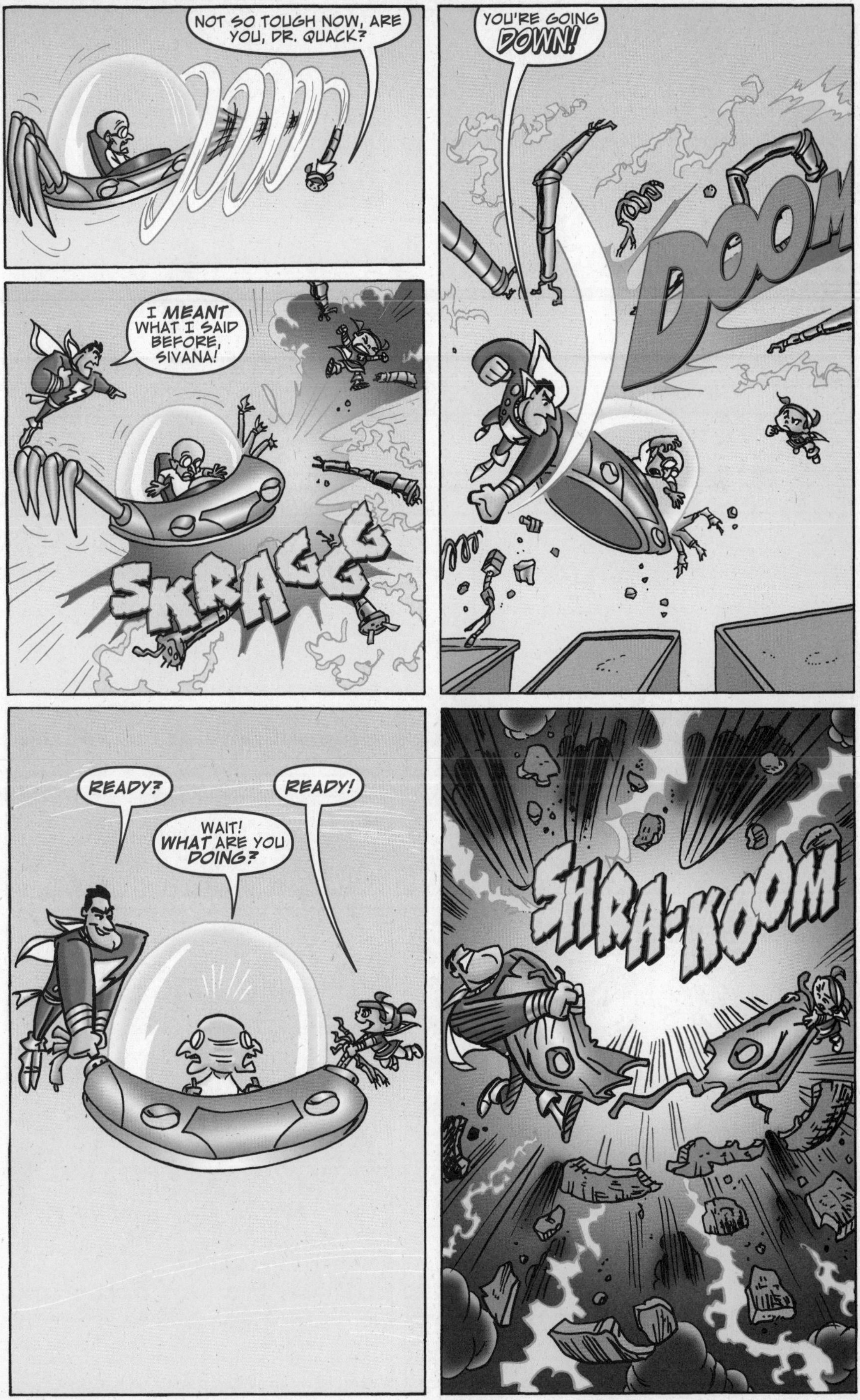
NOT SO TOUGH NOW, ARE YOU, DR. QUACK?
YOU'RE GOING DOWN!
DOOM
I MEANT WHAT I SAID BEFORE, SIVANA!
SKRAGG
READY?
READY!
WAIT! WHAT ARE YOU DOING?
SHRA-KOOM

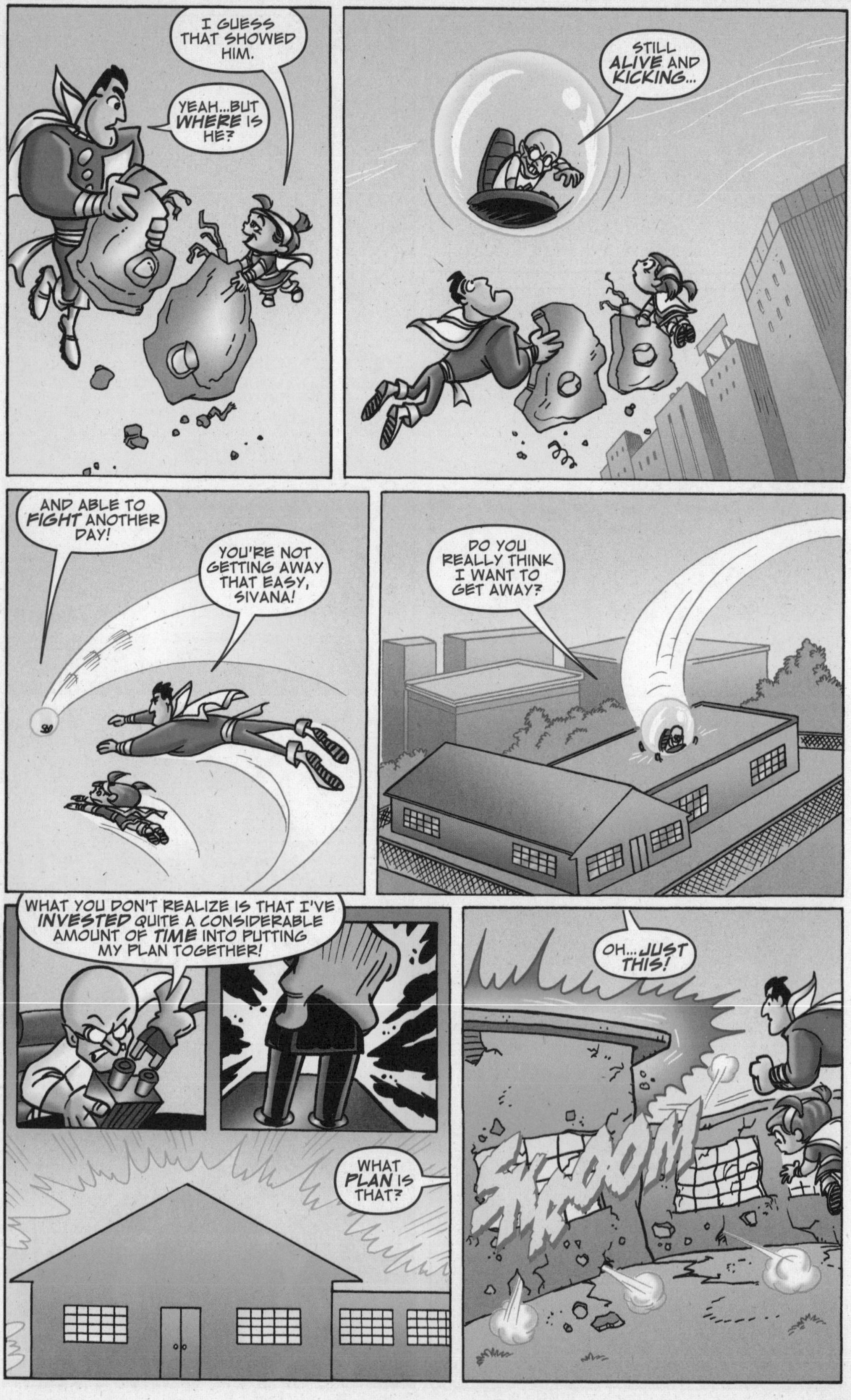
I GUESS THAT SHOWED HIM.
YEAH...BUT WHERE IS HE?
STILL ALIVE AND KICKING...
AND ABLE TO FIGHT ANOTHER DAY!
YOU'RE NOT GETTING AWAY THAT EASY, SIVANA!
DO YOU REALLY THINK I WANT TO GET AWAY?
WHAT YOU DON'T REALIZE IS THAT I'VE INVESTED QUITE A CONSIDERABLE AMOUNT OF TIME INTO PUTTING MY PLAN TOGETHER!
WHAT PLAN IS THAT?
OH...JUST THIS!
SKROOM

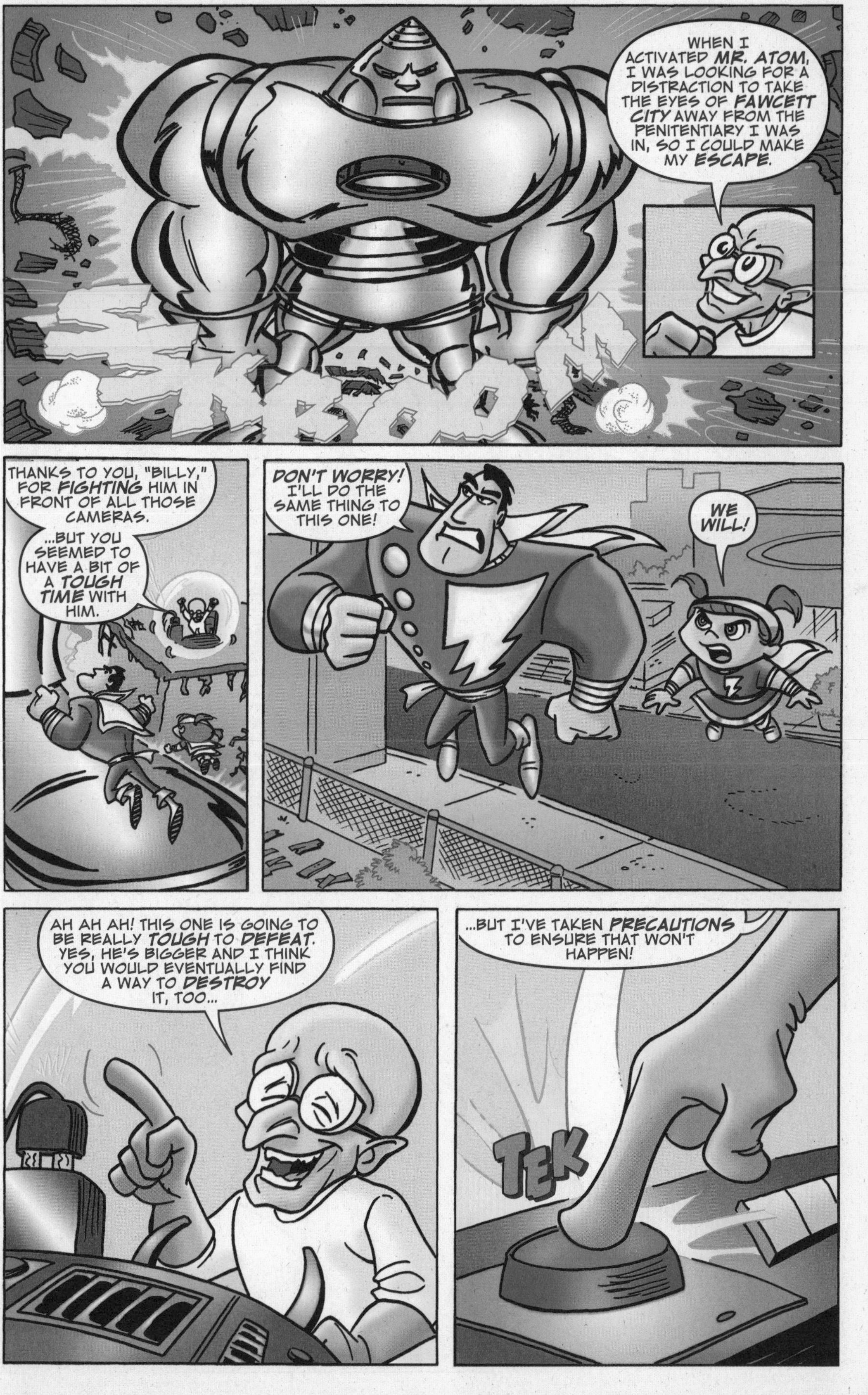
WHEN I ACTIVATED MR. ATOM, I WAS LOOKING FOR A DISTRACTION TO TAKE THE EYES OF FAWCETT CITY AWAY FROM THE PENITENTIARY I WAS IN, SO I COULD MAKE MY ESCAPE.
KRROOM
THANKS TO YOU, "BILLY," FOR FIGHTING HIM IN FRONT OF ALL THOSE CAMERAS.
...BUT YOU SEEMED TO HAVE A BIT OF A TOUGH TIME WITH HIM.
DON'T WORRY! I'LL DO THE SAME THING TO THIS ONE!
WE WILL!
AH AH AH! THIS ONE IS GOING TO BE REALLY TOUGH TO DEFEAT. YES, HE'S BIGGER AND I THINK YOU WOULD EVENTUALLY FIND A WAY TO DESTROY IT, TOO...
...BUT I'VE TAKEN PRECAUTIONS TO ENSURE THAT WON'T HAPPEN!
TEK

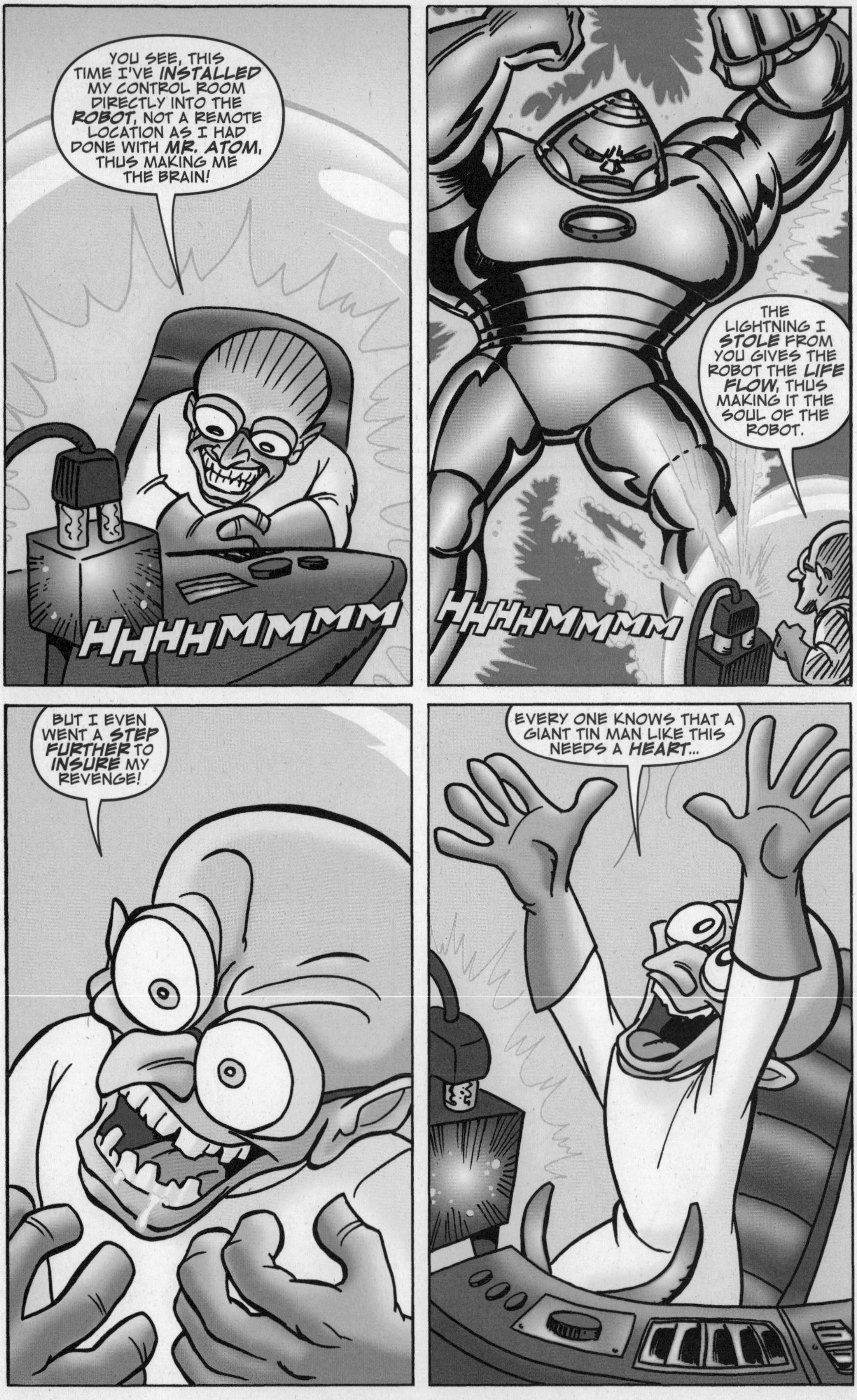
YOU SEE, THIS TIME I'VE INSTALLED MY CONTROL ROOM DIRECTLY INTO THE ROBOT, NOT A REMOTE LOCATION AS I HAD DONE WITH MR. ATOM, THUS MAKING ME THE BRAIN!
HHHHMMMMM
THE LIGHTNING I STOLE FROM YOU GIVES THE ROBOT THE LIFE FLOW, THUS MAKING IT THE SOUL OF THE ROBOT.
HHHHMMMMM
BUT I EVEN WENT A STEP FURTHER TO INSURE MY REVENGE!
EVERY ONE KNOWS THAT A GIANT TIN MAN LIKE THIS NEEDS A HEART...

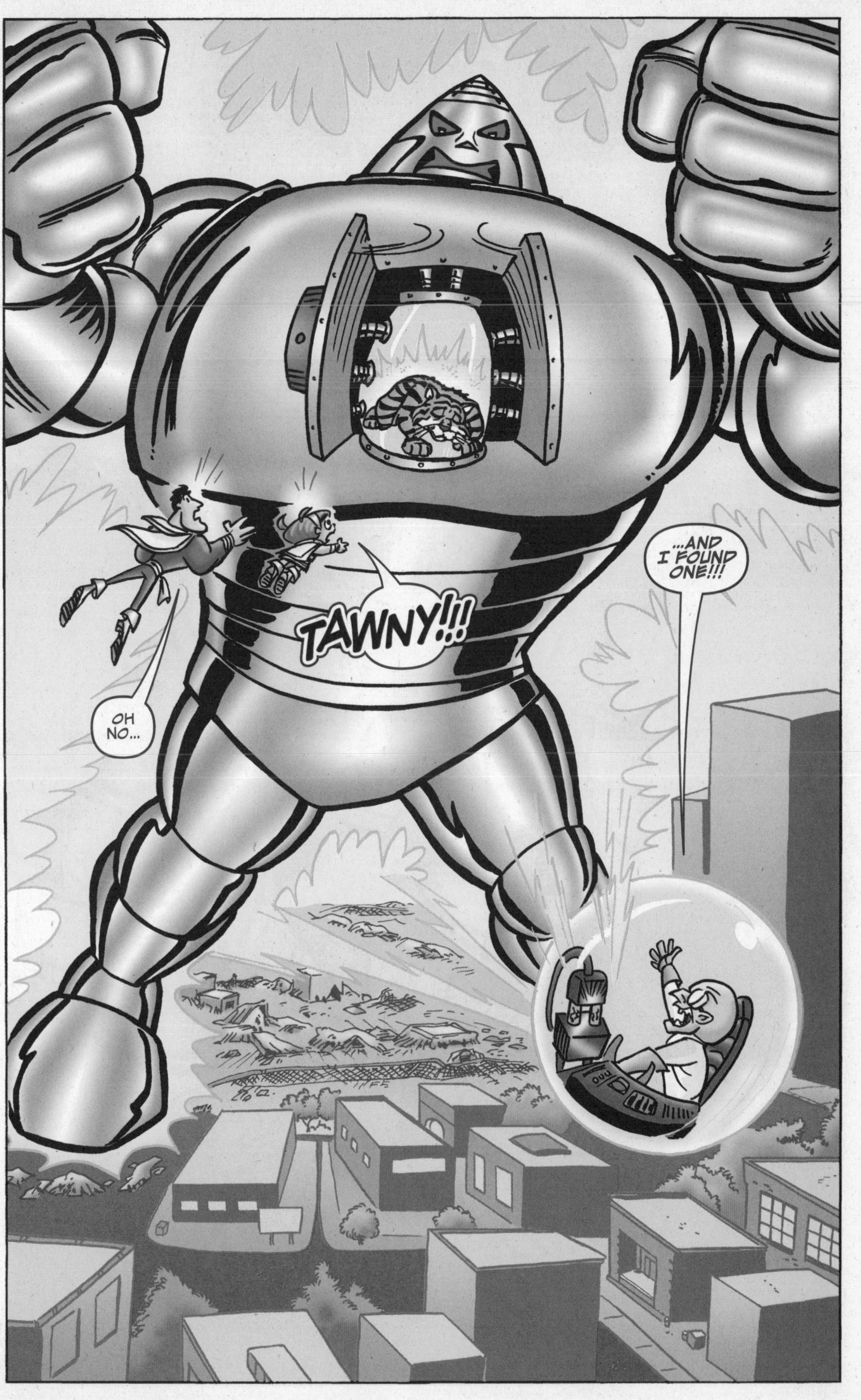
TAWNY!!!
OH NO...
...AND I FOUND ONE!!!

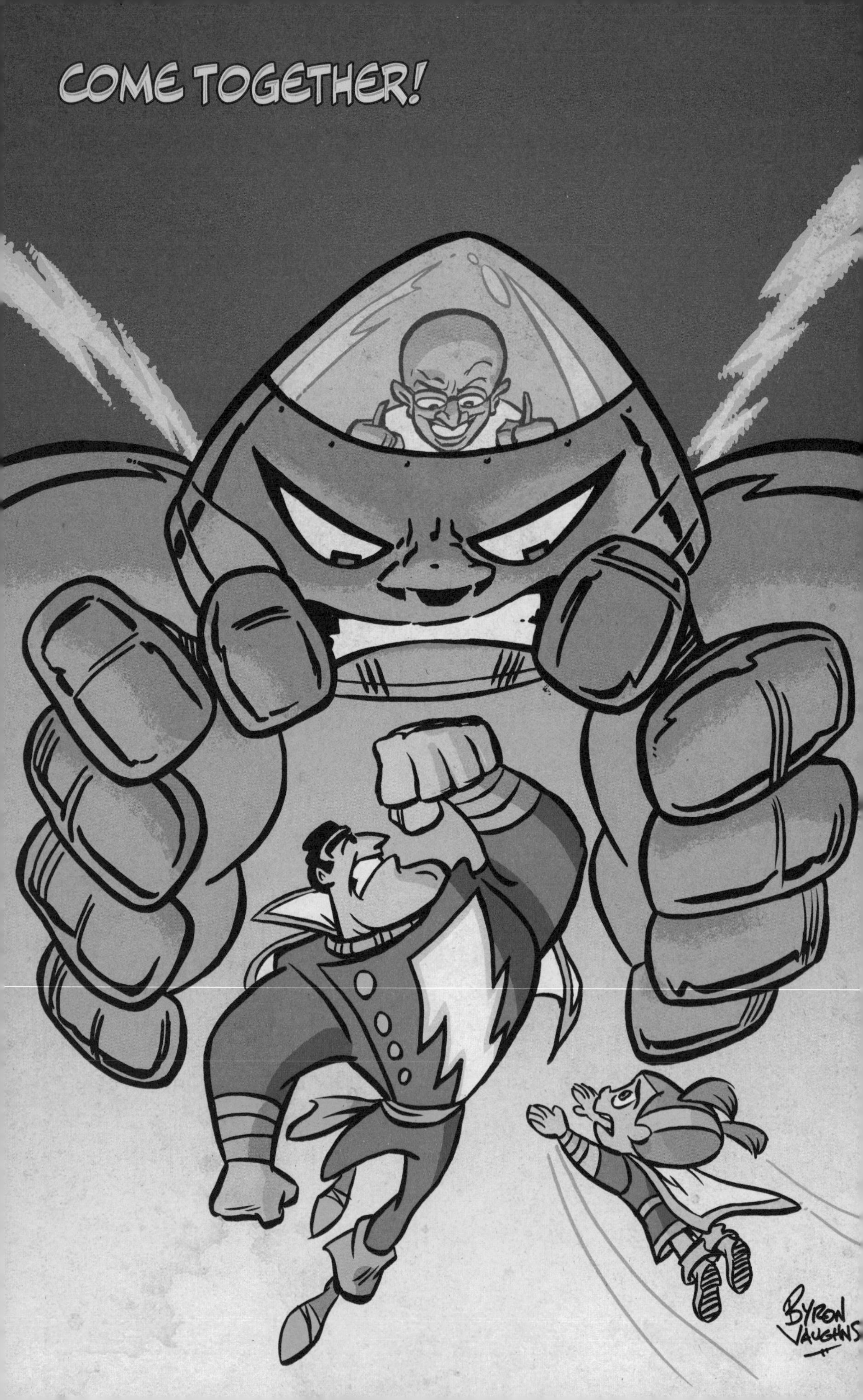
COME TOGETHER!
BYRON VAUGHNS

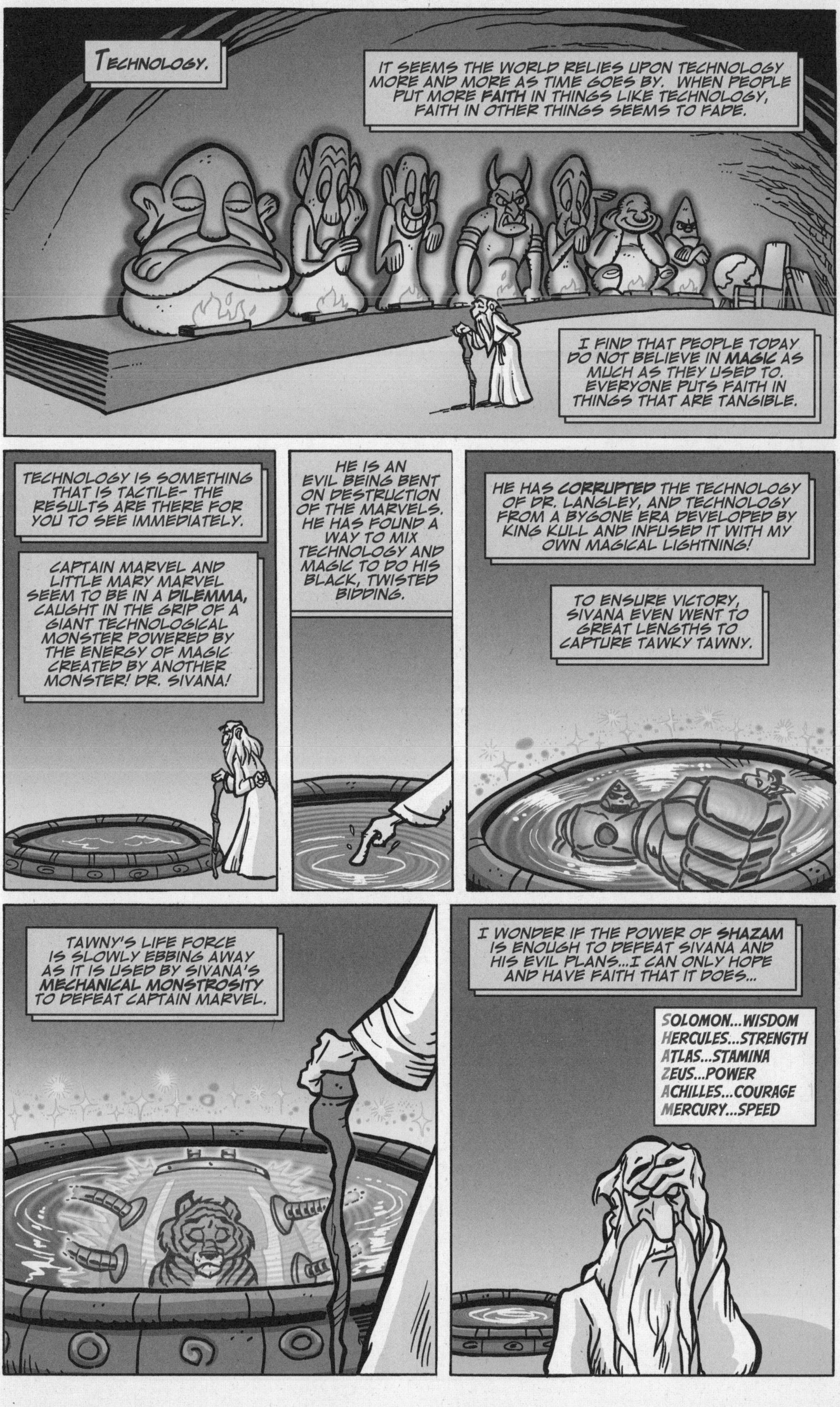
TECHNOLOGY.
IT SEEMS THE WORLD RELIES UPON TECHNOLOGY MORE AND MORE AS TIME GOES BY. WHEN PEOPLE PUT MORE **FAITH** IN THINGS LIKE TECHNOLOGY, FAITH IN OTHER THINGS SEEMS TO FADE.
I FIND THAT PEOPLE TODAY DO NOT BELIEVE IN **MAGIC** AS MUCH AS THEY USED TO. EVERYONE PUTS FAITH IN THINGS THAT ARE TANGIBLE.
TECHNOLOGY IS SOMETHING THAT IS TACTILE- THE RESULTS ARE THERE FOR YOU TO SEE IMMEDIATELY.
CAPTAIN MARVEL AND LITTLE MARY MARVEL SEEM TO BE IN A **DILEMMA,** CAUGHT IN THE GRIP OF A GIANT TECHNOLOGICAL MONSTER POWERED BY THE ENERGY OF MAGIC CREATED BY ANOTHER MONSTER! DR. SIVANA!
HE IS AN EVIL BEING BENT ON DESTRUCTION OF THE MARVELS. HE HAS FOUND A WAY TO MIX TECHNOLOGY AND MAGIC TO DO HIS BLACK, TWISTED BIDDING.
HE HAS **CORRUPTED** THE TECHNOLOGY OF DR. LANGLEY, AND TECHNOLOGY FROM A BYGONE ERA DEVELOPED BY KING KULL AND INFUSED IT WITH MY OWN MAGICAL LIGHTNING!
TO ENSURE VICTORY, SIVANA EVEN WENT TO GREAT LENGTHS TO CAPTURE TAWKY TAWNY.
TAWNY'S LIFE FORCE IS SLOWLY EBBING AWAY AS IT IS USED BY SIVANA'S **MECHANICAL MONSTROSITY** TO DEFEAT CAPTAIN MARVEL.
I WONDER IF THE POWER OF **SHAZAM** IS ENOUGH TO DEFEAT SIVANA AND HIS EVIL PLANS...I CAN ONLY HOPE AND HAVE FAITH THAT IT DOES...
SOLOMON...WISDOM
HERCULES...STRENGTH
ATLAS...STAMINA
ZEUS...POWER
ACHILLES...COURAGE
MERCURY...SPEED

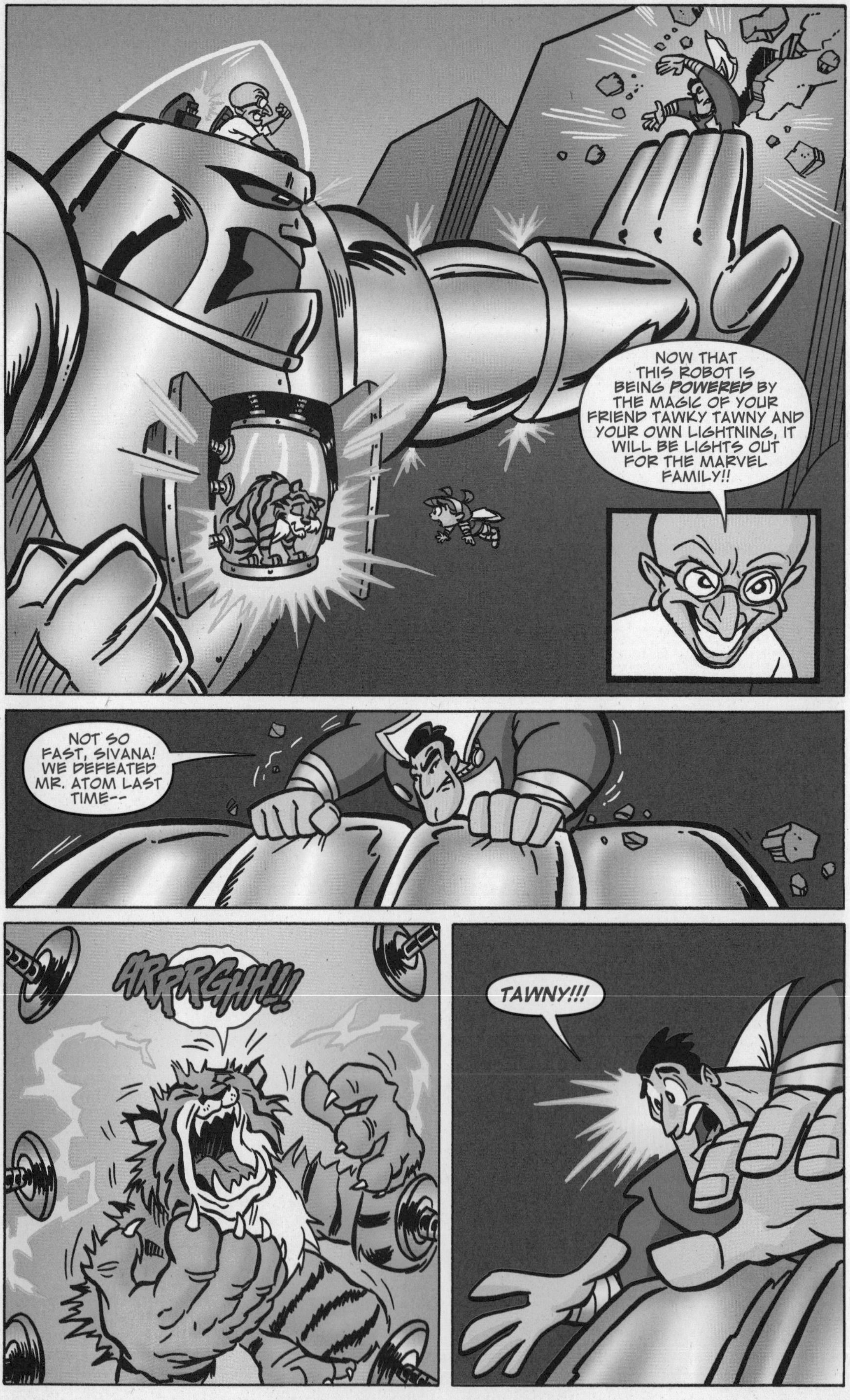
NOW THAT THIS ROBOT IS BEING *POWERED* BY THE MAGIC OF YOUR FRIEND TAWKY TAWNY AND YOUR OWN LIGHTNING, IT WILL BE LIGHTS OUT FOR THE MARVEL FAMILY!!
NOT SO FAST, SIVANA! WE DEFEATED MR. ATOM LAST TIME--
ARRRGHH!!!
TAWNY!!!

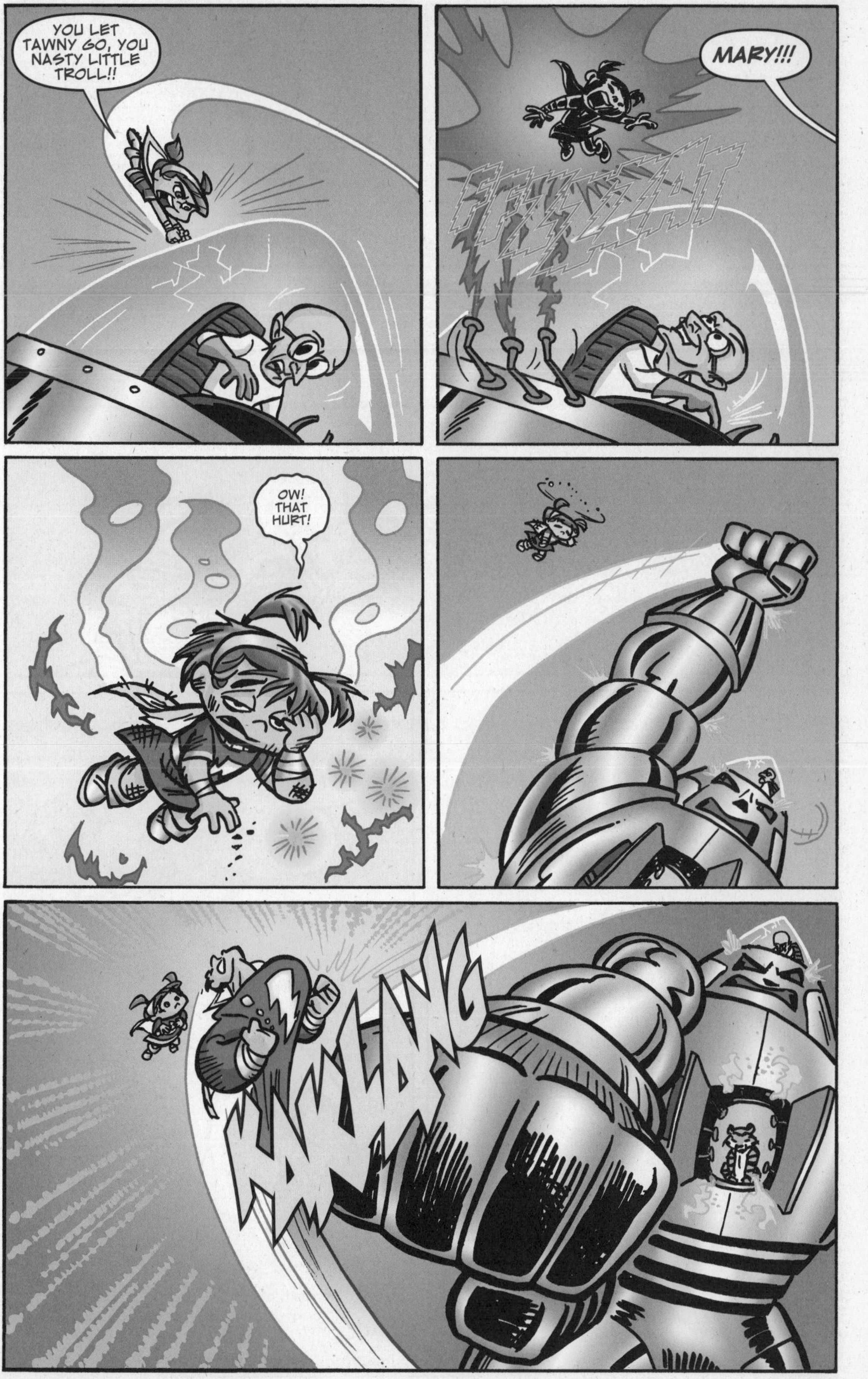
YOU LET TAWNY GO, YOU NASTY LITTLE TROLL!!
MARY!!!
OW! THAT HURT!

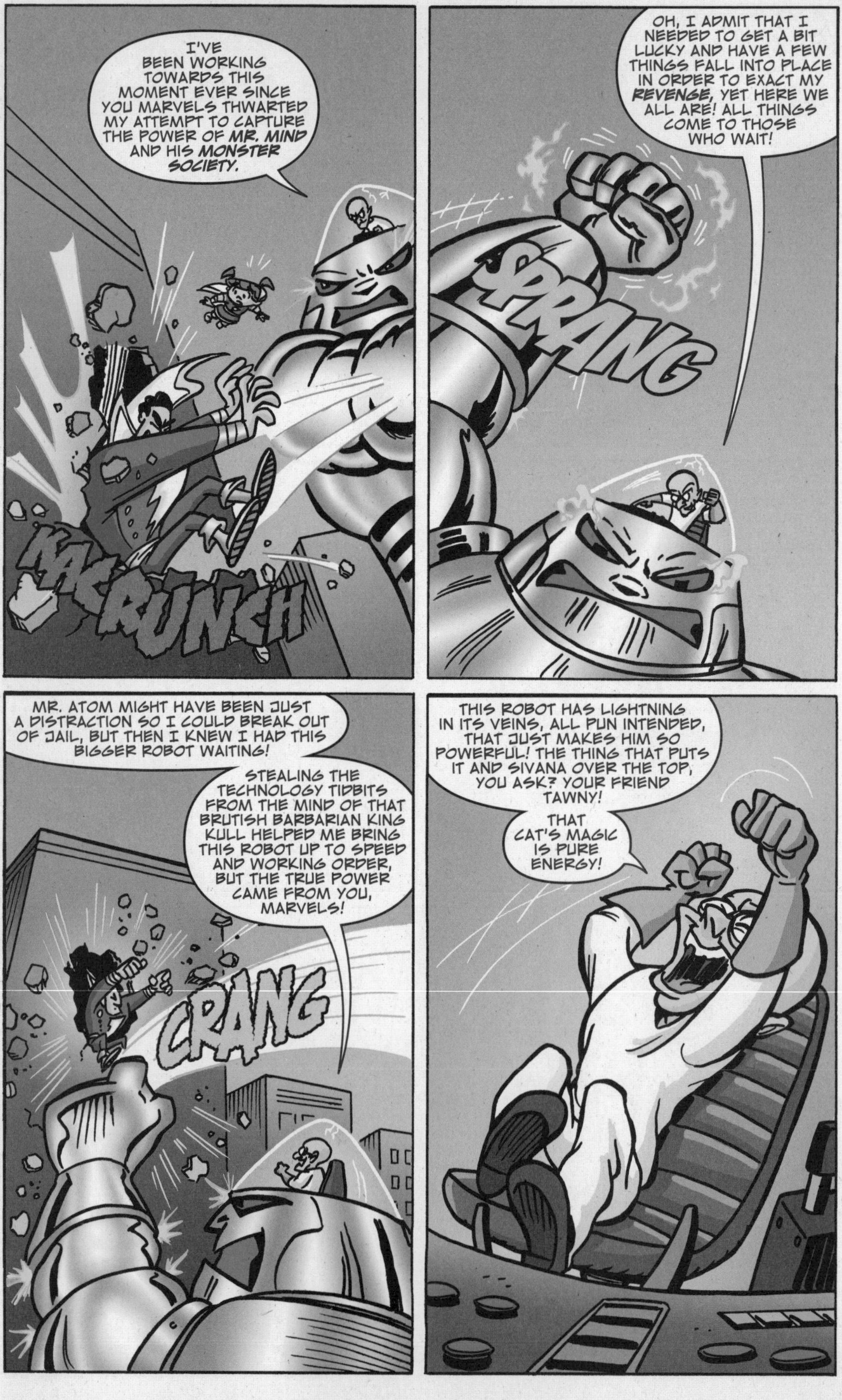
I'VE BEEN WORKING TOWARDS THIS MOMENT EVER SINCE YOU MARVELS THWARTED MY ATTEMPT TO CAPTURE THE POWER OF MR. MIND AND HIS MONSTER SOCIETY.
OH, I ADMIT THAT I NEEDED TO GET A BIT LUCKY AND HAVE A FEW THINGS FALL INTO PLACE IN ORDER TO EXACT MY REVENGE, YET HERE WE ALL ARE! ALL THINGS COME TO THOSE WHO WAIT!
SPRANG
MR. ATOM MIGHT HAVE BEEN JUST A DISTRACTION SO I COULD BREAK OUT OF JAIL, BUT THEN I KNEW I HAD THIS BIGGER ROBOT WAITING!
STEALING THE TECHNOLOGY TIDBITS FROM THE MIND OF THAT BRUTISH BARBARIAN KING KULL HELPED ME BRING THIS ROBOT UP TO SPEED AND WORKING ORDER, BUT THE TRUE POWER CAME FROM YOU, MARVELS!
CRANG
THIS ROBOT HAS LIGHTNING IN ITS VEINS, ALL PUN INTENDED, THAT JUST MAKES HIM SO POWERFUL! THE THING THAT PUTS IT AND SIVANA OVER THE TOP, YOU ASK? YOUR FRIEND TAWNY!
THAT CAT'S MAGIC IS PURE ENERGY!

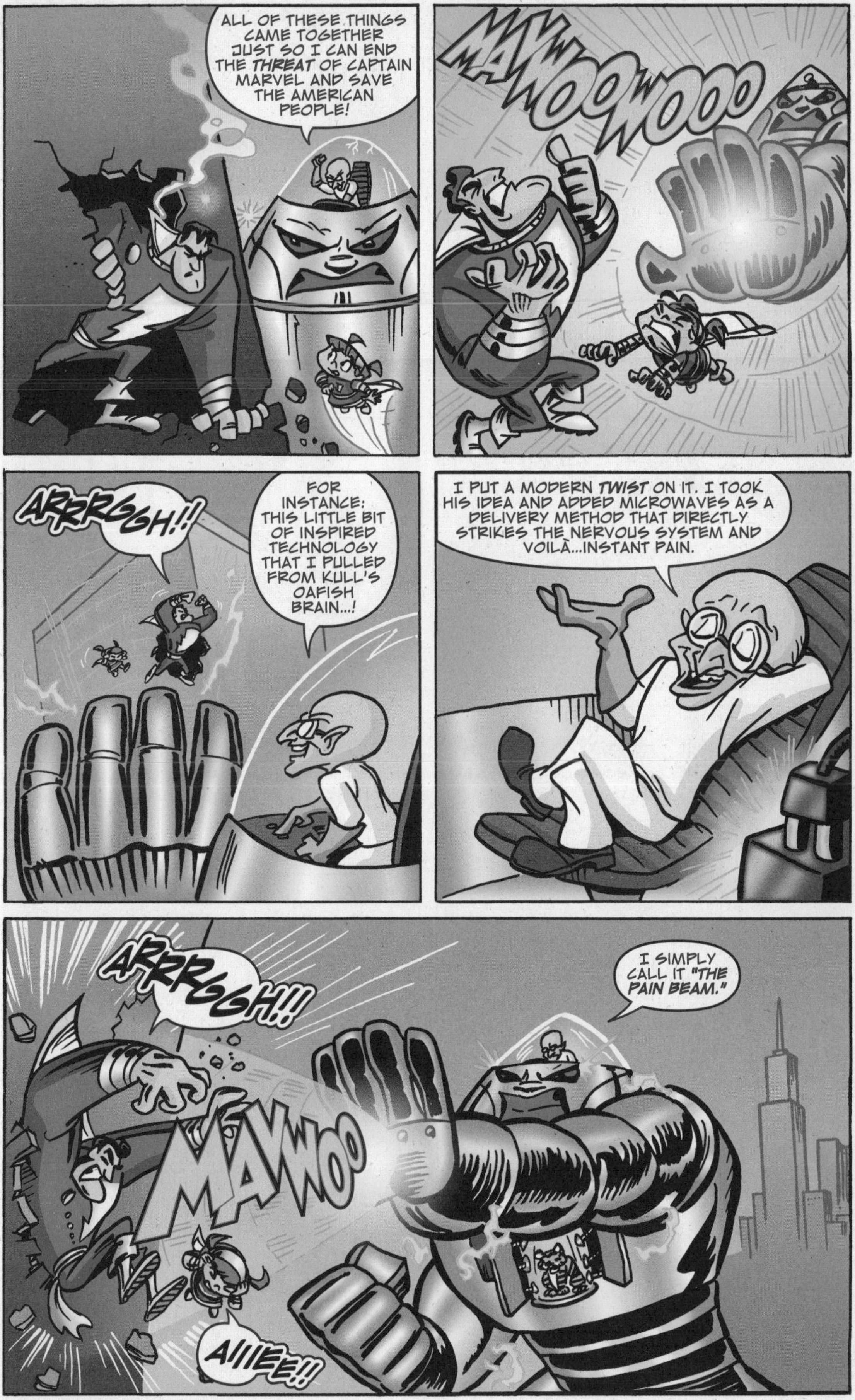
ALL OF THESE THINGS CAME TOGETHER JUST SO I CAN END THE *THREAT* OF CAPTAIN MARVEL AND SAVE THE AMERICAN PEOPLE!
MAWOOWOOO
ARRRGGH!!
FOR INSTANCE: THIS LITTLE BIT OF INSPIRED TECHNOLOGY THAT I PULLED FROM KULL'S OAFISH BRAIN...!
I PUT A MODERN *TWIST* ON IT. I TOOK HIS IDEA AND ADDED MICROWAVES AS A DELIVERY METHOD THAT DIRECTLY STRIKES THE NERVOUS SYSTEM AND VOILÀ...INSTANT PAIN.
ARRRGGH!!
I SIMPLY CALL IT *"THE PAIN BEAM."*
MAWOO
AIIIEE!!

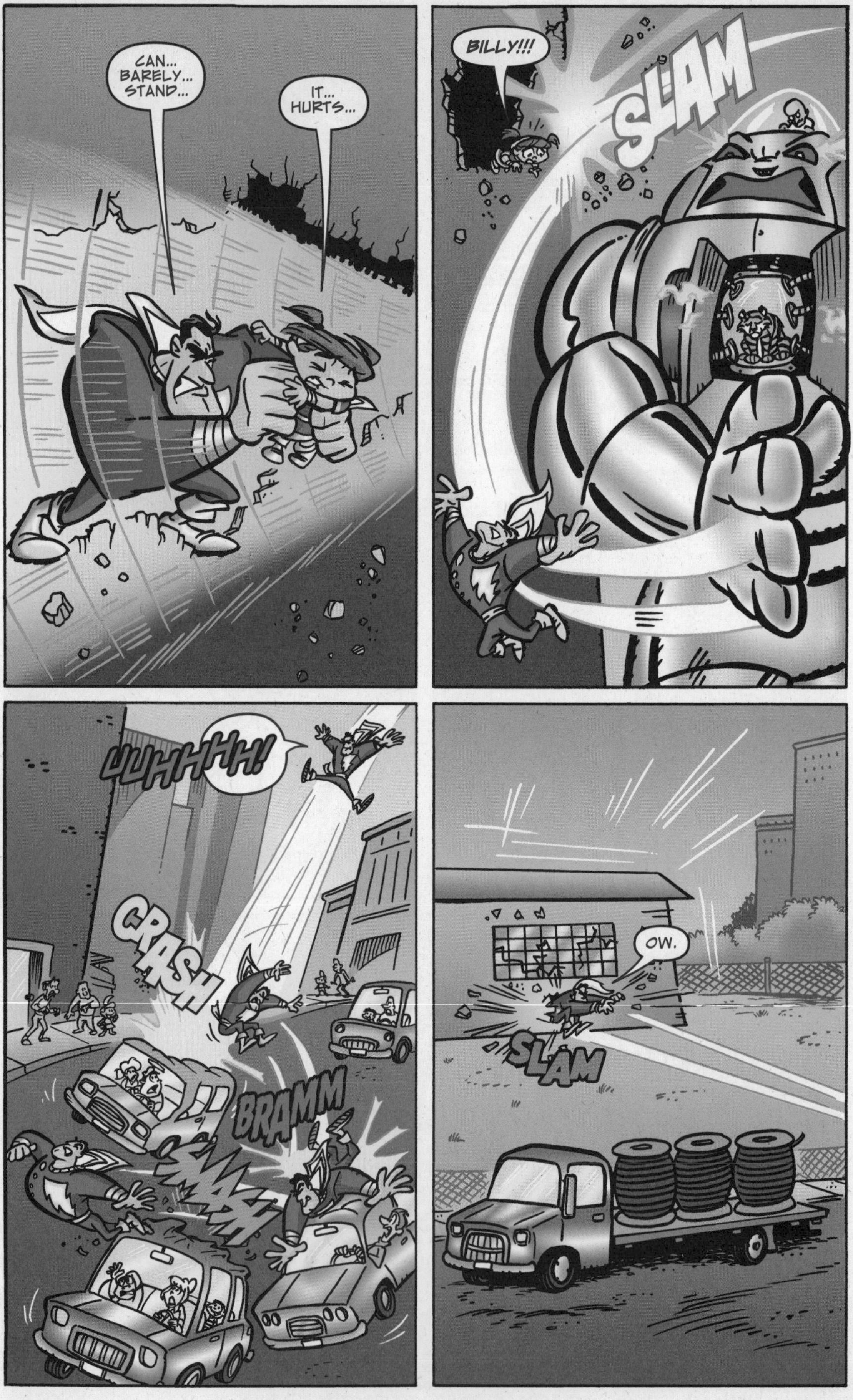
CAN... BARELY... STAND...
IT... HURTS...
BILLY!!!
SLAM
UUHHHH!
CRASH
BRAMM
OW.
SLAM

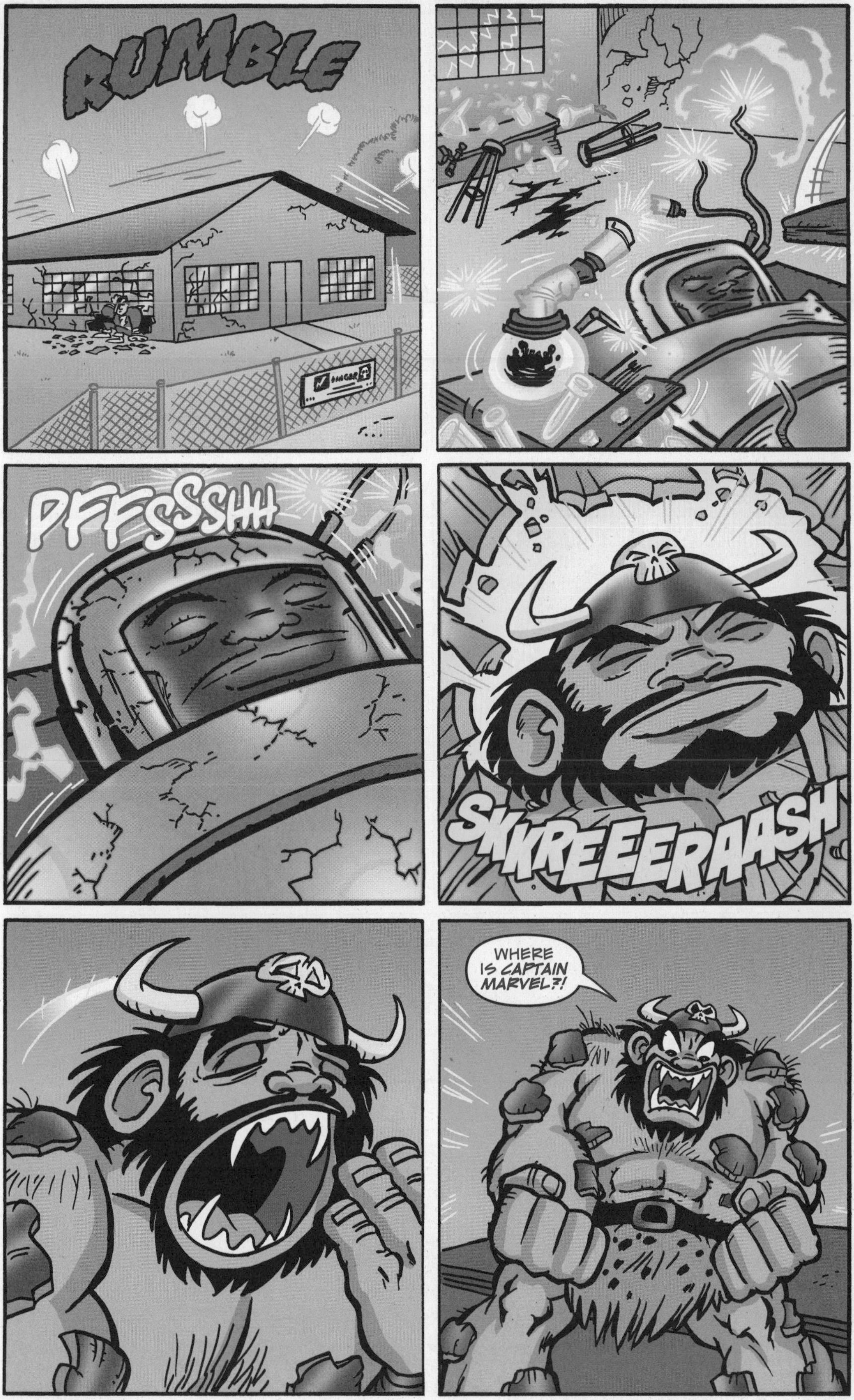
RUMBLE
PFFSSSHH
SKKREEERAASH
WHERE IS CAPTAIN MARVEL?!

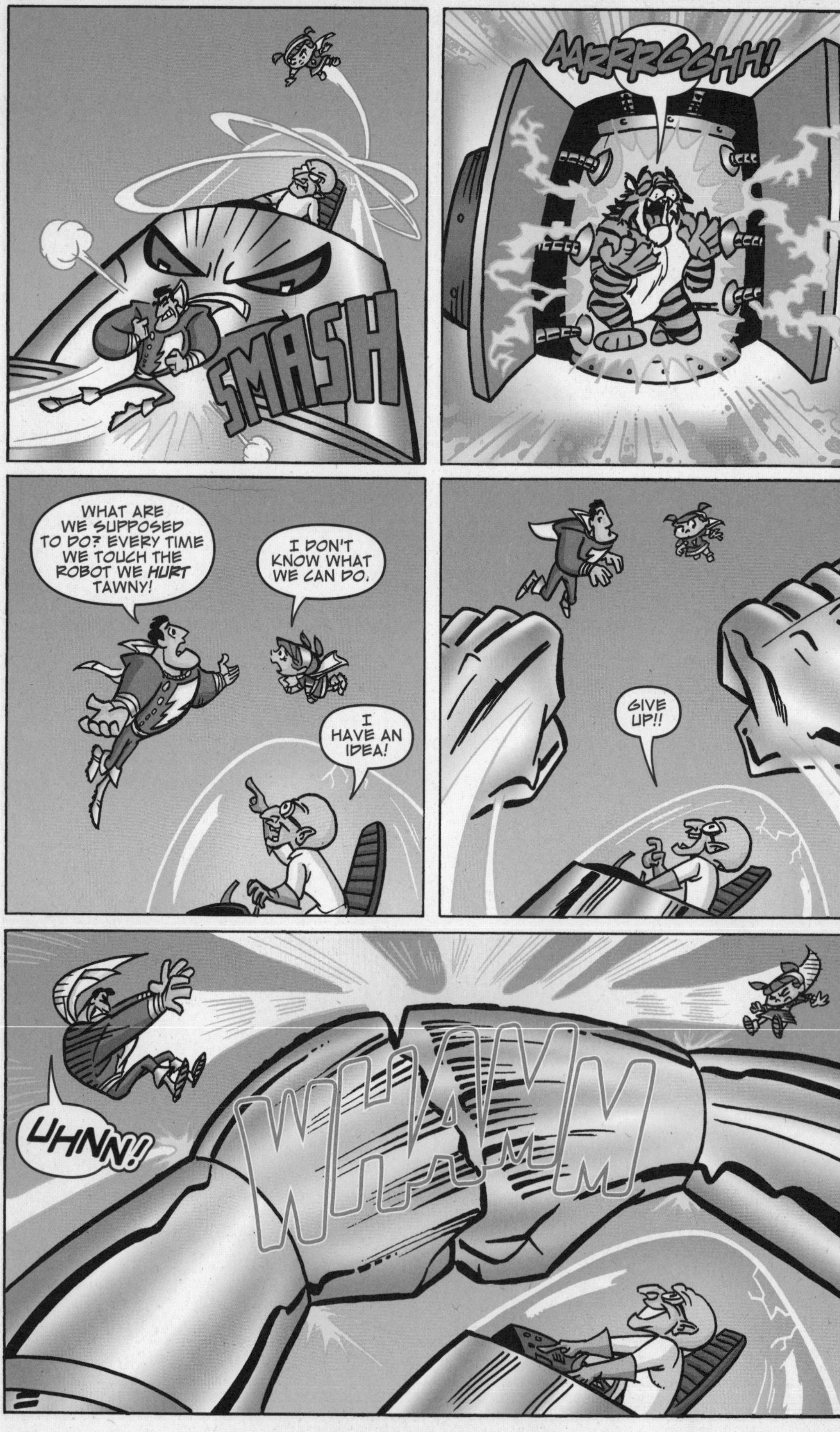
SMASH
AARRRGGHH!
WHAT ARE WE SUPPOSED TO DO? EVERY TIME WE TOUCH THE ROBOT WE HURT TAWNY!
I DON'T KNOW WHAT WE CAN DO.
I HAVE AN IDEA!
GIVE UP!!
UHNN!
WHAMM

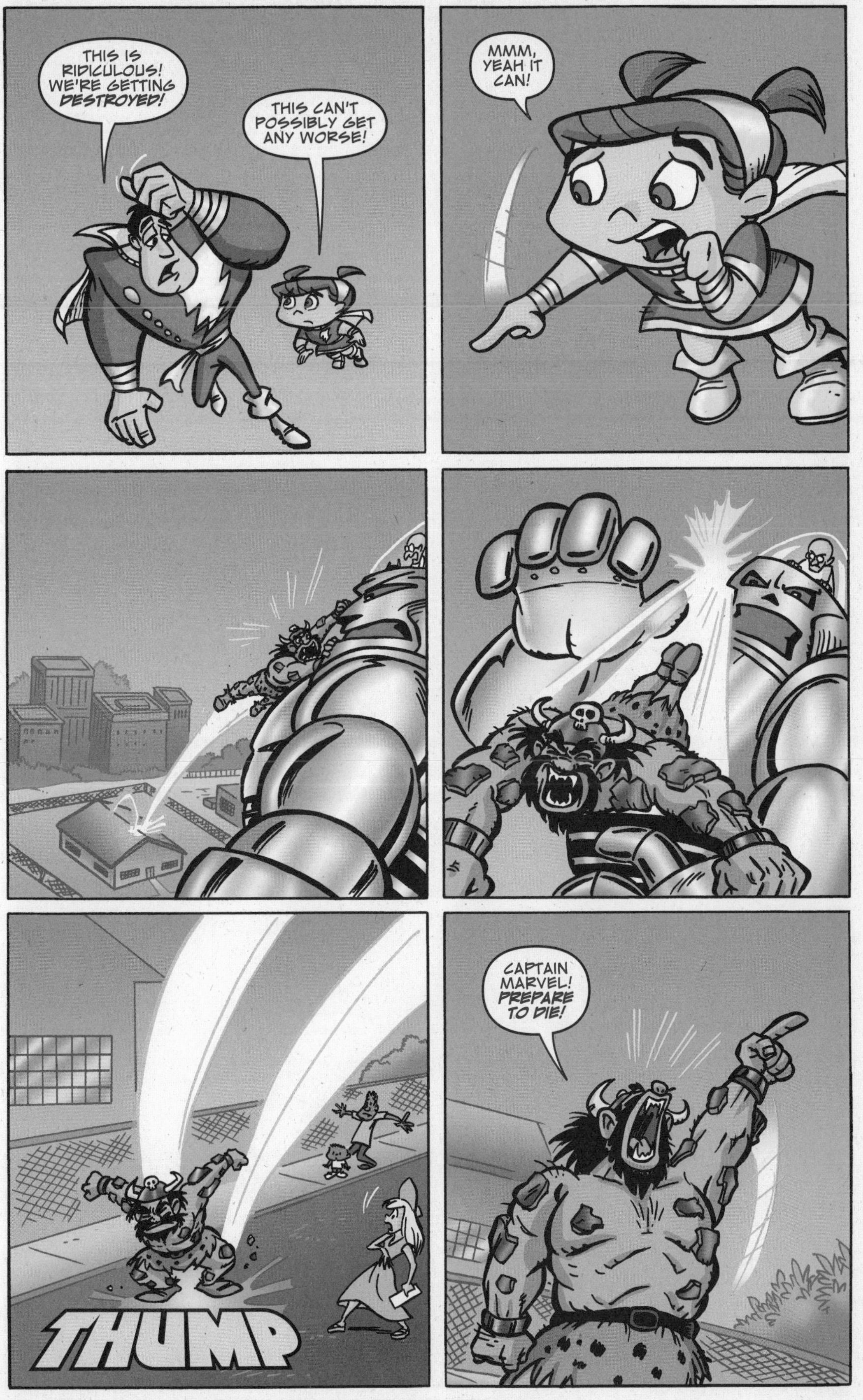
THIS IS RIDICULOUS! WE'RE GETTING DESTROYED!
THIS CAN'T POSSIBLY GET ANY WORSE!
MMM, YEAH IT CAN!
THUMP
CAPTAIN MARVEL! PREPARE TO DIE!

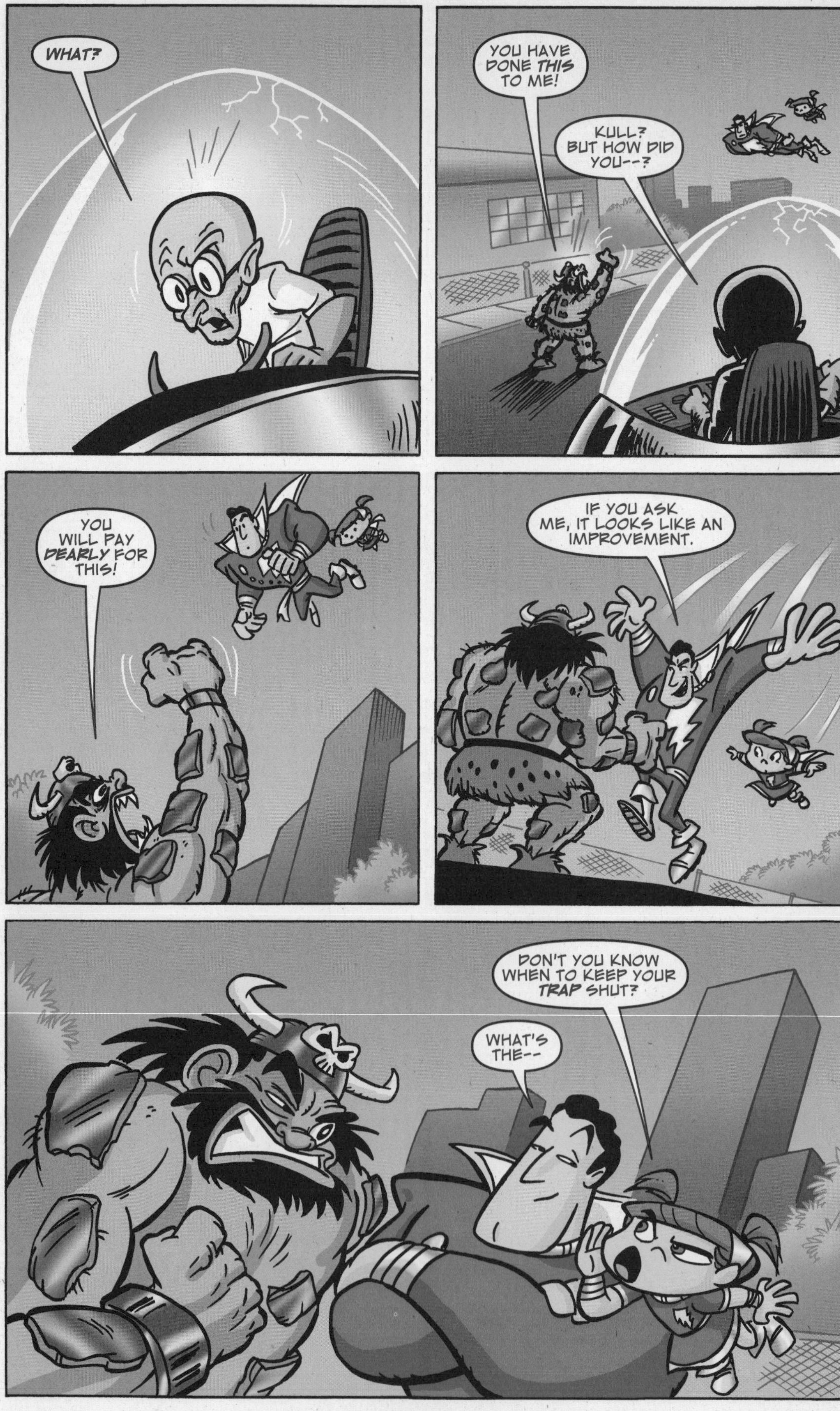
WHAT?
YOU HAVE DONE THIS TO ME!
KULL? BUT HOW DID YOU--?
YOU WILL PAY DEARLY FOR THIS!
IF YOU ASK ME, IT LOOKS LIKE AN IMPROVEMENT.
DON'T YOU KNOW WHEN TO KEEP YOUR TRAP SHUT?
WHAT'S THE--

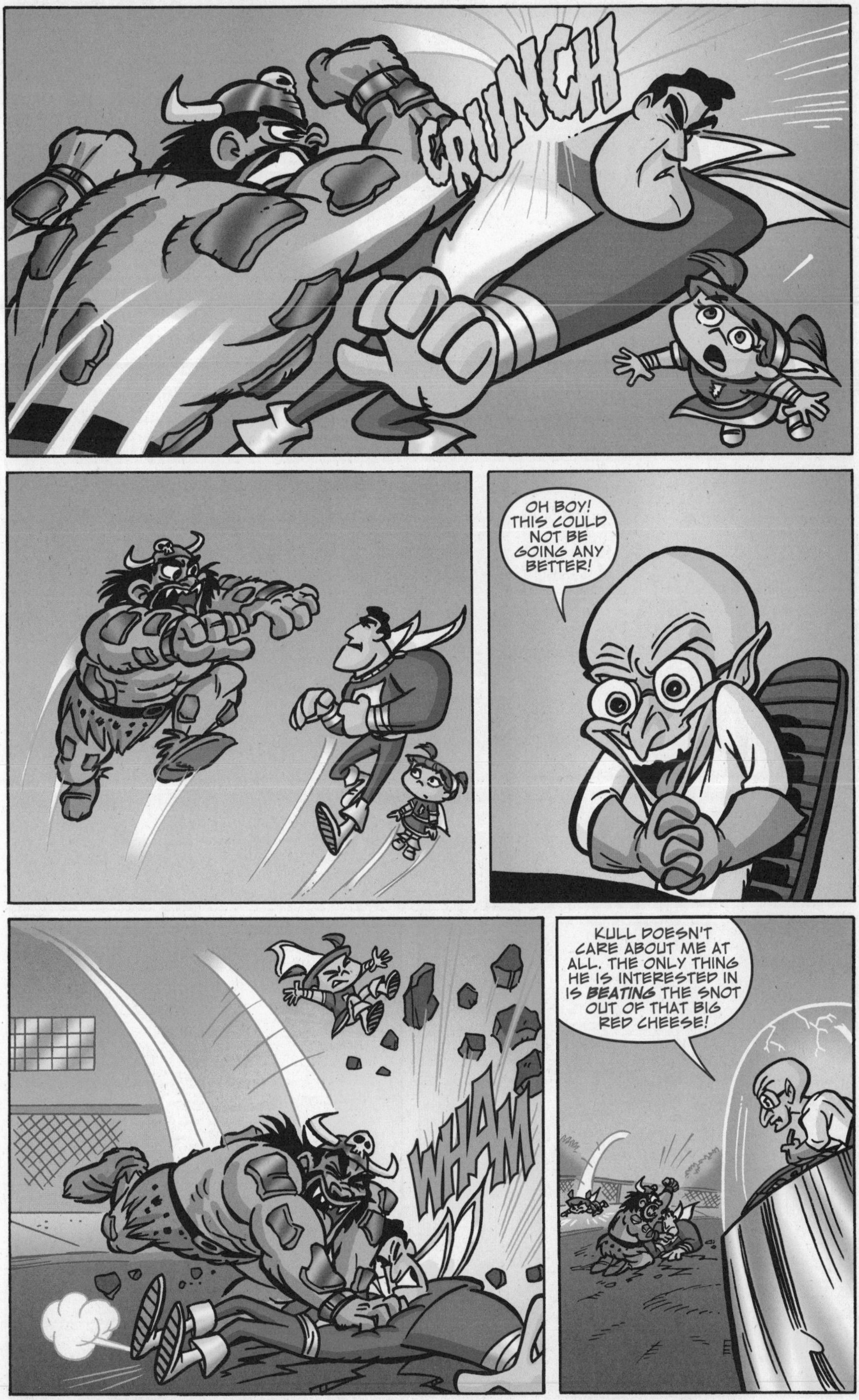
CRUNCH
OH BOY! THIS COULD NOT BE GOING ANY BETTER!
WHAM
KULL DOESN'T CARE ABOUT ME AT ALL. THE ONLY THING HE IS INTERESTED IN IS *BEATING* THE SNOT OUT OF THAT BIG RED CHEESE!

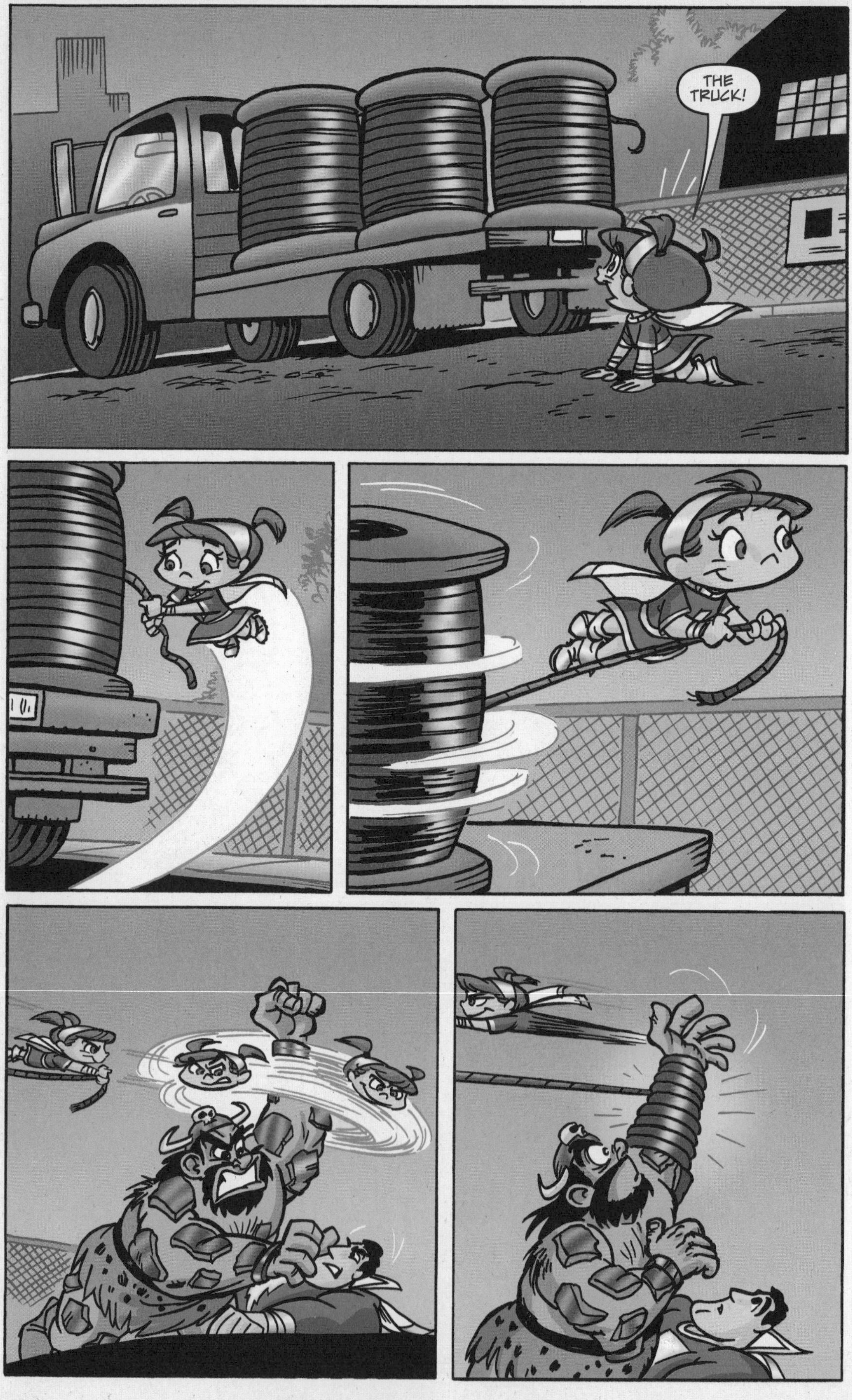
THE TRUCK!

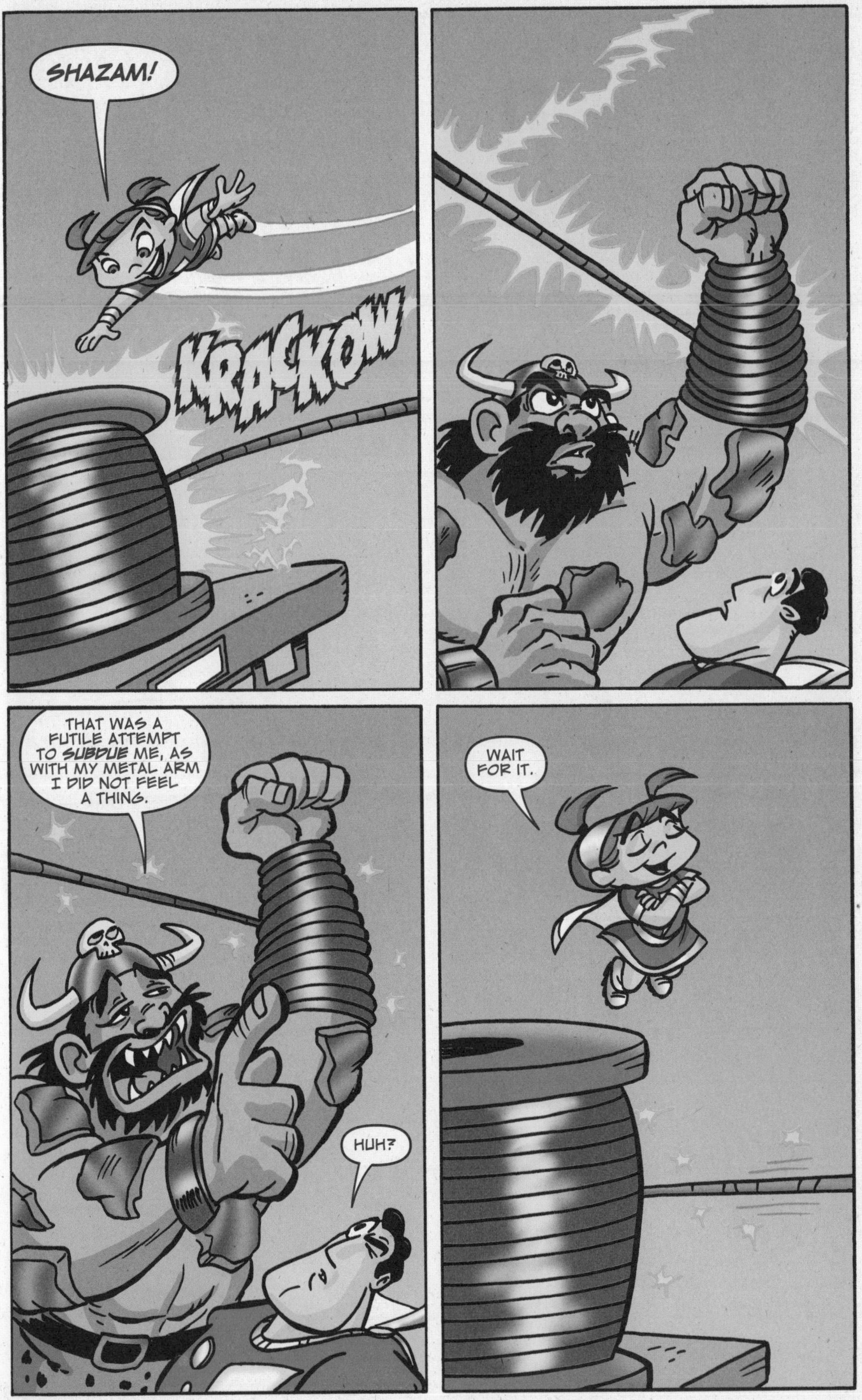
SHAZAM!
KRACKOW
THAT WAS A FUTILE ATTEMPT TO SUBDUE ME, AS WITH MY METAL ARM I DID NOT FEEL A THING.
HUH?
WAIT FOR IT.

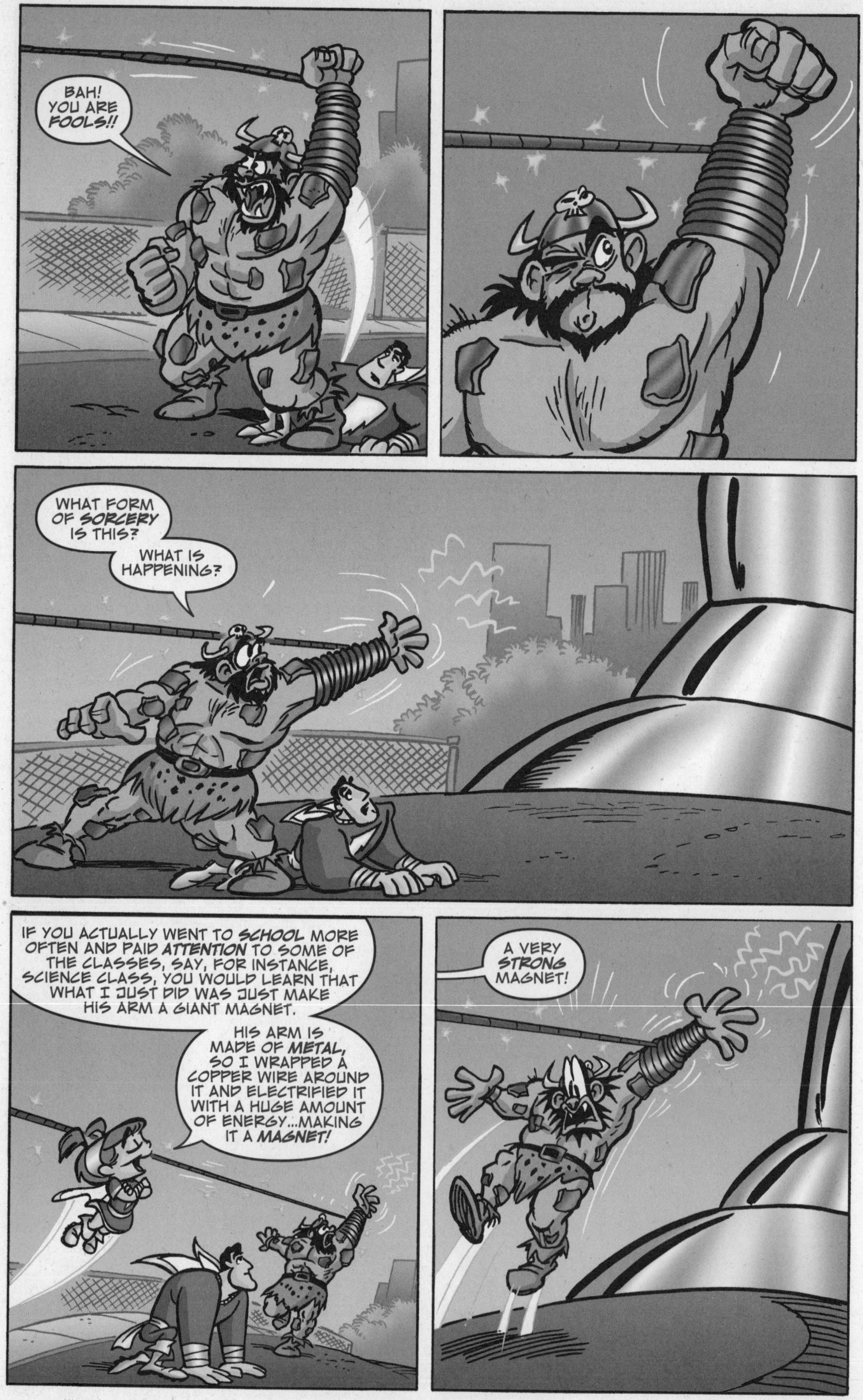
BAH! YOU ARE FOOLS!!
WHAT FORM OF SORCERY IS THIS?
WHAT IS HAPPENING?
IF YOU ACTUALLY WENT TO SCHOOL MORE OFTEN AND PAID ATTENTION TO SOME OF THE CLASSES, SAY, FOR INSTANCE, SCIENCE CLASS, YOU WOULD LEARN THAT WHAT I JUST DID WAS JUST MAKE HIS ARM A GIANT MAGNET.
HIS ARM IS MADE OF METAL, SO I WRAPPED A COPPER WIRE AROUND IT AND ELECTRIFIED IT WITH A HUGE AMOUNT OF ENERGY...MAKING IT A MAGNET!
A VERY STRONG MAGNET!

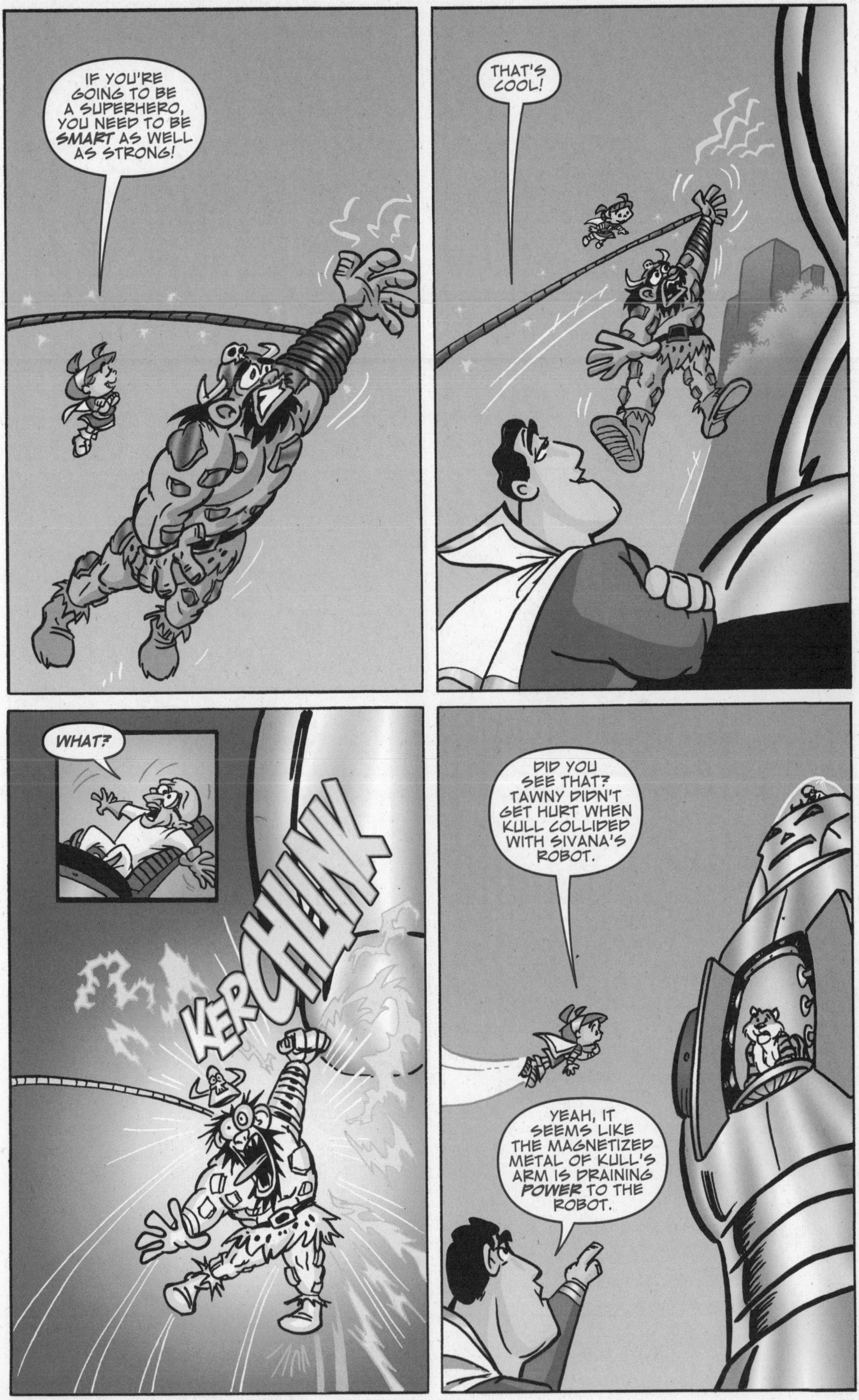

IF YOU'RE GOING TO BE A SUPERHERO, YOU NEED TO BE SMART AS WELL AS STRONG!
THAT'S COOL!
WHAT?
KERCHUNK
DID YOU SEE THAT? TAWNY DIDN'T GET HURT WHEN KULL COLLIDED WITH SIVANA'S ROBOT.
YEAH, IT SEEMS LIKE THE MAGNETIZED METAL OF KULL'S ARM IS DRAINING POWER TO THE ROBOT.

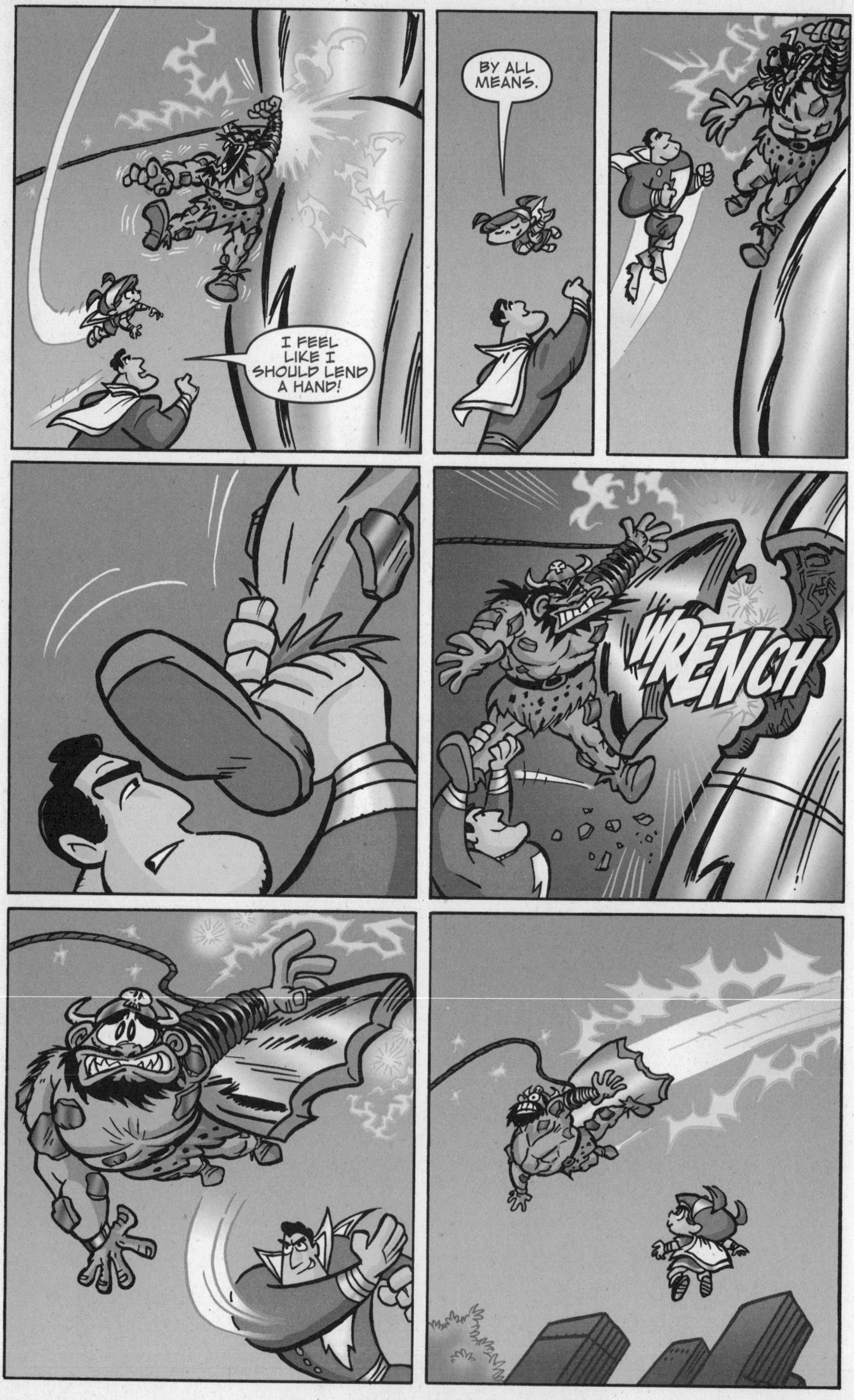
I FEEL LIKE I SHOULD LEND A HAND!
BY ALL MEANS.
WRENCH

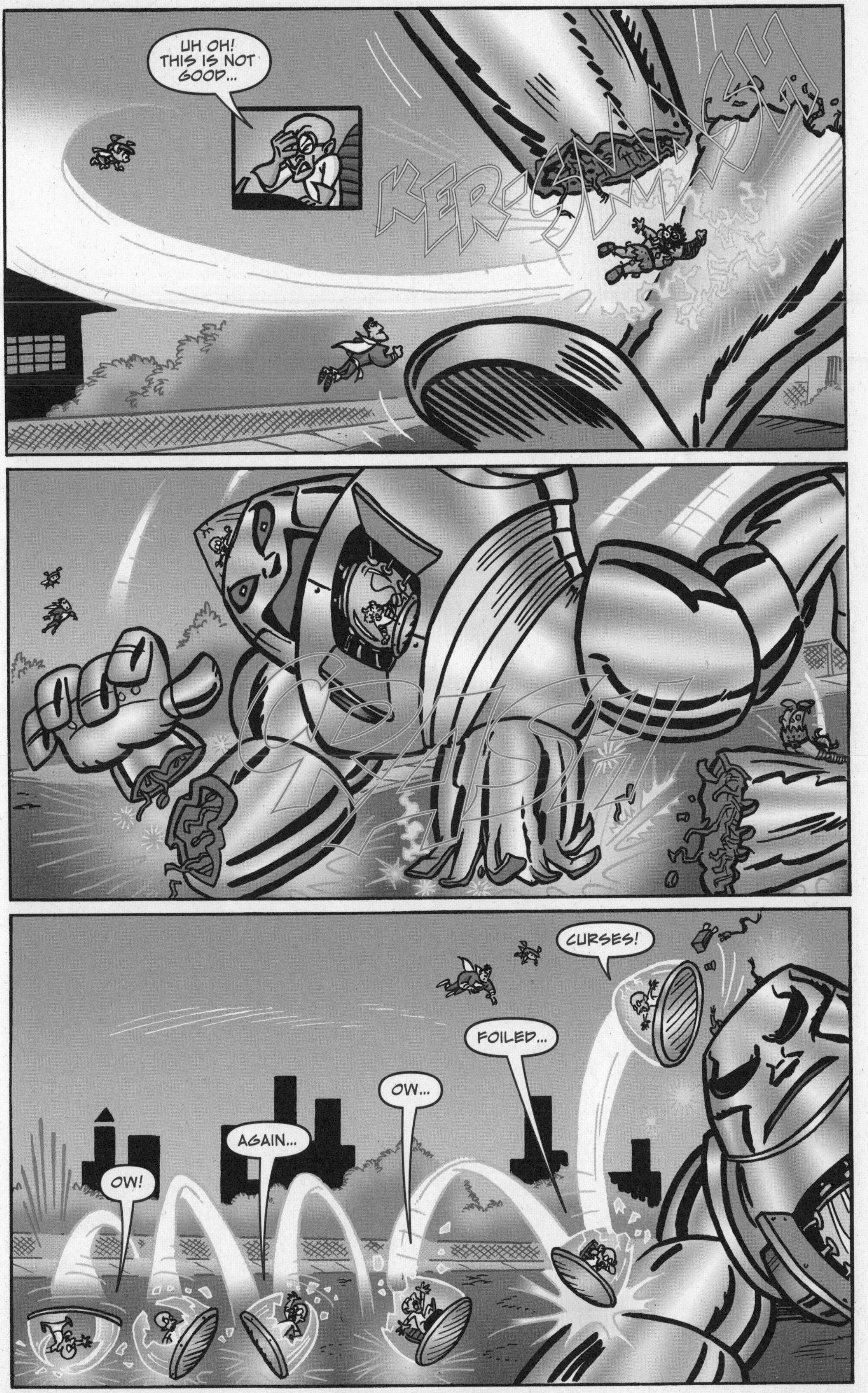
UH OH! THIS IS NOT GOOD...
KER-SMASH
CRASH!
OW!
AGAIN...
OW...
FOILED...
CURSES!

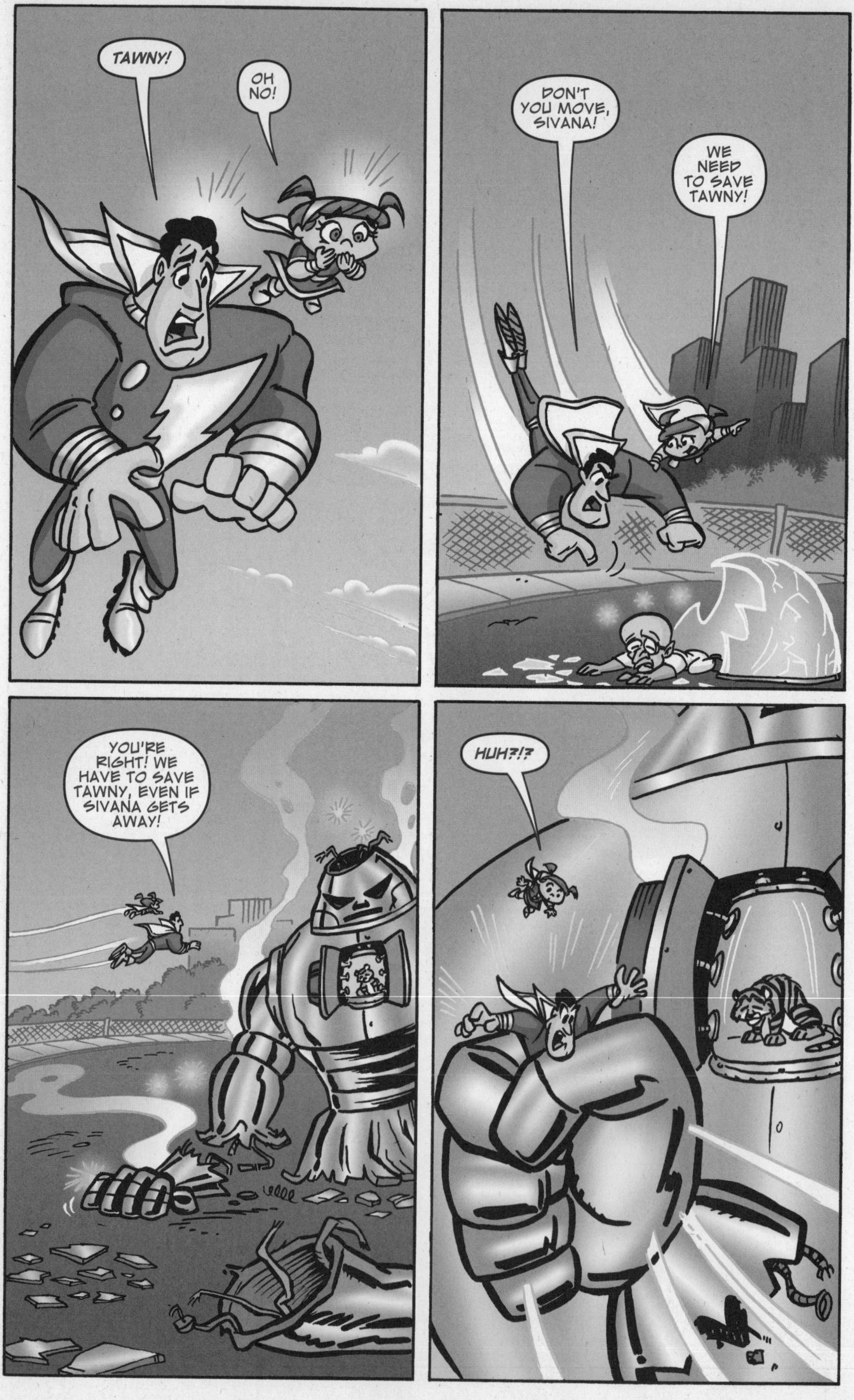
TAWNY!
OH NO!
DON'T YOU MOVE, SIVANA!
WE NEED TO SAVE TAWNY!
YOU'RE RIGHT! WE HAVE TO SAVE TAWNY, EVEN IF SIVANA GETS AWAY!
HUH?!?

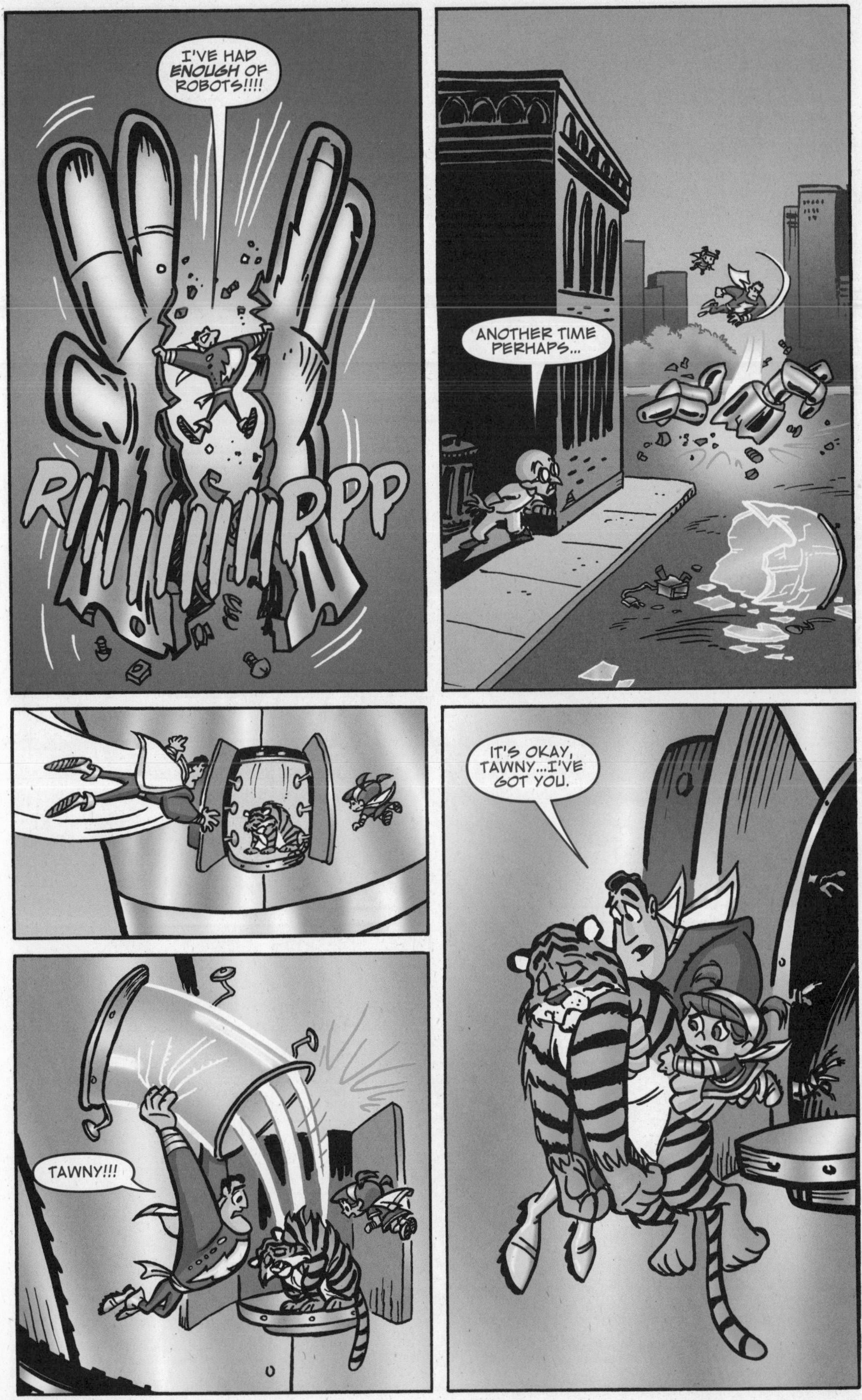
I'VE HAD ENOUGH OF ROBOTS!!!!
RIIIIIIIIIPPP
ANOTHER TIME PERHAPS...
TAWNY!!!
IT'S OKAY, TAWNY...I'VE GOT YOU.

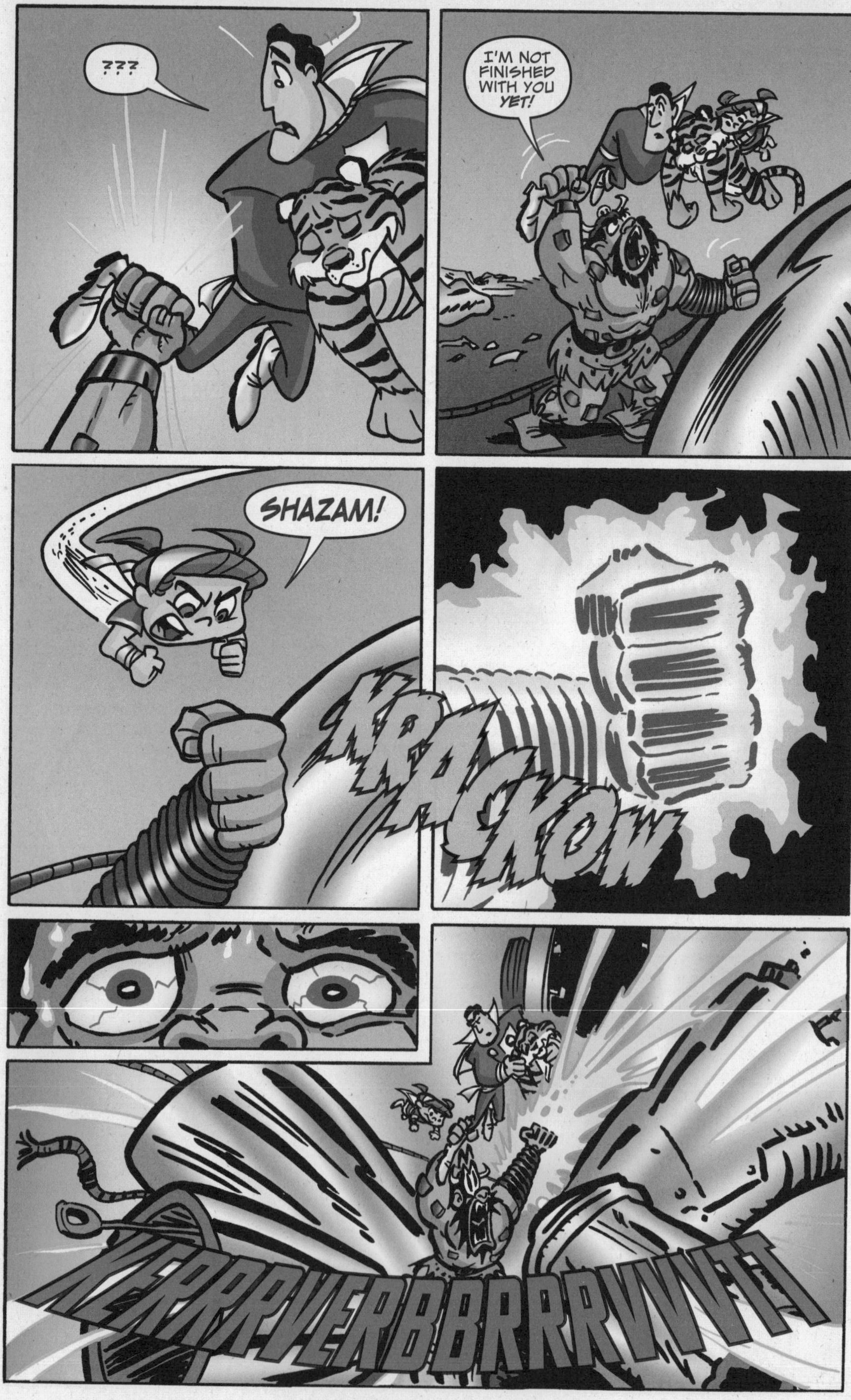
???
I'M NOT FINISHED WITH YOU *YET!*
SHAZAM!
KRACKOW
KERRRVERBBRRRVVVTT

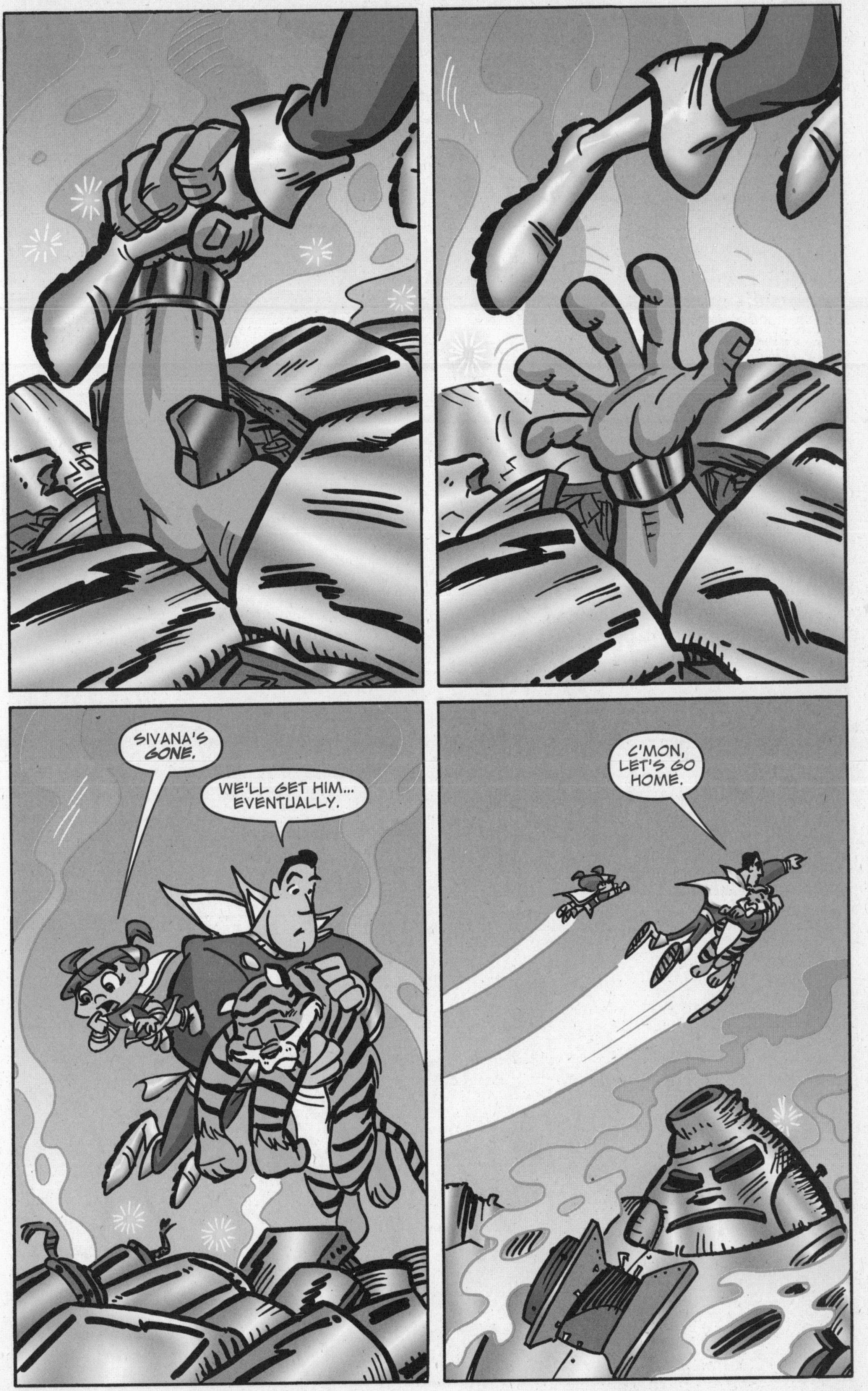
SIVANA'S GONE.
WE'LL GET HIM... EVENTUALLY.
C'MON, LET'S GO HOME.

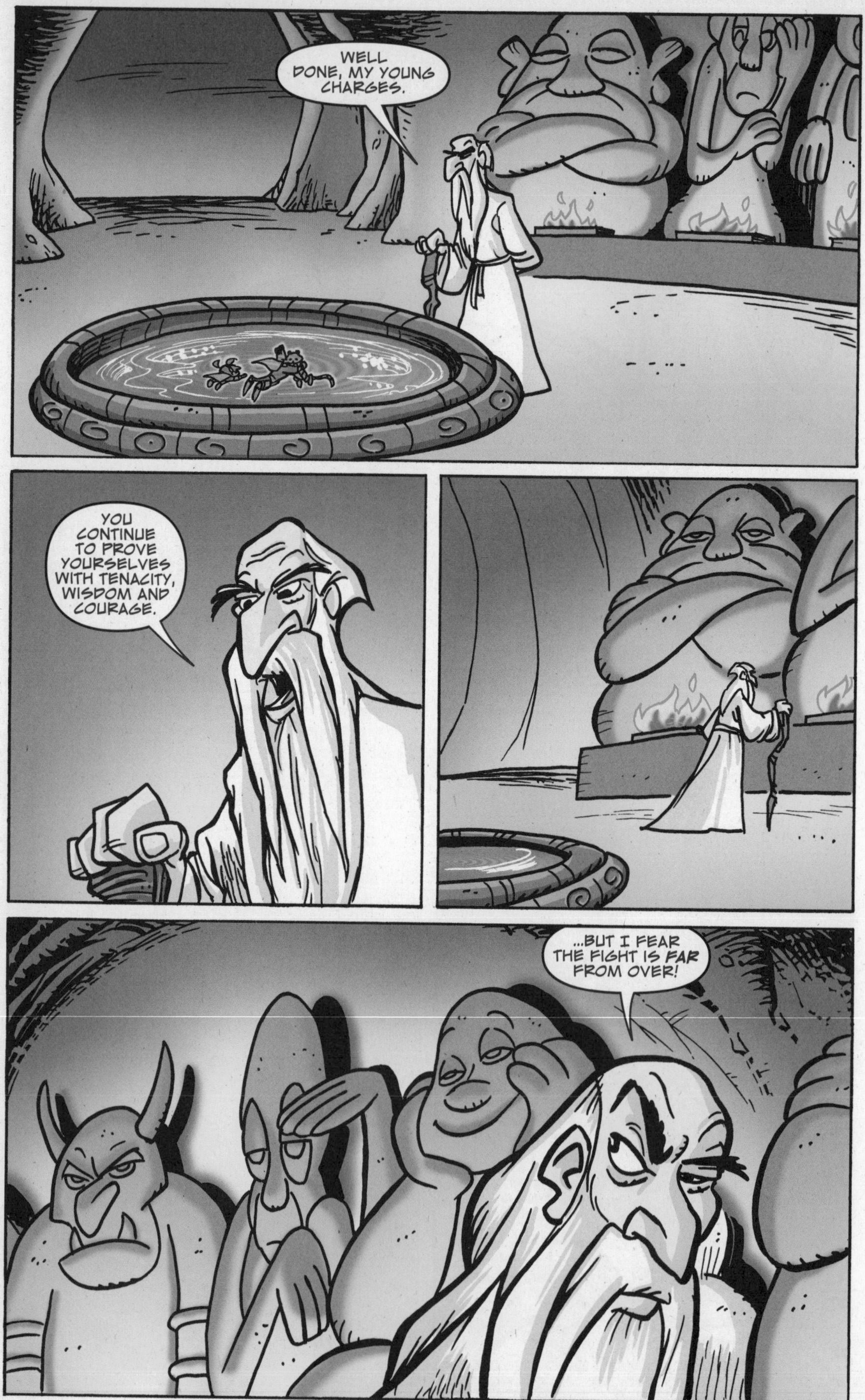
WELL DONE, MY YOUNG CHARGES.
YOU CONTINUE TO PROVE YOURSELVES WITH TENACITY, WISDOM AND COURAGE.
...BUT I FEAR THE FIGHT IS **FAR** FROM OVER!

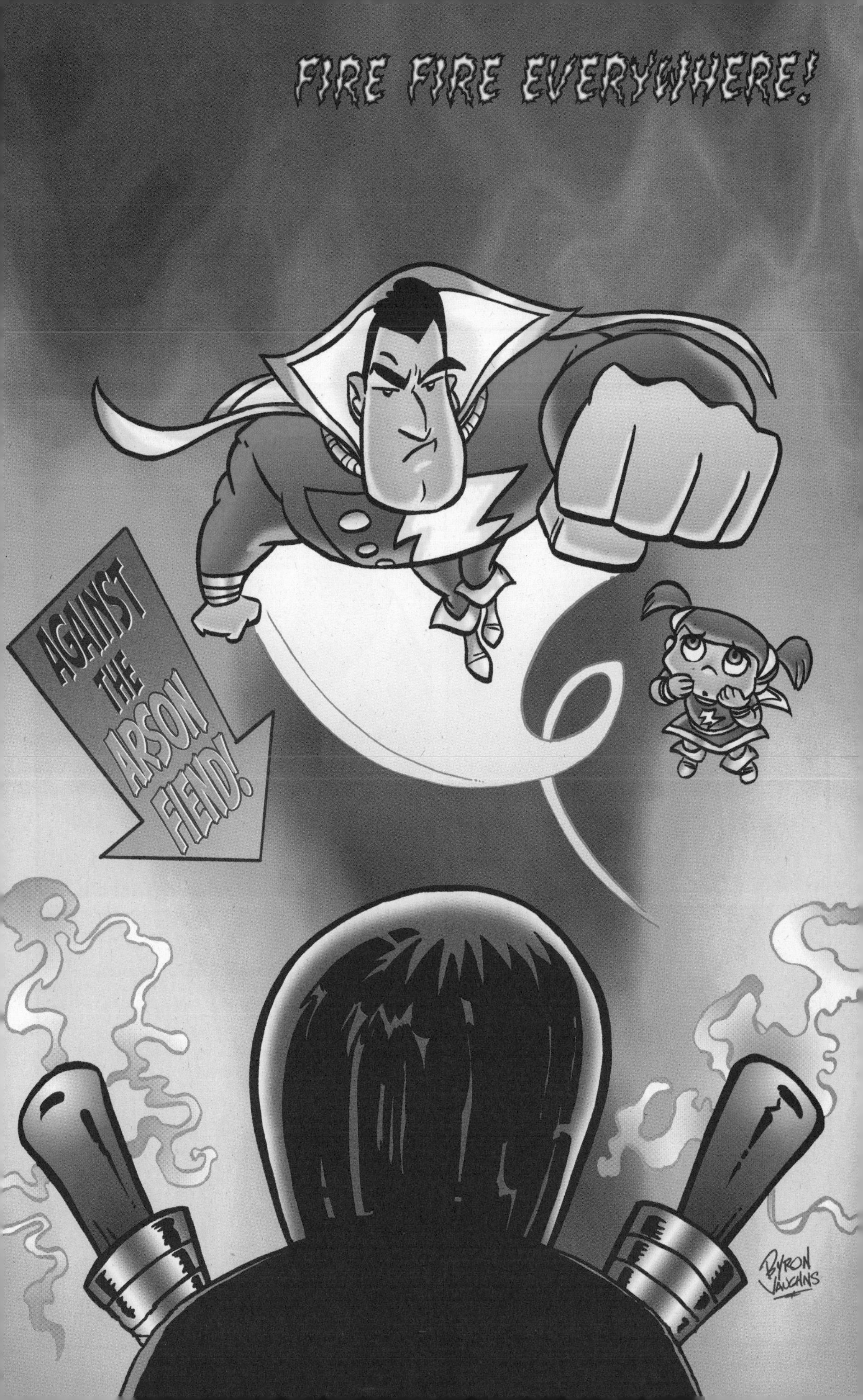
FIRE FIRE EVERYWHERE!
AGAINST THE ARSON FIEND!
BYRON VAUGHNS

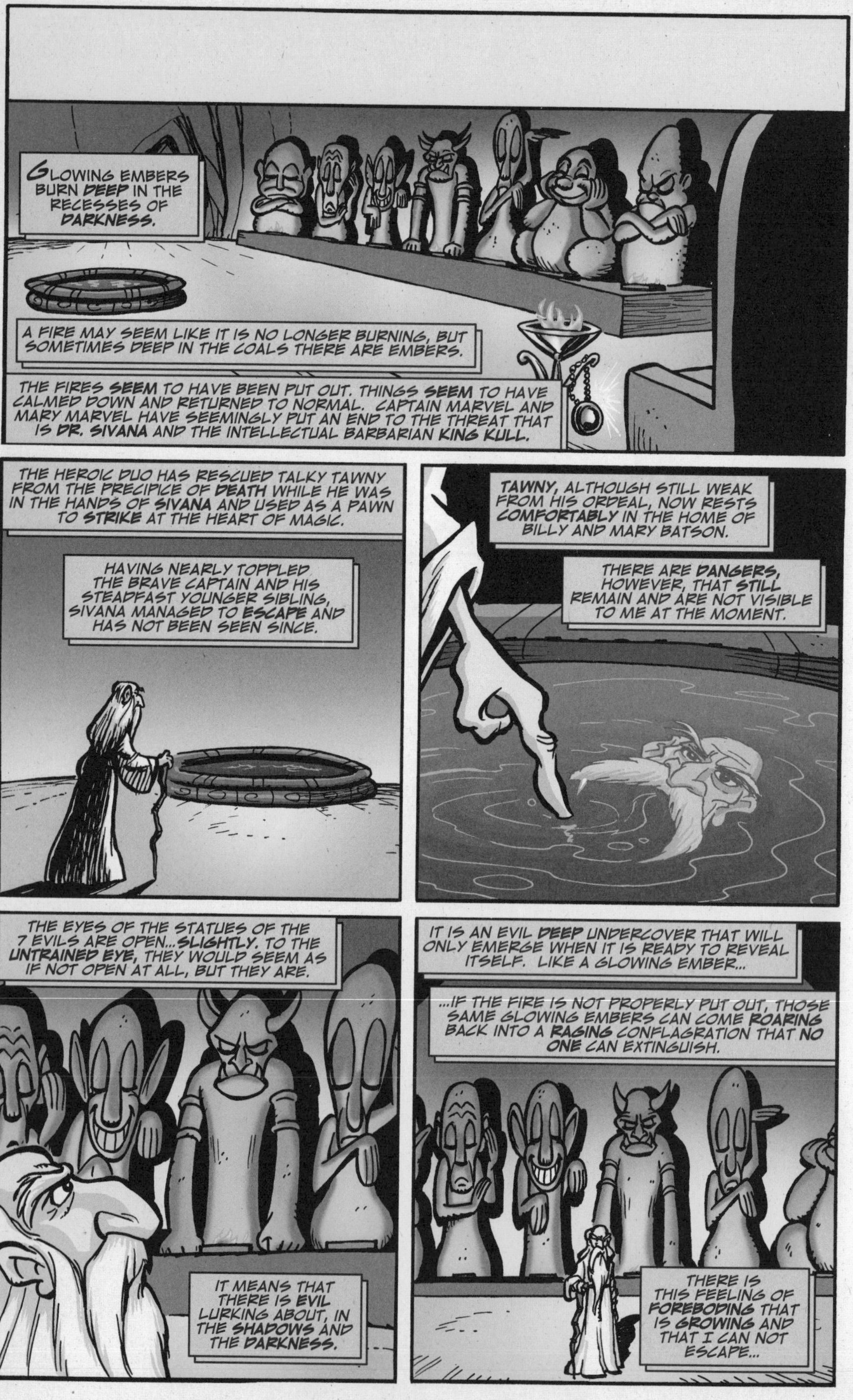
GLOWING EMBERS BURN DEEP IN THE RECESSES OF DARKNESS.
A FIRE MAY SEEM LIKE IT IS NO LONGER BURNING, BUT SOMETIMES DEEP IN THE COALS THERE ARE EMBERS.
THE FIRES SEEM TO HAVE BEEN PUT OUT. THINGS SEEM TO HAVE CALMED DOWN AND RETURNED TO NORMAL. CAPTAIN MARVEL AND MARY MARVEL HAVE SEEMINGLY PUT AN END TO THE THREAT THAT IS DR. SIVANA AND THE INTELLECTUAL BARBARIAN KING KULL.
THE HEROIC DUO HAS RESCUED TALKY TAWNY FROM THE PRECIPICE OF DEATH WHILE HE WAS IN THE HANDS OF SIVANA AND USED AS A PAWN TO STRIKE AT THE HEART OF MAGIC.
HAVING NEARLY TOPPLED THE BRAVE CAPTAIN AND HIS STEADFAST YOUNGER SIBLING, SIVANA MANAGED TO ESCAPE AND HAS NOT BEEN SEEN SINCE.
TAWNY, ALTHOUGH STILL WEAK FROM HIS ORDEAL, NOW RESTS COMFORTABLY IN THE HOME OF BILLY AND MARY BATSON.
THERE ARE DANGERS, HOWEVER, THAT STILL REMAIN AND ARE NOT VISIBLE TO ME AT THE MOMENT.
THE EYES OF THE STATUES OF THE 7 EVILS ARE OPEN...SLIGHTLY. TO THE UNTRAINED EYE, THEY WOULD SEEM AS IF NOT OPEN AT ALL, BUT THEY ARE.
IT MEANS THAT THERE IS EVIL LURKING ABOUT, IN THE SHADOWS AND THE DARKNESS.
IT IS AN EVIL DEEP UNDERCOVER THAT WILL ONLY EMERGE WHEN IT IS READY TO REVEAL ITSELF. LIKE A GLOWING EMBER...
...IF THE FIRE IS NOT PROPERLY PUT OUT, THOSE SAME GLOWING EMBERS CAN COME ROARING BACK INTO A RAGING CONFLAGRATION THAT NO ONE CAN EXTINGUISH.
THERE IS THIS FEELING OF FOREBODING THAT IS GROWING AND THAT I CAN NOT ESCAPE...

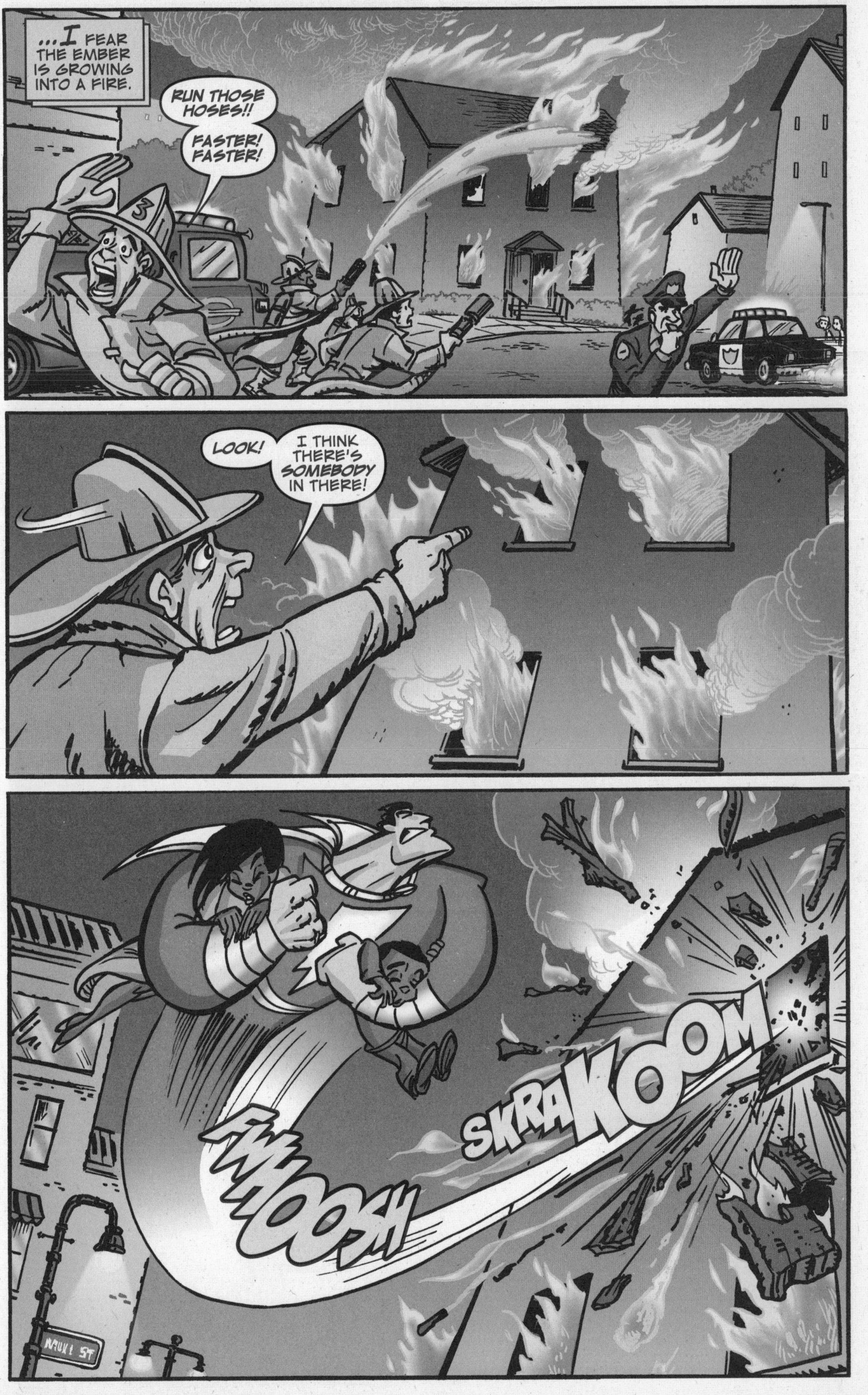
...I FEAR THE EMBER IS GROWING INTO A FIRE.
RUN THOSE HOSES!!
FASTER! FASTER!
LOOK!
I THINK THERE'S SOMEBODY IN THERE!
FWOOOSH
SKRAKOOOM

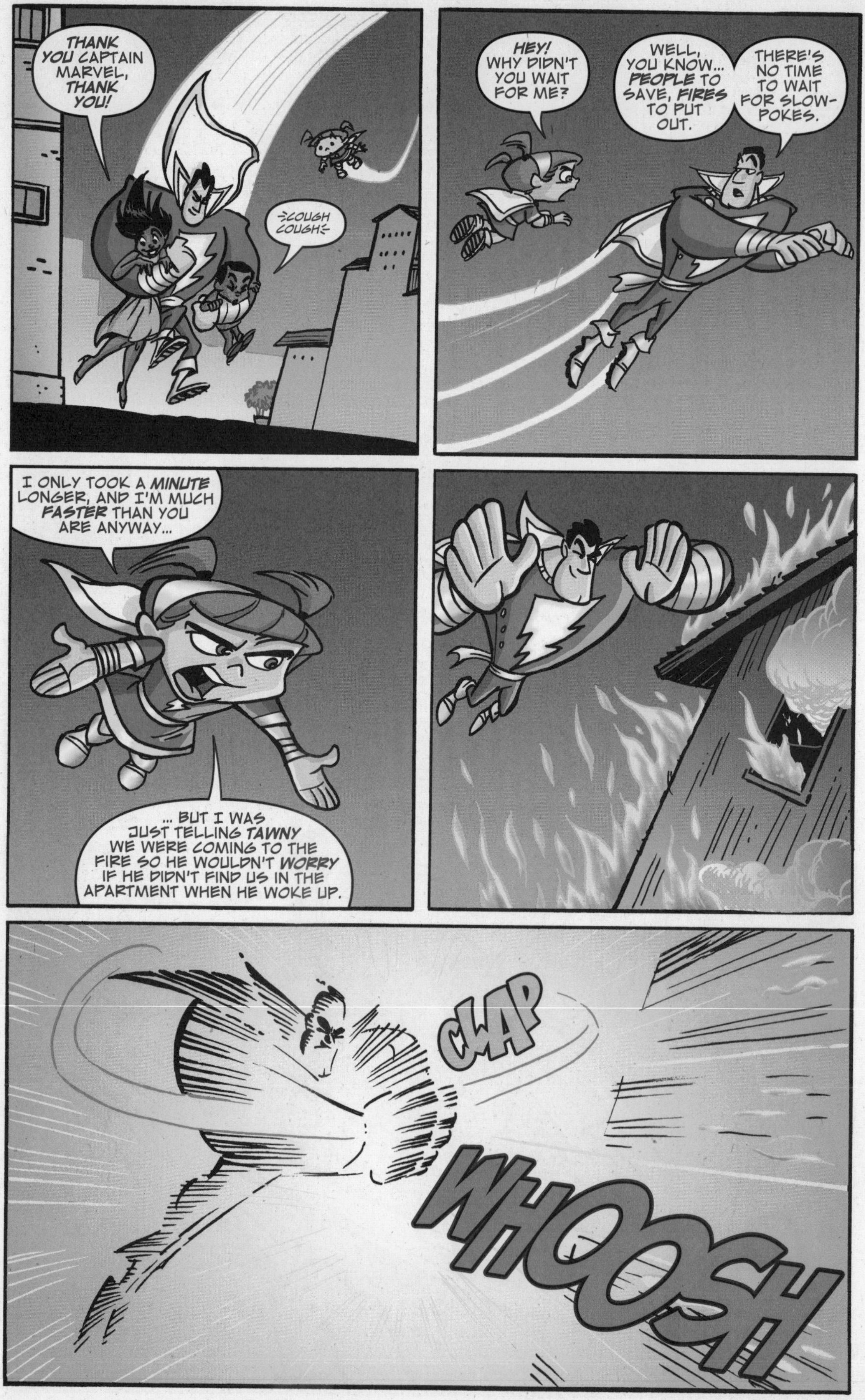
THANK YOU CAPTAIN MARVEL, THANK YOU!
COUGH COUGH
HEY! WHY DIDN'T YOU WAIT FOR ME?
WELL, YOU KNOW... PEOPLE TO SAVE, FIRES TO PUT OUT.
THERE'S NO TIME TO WAIT FOR SLOW-POKES.
I ONLY TOOK A MINUTE LONGER, AND I'M MUCH FASTER THAN YOU ARE ANYWAY...
... BUT I WAS JUST TELLING TAWNY WE WERE COMING TO THE FIRE SO HE WOULDN'T WORRY IF HE DIDN'T FIND US IN THE APARTMENT WHEN HE WOKE UP.
CLAP
WHOOSH

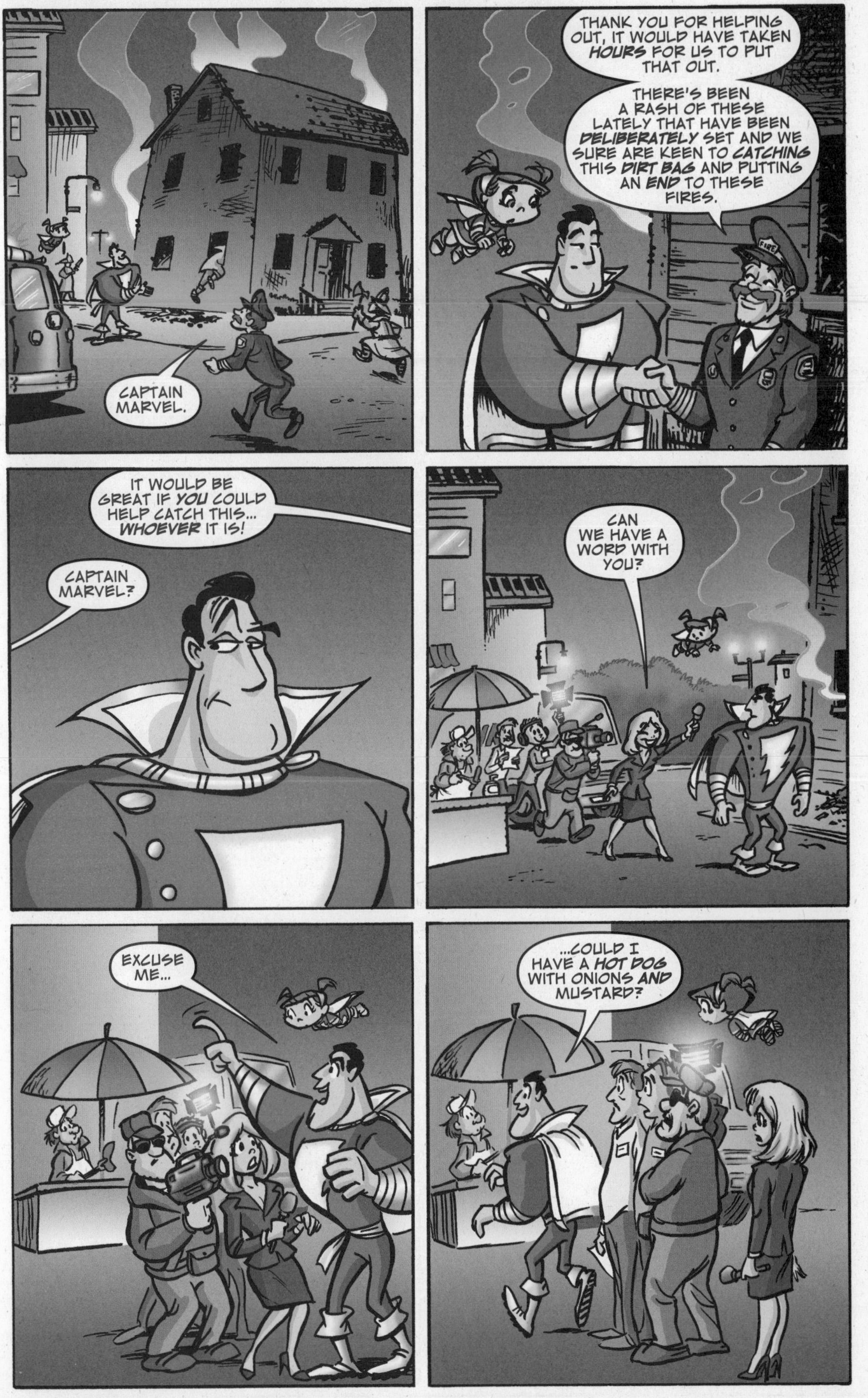
CAPTAIN MARVEL.
THANK YOU FOR HELPING OUT, IT WOULD HAVE TAKEN HOURS FOR US TO PUT THAT OUT.
THERE'S BEEN A RASH OF THESE LATELY THAT HAVE BEEN DELIBERATELY SET AND WE SURE ARE KEEN TO CATCHING THIS DIRT BAG AND PUTTING AN END TO THESE FIRES.
IT WOULD BE GREAT IF YOU COULD HELP CATCH THIS... WHOEVER IT IS!
CAPTAIN MARVEL?
CAN WE HAVE A WORD WITH YOU?
EXCUSE ME...
...COULD I HAVE A HOT DOG WITH ONIONS AND MUSTARD?
FIRE

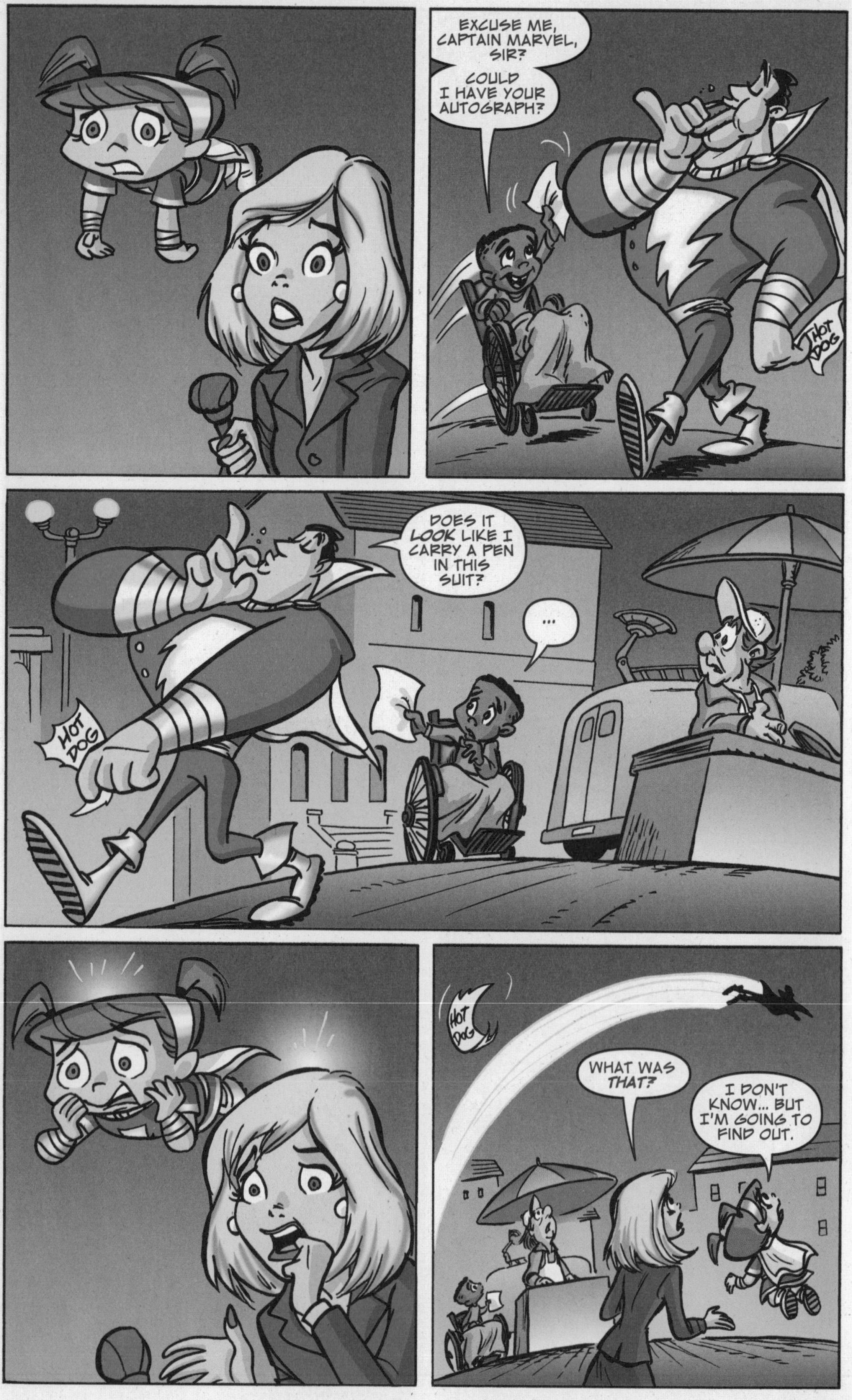
EXCUSE ME, CAPTAIN MARVEL, SIR?
COULD I HAVE YOUR AUTOGRAPH?
HOT DOG
DOES IT LOOK LIKE I CARRY A PEN IN THIS SUIT?
...
HOT DOG
HOT DOG
WHAT WAS THAT?
I DON'T KNOW... BUT I'M GOING TO FIND OUT.

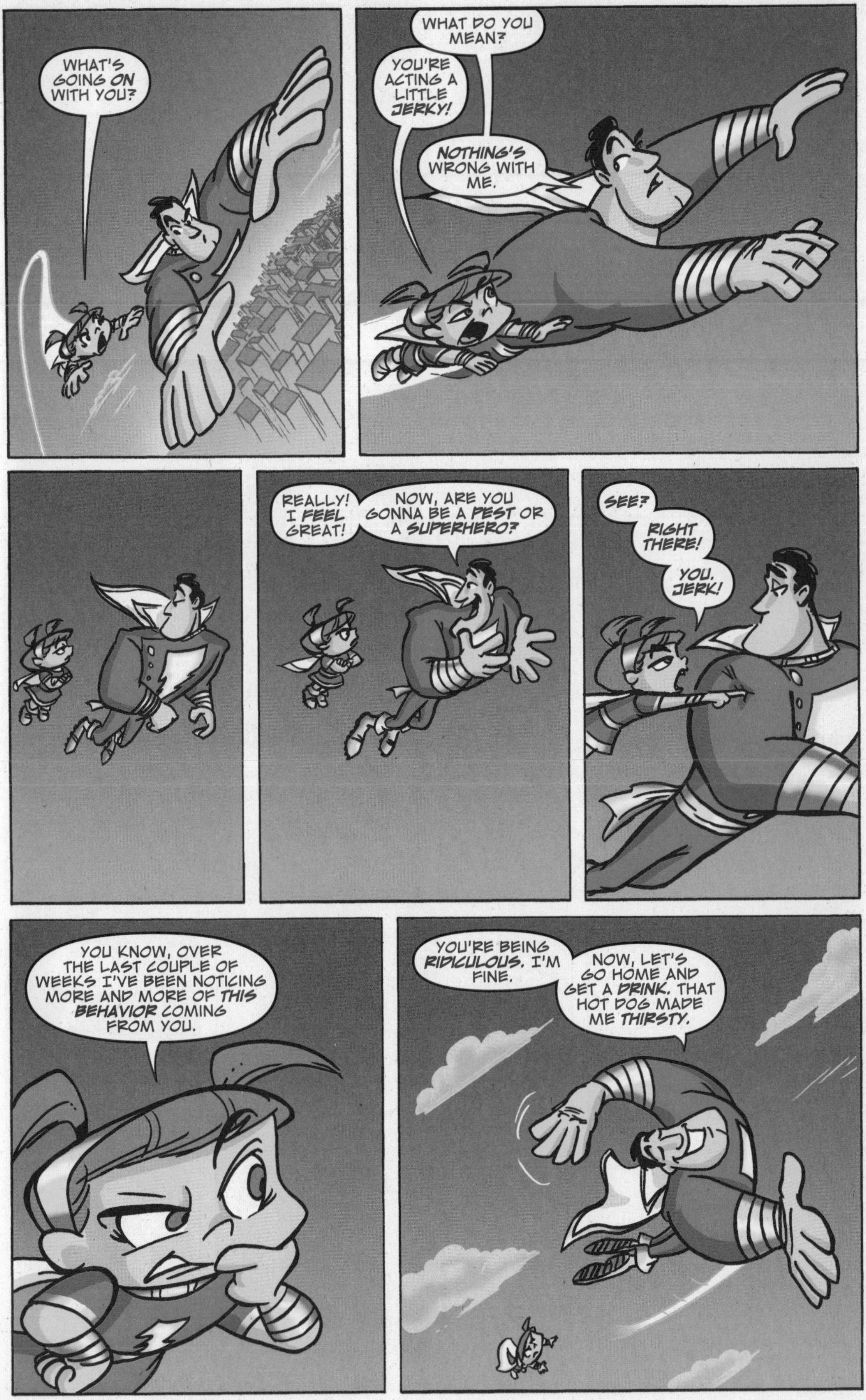
WHAT'S GOING ON WITH YOU?
WHAT DO YOU MEAN?
YOU'RE ACTING A LITTLE JERKY!
NOTHING'S WRONG WITH ME.
REALLY! I FEEL GREAT!
NOW, ARE YOU GONNA BE A PEST OR A SUPERHERO?
SEE?
RIGHT THERE!
YOU. JERK!
YOU KNOW, OVER THE LAST COUPLE OF WEEKS I'VE BEEN NOTICING MORE AND MORE OF THIS BEHAVIOR COMING FROM YOU.
YOU'RE BEING RIDICULOUS. I'M FINE.
NOW, LET'S GO HOME AND GET A DRINK. THAT HOT DOG MADE ME THIRSTY.

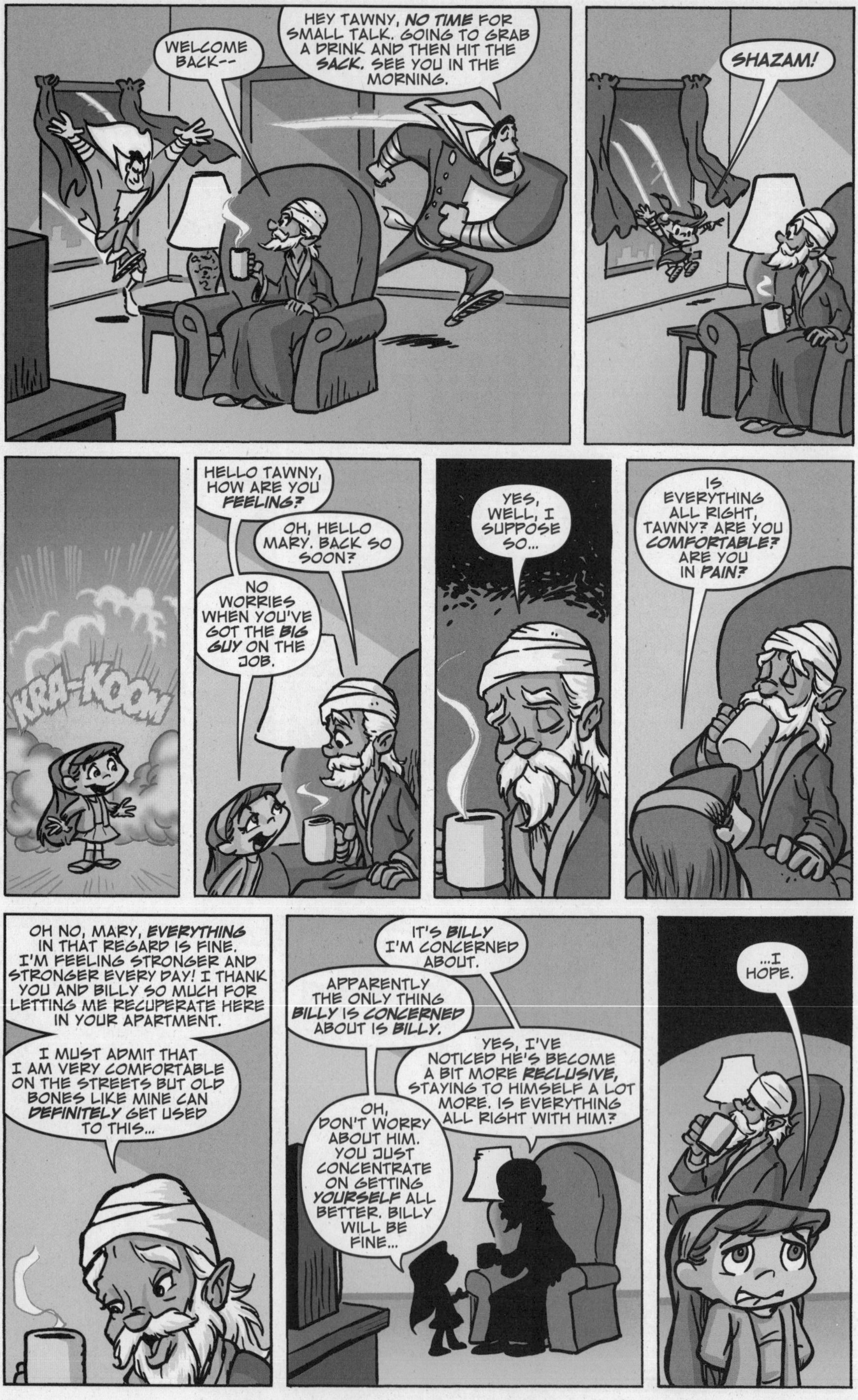
WELCOME BACK--
HEY TAWNY, NO TIME FOR SMALL TALK. GOING TO GRAB A DRINK AND THEN HIT THE SACK. SEE YOU IN THE MORNING.
SHAZAM!
KRA-KOOM
HELLO TAWNY, HOW ARE YOU FEELING?
OH, HELLO MARY. BACK SO SOON?
NO WORRIES WHEN YOU'VE GOT THE BIG GUY ON THE JOB.
YES, WELL, I SUPPOSE SO...
IS EVERYTHING ALL RIGHT, TAWNY? ARE YOU COMFORTABLE? ARE YOU IN PAIN?
OH NO, MARY, EVERYTHING IN THAT REGARD IS FINE. I'M FEELING STRONGER AND STRONGER EVERY DAY! I THANK YOU AND BILLY SO MUCH FOR LETTING ME RECUPERATE HERE IN YOUR APARTMENT.
I MUST ADMIT THAT I AM VERY COMFORTABLE ON THE STREETS BUT OLD BONES LIKE MINE CAN DEFINITELY GET USED TO THIS...
IT'S BILLY I'M CONCERNED ABOUT.
APPARENTLY THE ONLY THING BILLY IS CONCERNED ABOUT IS BILLY.
YES, I'VE NOTICED HE'S BECOME A BIT MORE RECLUSIVE, STAYING TO HIMSELF A LOT MORE. IS EVERYTHING ALL RIGHT WITH HIM?
OH, DON'T WORRY ABOUT HIM. YOU JUST CONCENTRATE ON GETTING YOURSELF ALL BETTER. BILLY WILL BE FINE...
...I HOPE.

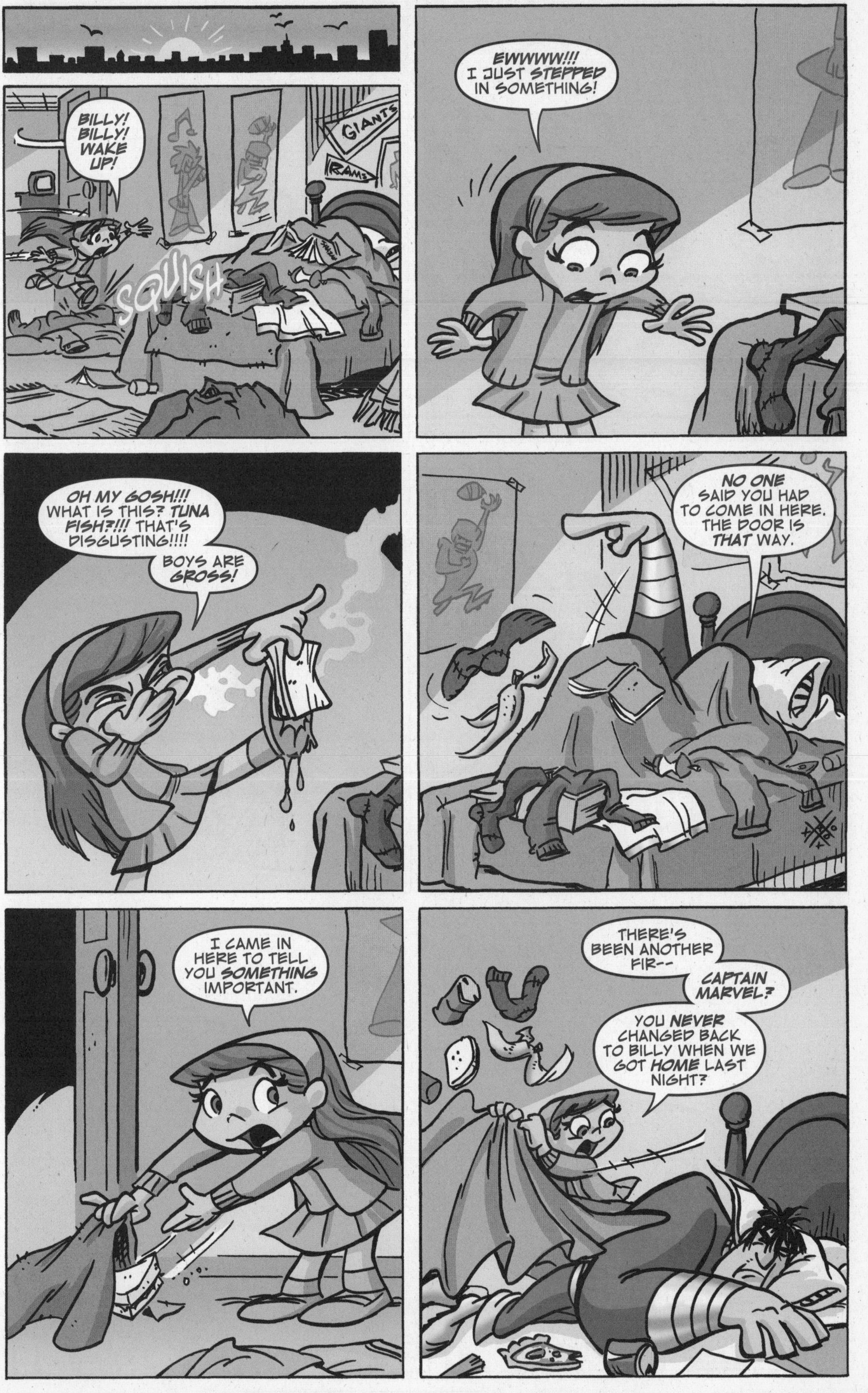
BILLY! BILLY! WAKE UP!
GIANTS
RAMS
SQUISH
EWWWW!!! I JUST STEPPED IN SOMETHING!
OH MY GOSH!!! WHAT IS THIS? TUNA FISH?!!! THAT'S DISGUSTING!!!!
BOYS ARE GROSS!
NO ONE SAID YOU HAD TO COME IN HERE. THE DOOR IS THAT WAY.
I CAME IN HERE TO TELL YOU SOMETHING IMPORTANT.
THERE'S BEEN ANOTHER FIR--
CAPTAIN MARVEL?
YOU NEVER CHANGED BACK TO BILLY WHEN WE GOT HOME LAST NIGHT?

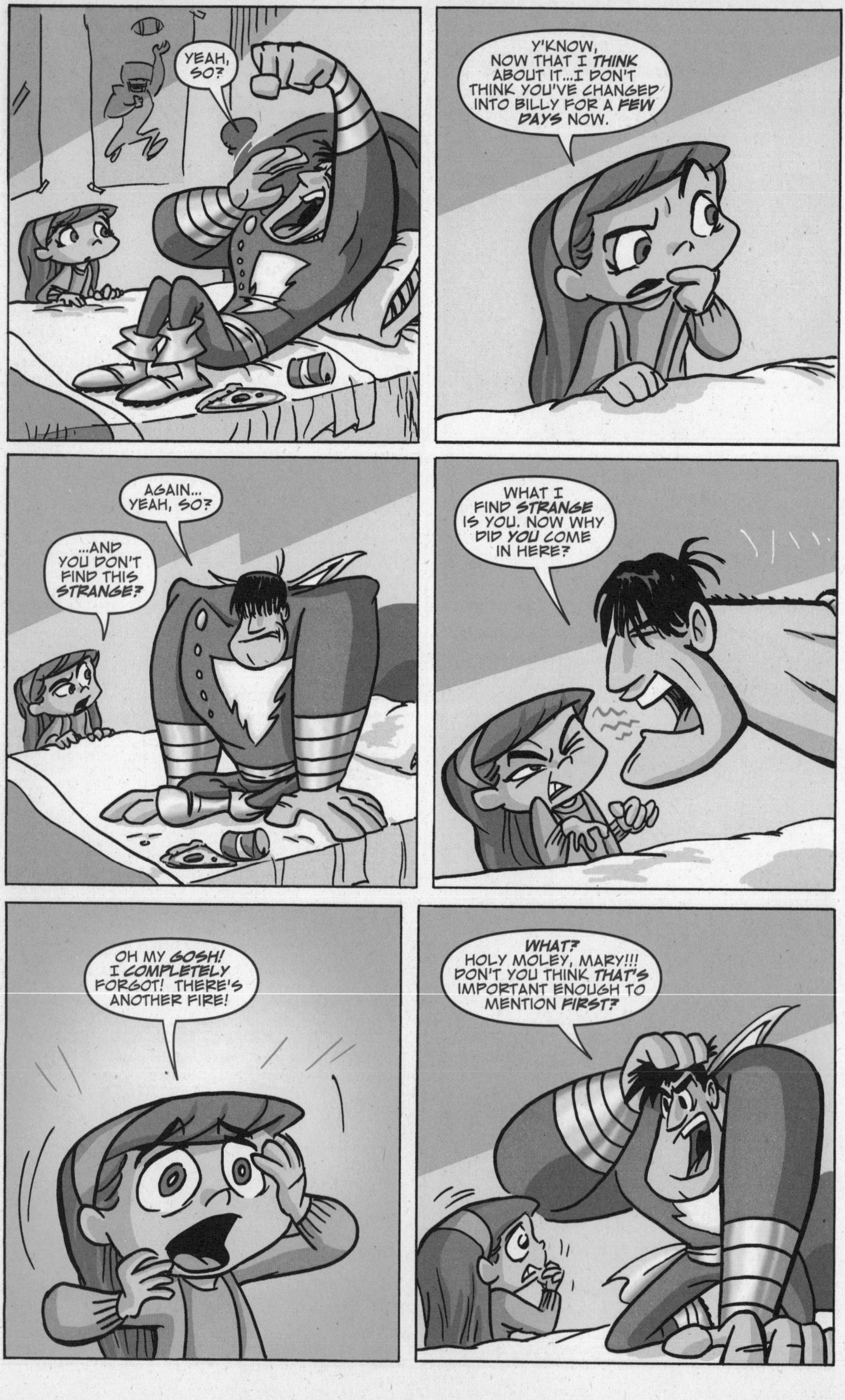
YEAH, SO?
Y'KNOW, NOW THAT I THINK ABOUT IT...I DON'T THINK YOU'VE CHANGED INTO BILLY FOR A FEW DAYS NOW.
...AND YOU DON'T FIND THIS STRANGE?
AGAIN... YEAH, SO?
WHAT I FIND STRANGE IS YOU. NOW WHY DID YOU COME IN HERE?
OH MY GOSH! I COMPLETELY FORGOT! THERE'S ANOTHER FIRE!
WHAT? HOLY MOLEY, MARY!!! DON'T YOU THINK THAT'S IMPORTANT ENOUGH TO MENTION FIRST?

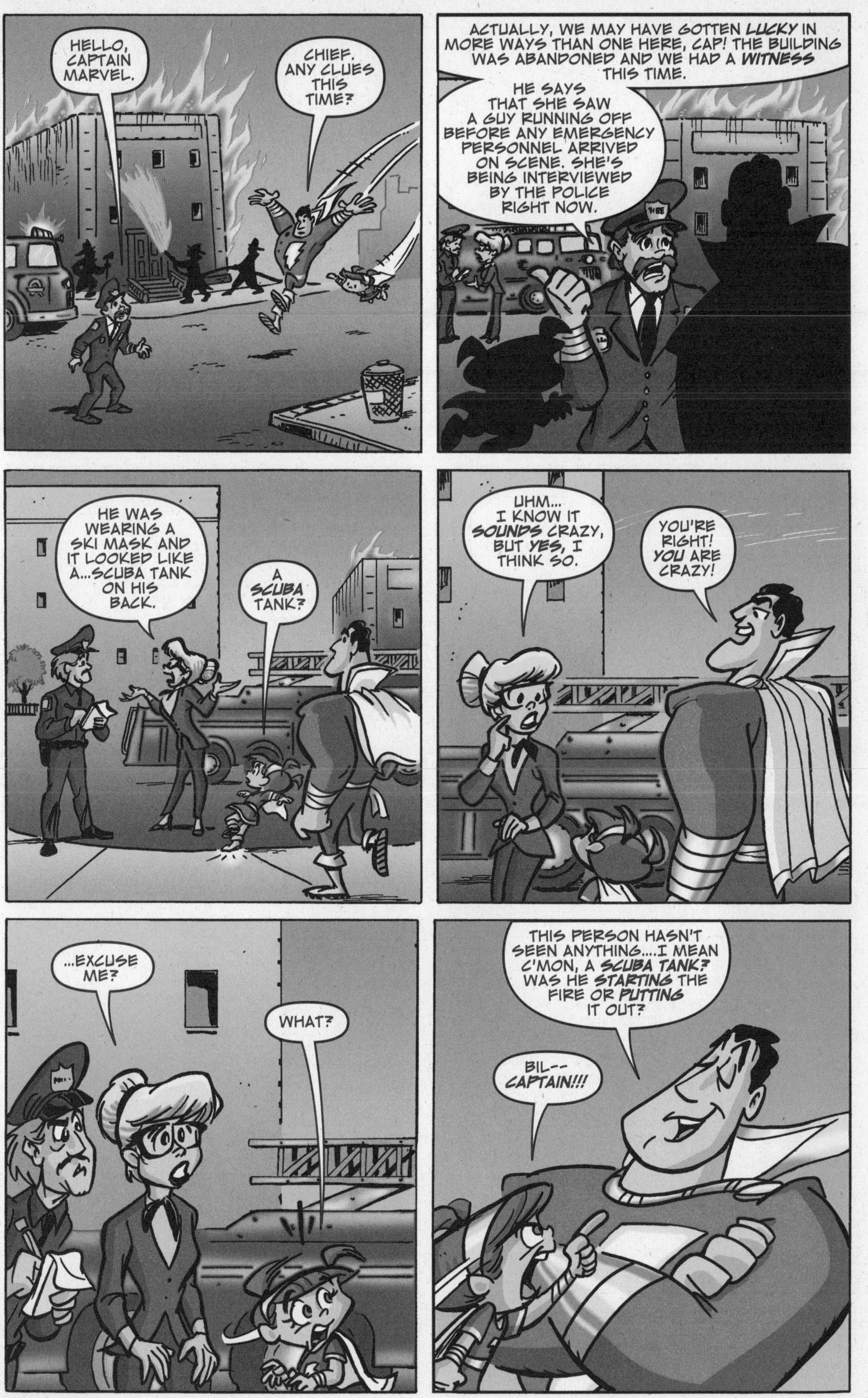
HELLO, CAPTAIN MARVEL.
CHIEF. ANY CLUES THIS TIME?
ACTUALLY, WE MAY HAVE GOTTEN LUCKY IN MORE WAYS THAN ONE HERE, CAP! THE BUILDING WAS ABANDONED AND WE HAD A WITNESS THIS TIME.
HE SAYS THAT SHE SAW A GUY RUNNING OFF BEFORE ANY EMERGENCY PERSONNEL ARRIVED ON SCENE. SHE'S BEING INTERVIEWED BY THE POLICE RIGHT NOW.
HE WAS WEARING A SKI MASK AND IT LOOKED LIKE A...SCUBA TANK ON HIS BACK.
A SCUBA TANK?
UHM... I KNOW IT SOUNDS CRAZY, BUT YES, I THINK SO.
YOU'RE RIGHT! YOU ARE CRAZY!
...EXCUSE ME?
WHAT?
THIS PERSON HASN'T SEEN ANYTHING....I MEAN C'MON, A SCUBA TANK? WAS HE STARTING THE FIRE OR PUTTING IT OUT?
BIL-- CAPTAIN!!!

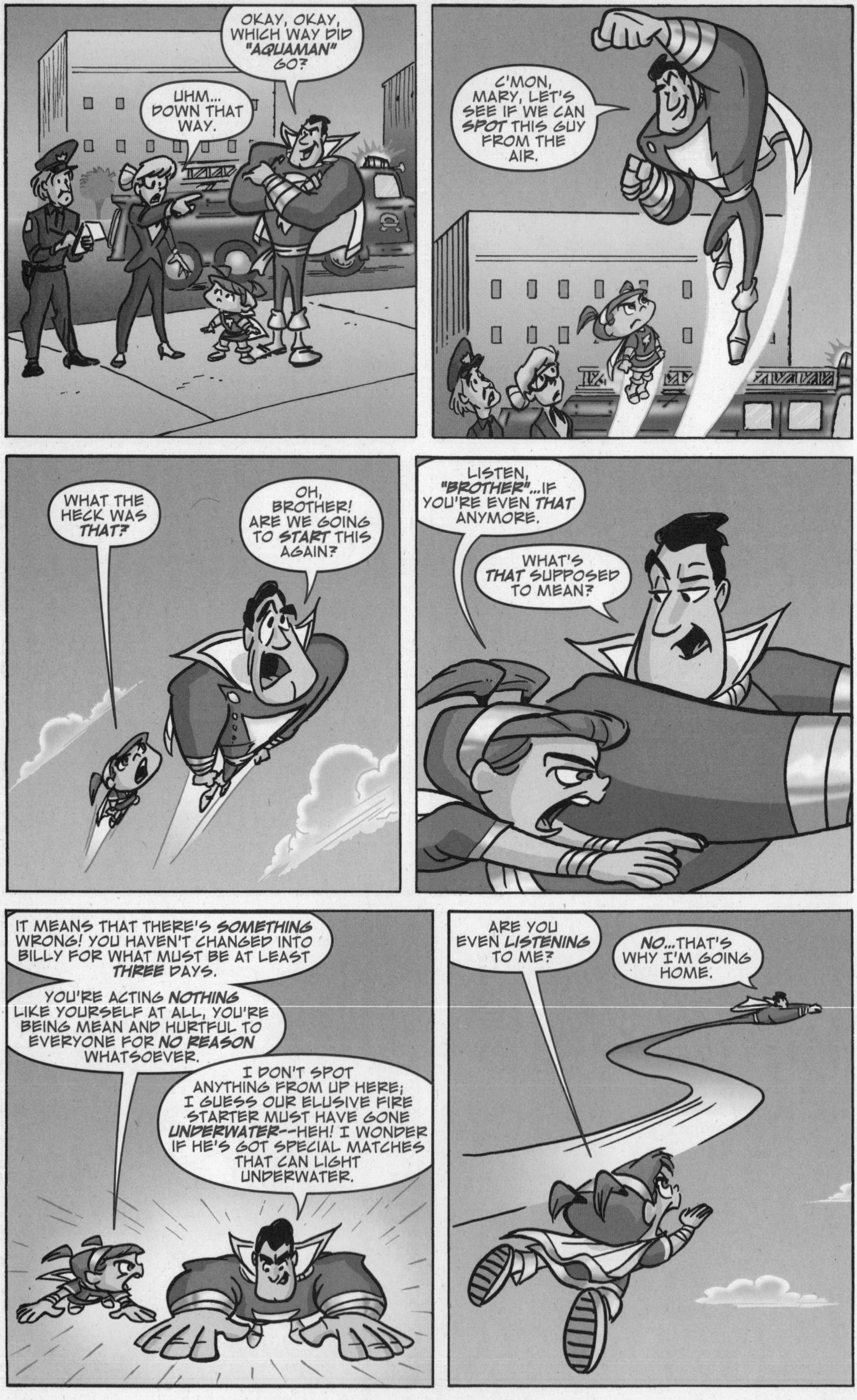
OKAY, OKAY, WHICH WAY DID "AQUAMAN" GO?
UHM... DOWN THAT WAY.
C'MON, MARY, LET'S SEE IF WE CAN SPOT THIS GUY FROM THE AIR.
WHAT THE HECK WAS THAT?
OH, BROTHER! ARE WE GOING TO START THIS AGAIN?
LISTEN, "BROTHER"...IF YOU'RE EVEN THAT ANYMORE.
WHAT'S THAT SUPPOSED TO MEAN?
IT MEANS THAT THERE'S SOMETHING WRONG! YOU HAVEN'T CHANGED INTO BILLY FOR WHAT MUST BE AT LEAST THREE DAYS.
YOU'RE ACTING NOTHING LIKE YOURSELF AT ALL, YOU'RE BEING MEAN AND HURTFUL TO EVERYONE FOR NO REASON WHATSOEVER.
I DON'T SPOT ANYTHING FROM UP HERE; I GUESS OUR ELUSIVE FIRE STARTER MUST HAVE GONE UNDERWATER--HEH! I WONDER IF HE'S GOT SPECIAL MATCHES THAT CAN LIGHT UNDERWATER.
ARE YOU EVEN LISTENING TO ME?
NO...THAT'S WHY I'M GOING HOME.

SO--ANY *LUCK* WITH THIS "ARSON FIEND"?

¿Burp¿ NAH... APPARENTLY HE MUST BE HIDING IN HIS SECRET *UNDERWATER LAIR.*

ISN'T THAT *RIGHT,* MARY?

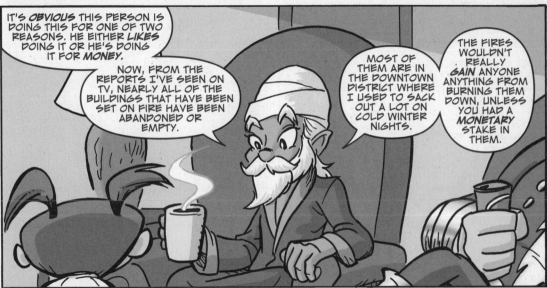

IT'S *OBVIOUS* THIS PERSON IS DOING THIS FOR ONE OF TWO REASONS. HE EITHER *LIKES* DOING IT OR HE'S DOING IT FOR *MONEY.*

NOW, FROM THE REPORTS I'VE SEEN ON TV, NEARLY ALL OF THE BUILDINGS THAT HAVE BEEN SET ON FIRE HAVE BEEN ABANDONED OR EMPTY.

MOST OF THEM ARE IN THE DOWNTOWN DISTRICT WHERE I USED TO SACK OUT A LOT ON COLD WINTER NIGHTS.

THE FIRES WOULDN'T REALLY *GAIN* ANYONE ANYTHING FROM BURNING THEM DOWN, UNLESS YOU HAD A *MONETARY* STAKE IN THEM.

SO?

I WOULD CONCENTRATE MY EFFORTS THERE... FIGHT FIRE WITH FIRE, SO TO SPEAK.

FIRE WITH FIRE? HA HA! THAT'S *RIDICULOUS!* YOU'RE ALMOST AS BAD AS THAT *LADY* THAT SAID THE GUY WAS WEARING A SCUBA TANK!

BILLY!

I. AM. NOT. BILLY!
...TAWNY WAS JUST TRYING TO HELP.
MAYBE IF YOU JUST CHANGE INTO BILLY...
THIS IS RIDICULOUS! THERE'S NOTHING WRONG WITH ME! PEOPLE THINK THEY KNOW WHAT'S BEST AND HOW TO CATCH THIS GUY, BUT YOU KNOW WHAT? I KNOW WHAT'S BEST!
AND THE BEST THING FOR ME IS TO BE ME AND THAT'S CAPTAIN MARVEL!
WHOOSH
TAWNY, I...I'M WORRIED.
GO. FIND HIM.
CONCENTRATE YOUR SEARCH DOWNTOWN!

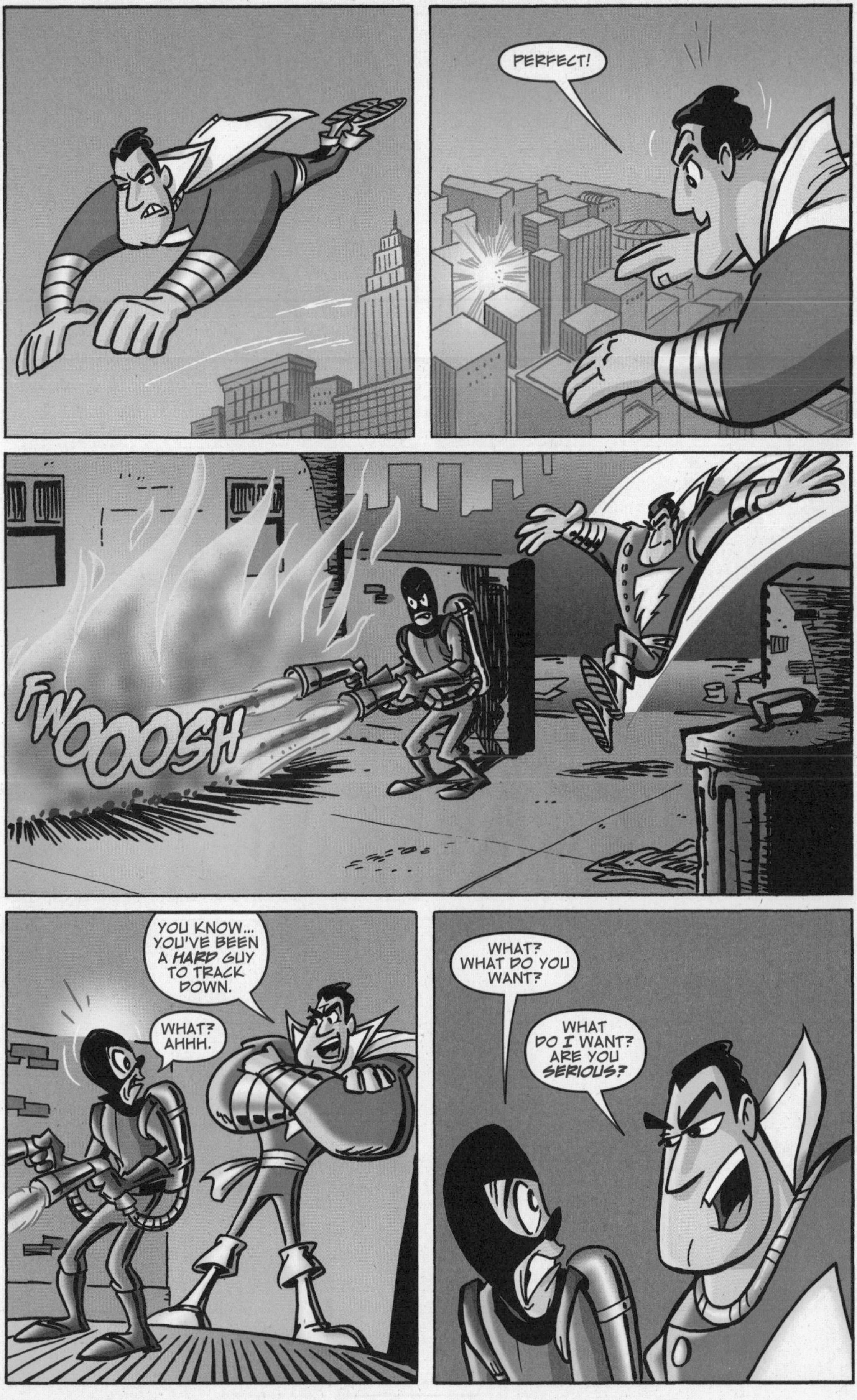
PERFECT!
FWOOOSH
YOU KNOW... YOU'VE BEEN A HARD GUY TO TRACK DOWN.
WHAT? AHHH.
WHAT? WHAT DO YOU WANT?
WHAT DO I WANT? ARE YOU SERIOUS?

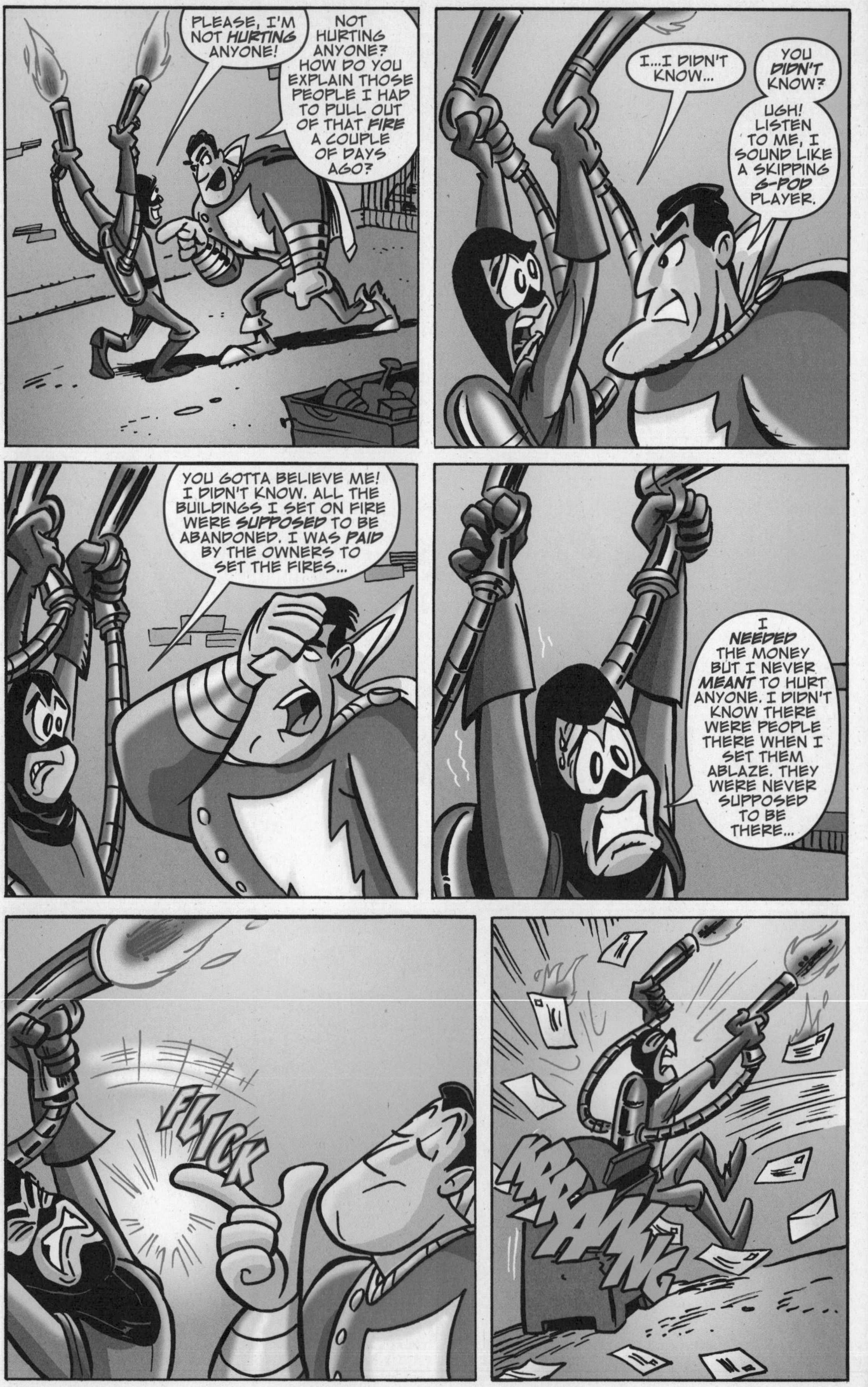
PLEASE, I'M NOT HURTING ANYONE!
NOT HURTING ANYONE? HOW DO YOU EXPLAIN THOSE PEOPLE I HAD TO PULL OUT OF THAT FIRE A COUPLE OF DAYS AGO?
I...I DIDN'T KNOW...
YOU DIDN'T KNOW?
UGH! LISTEN TO ME, I SOUND LIKE A SKIPPING G-POD PLAYER.
YOU GOTTA BELIEVE ME! I DIDN'T KNOW. ALL THE BUILDINGS I SET ON FIRE WERE SUPPOSED TO BE ABANDONED. I WAS PAID BY THE OWNERS TO SET THE FIRES...
I NEEDED THE MONEY BUT I NEVER MEANT TO HURT ANYONE. I DIDN'T KNOW THERE WERE PEOPLE THERE WHEN I SET THEM ABLAZE. THEY WERE NEVER SUPPOSED TO BE THERE...
FLICK
KRRANNG

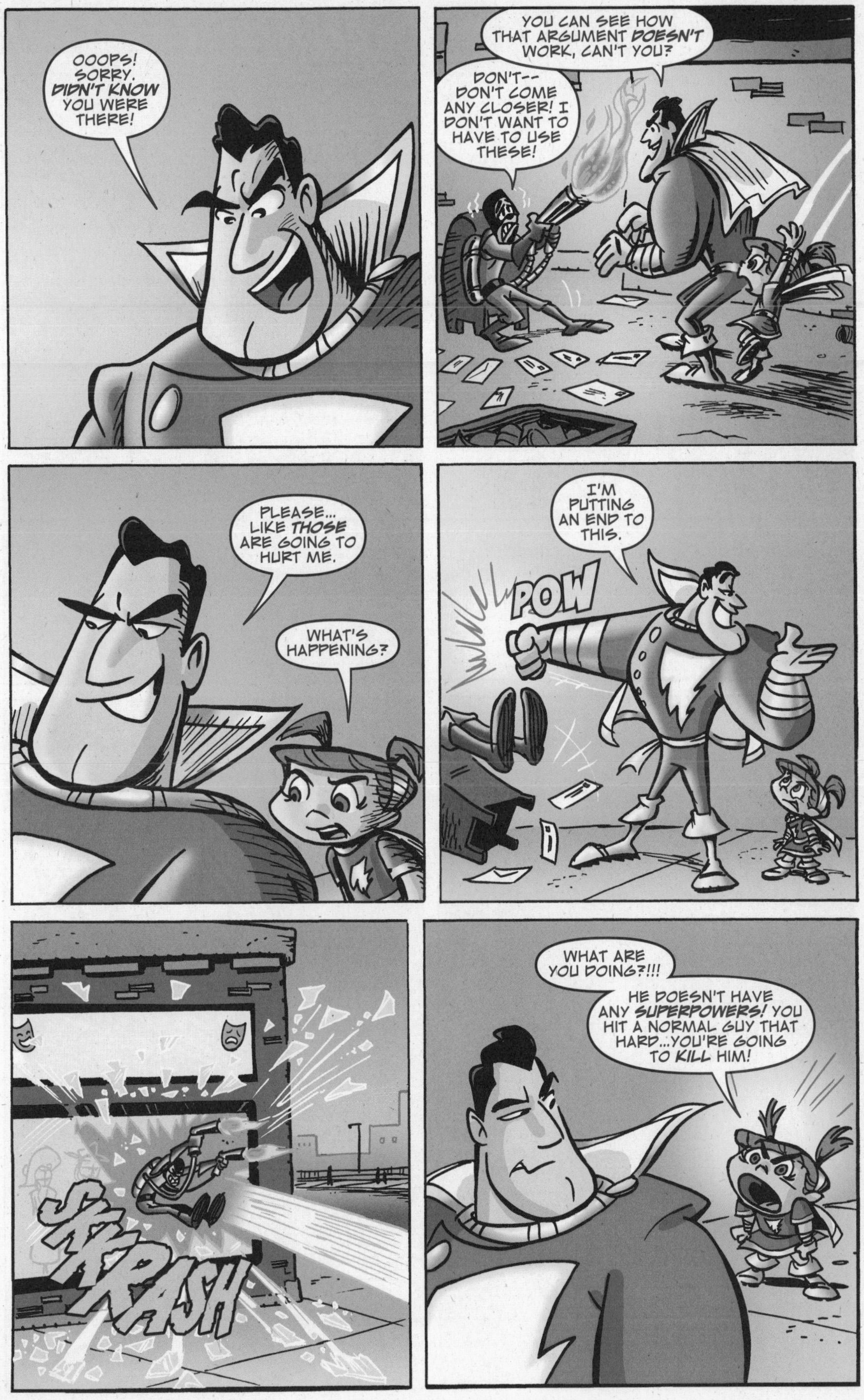

OOOPS! SORRY. DIDN'T KNOW YOU WERE THERE!
YOU CAN SEE HOW THAT ARGUMENT DOESN'T WORK, CAN'T YOU?
DON'T-- DON'T COME ANY CLOSER! I DON'T WANT TO HAVE TO USE THESE!
PLEASE... LIKE THOSE ARE GOING TO HURT ME.
WHAT'S HAPPENING?
I'M PUTTING AN END TO THIS.
POW
SKRASH
WHAT ARE YOU DOING?!!!
HE DOESN'T HAVE ANY SUPERPOWERS! YOU HIT A NORMAL GUY THAT HARD...YOU'RE GOING TO KILL HIM!

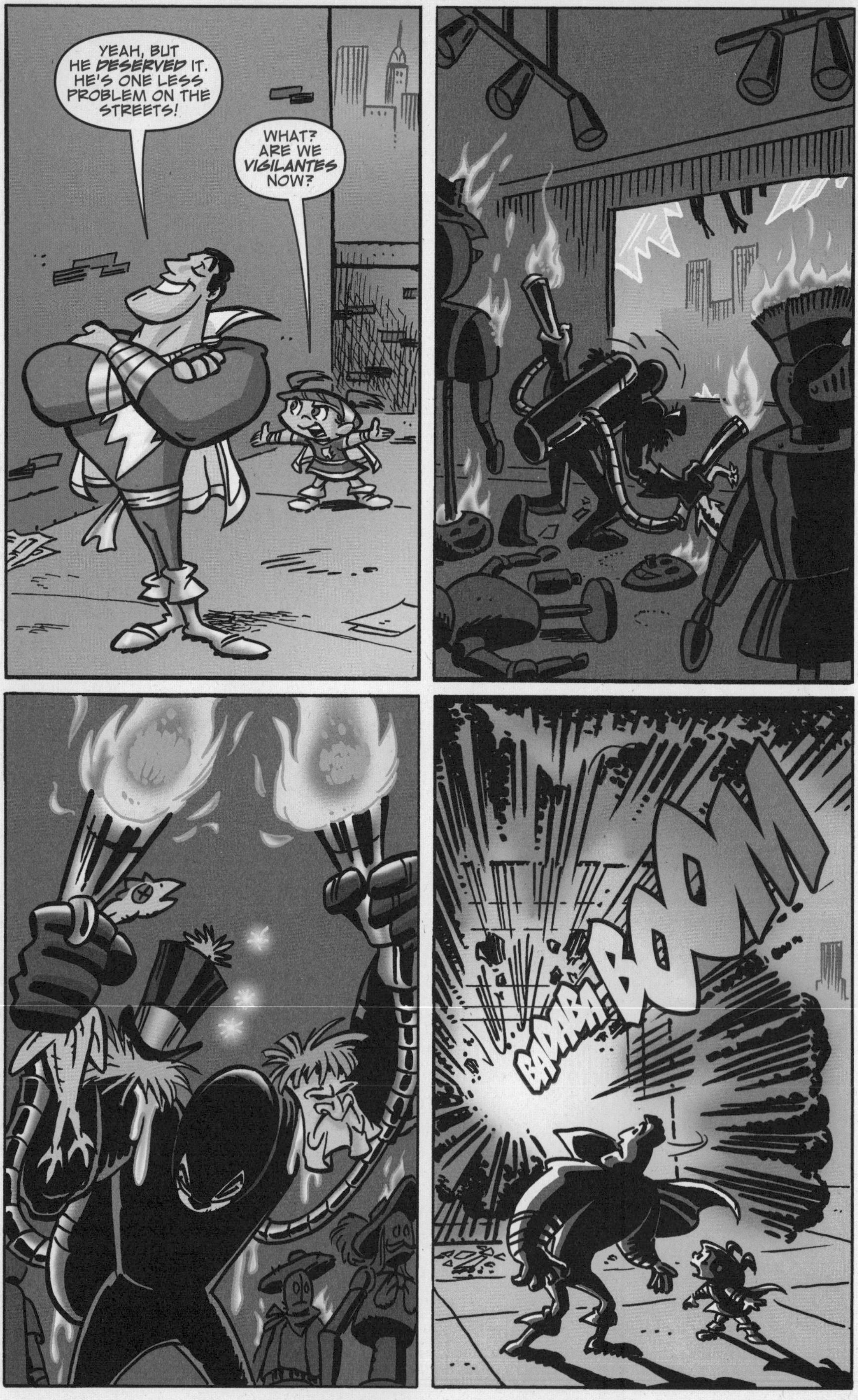
YEAH, BUT HE DESERVED IT. HE'S ONE LESS PROBLEM ON THE STREETS!
WHAT? ARE WE VIGILANTES NOW?
BADABA BOOM!

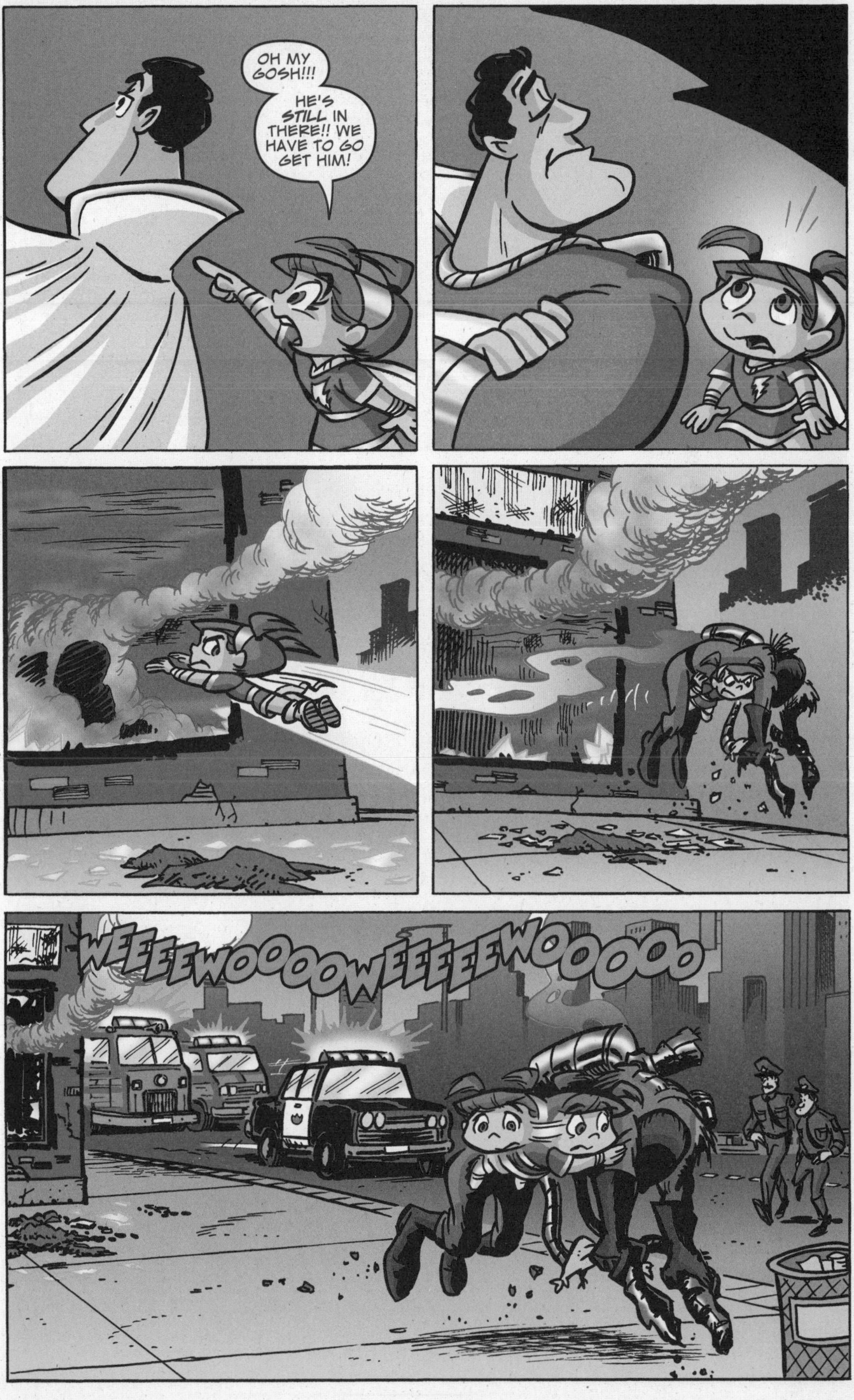
OH MY GOSH!!!
HE'S STILL IN THERE!! WE HAVE TO GO GET HIM!
WEEEEWOOOOOWEEEEEWOOOOO

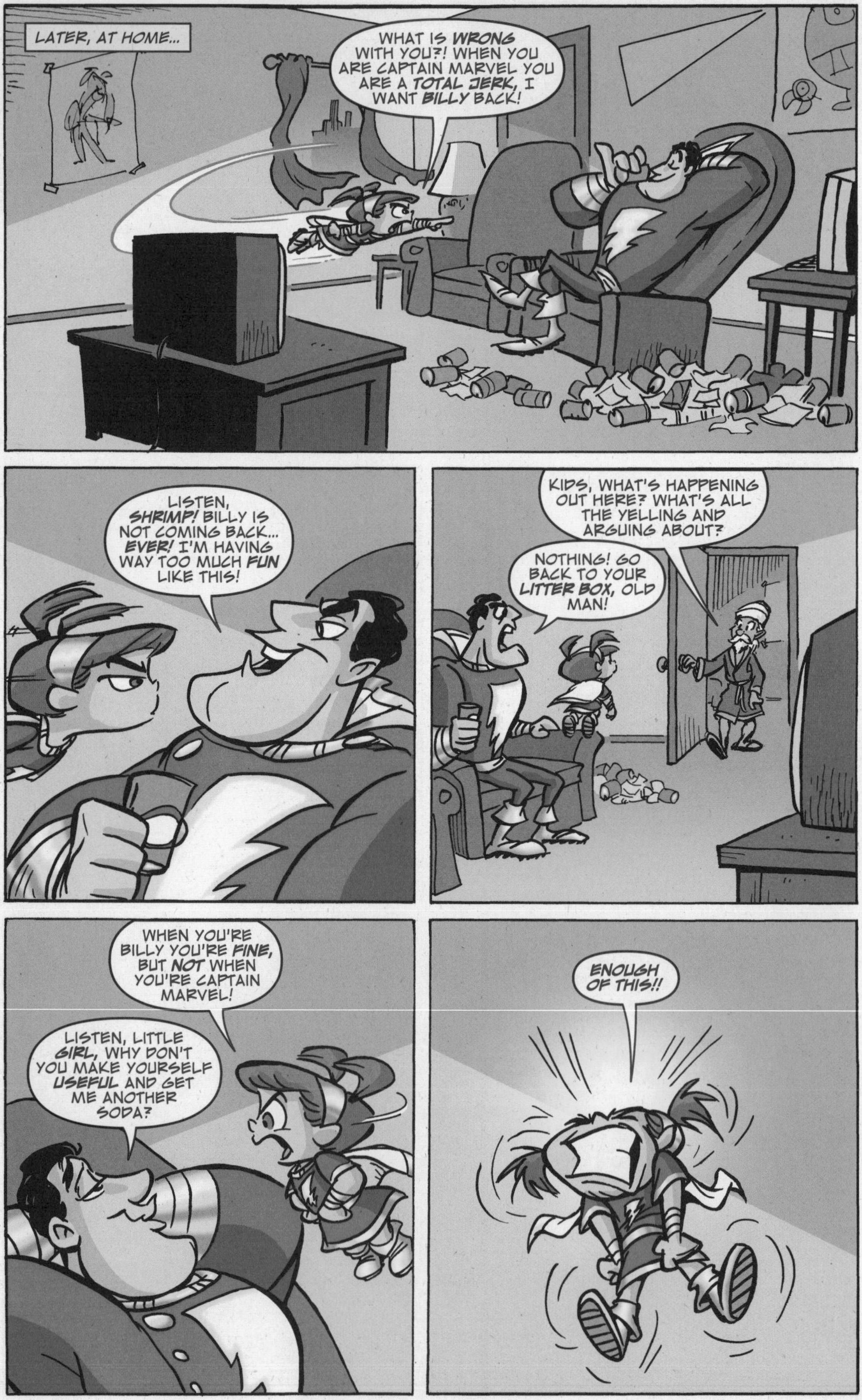
LATER, AT HOME...
WHAT IS WRONG WITH YOU?! WHEN YOU ARE CAPTAIN MARVEL YOU ARE A TOTAL JERK, I WANT BILLY BACK!
LISTEN, SHRIMP! BILLY IS NOT COMING BACK... EVER! I'M HAVING WAY TOO MUCH FUN LIKE THIS!
KIDS, WHAT'S HAPPENING OUT HERE? WHAT'S ALL THE YELLING AND ARGUING ABOUT?
NOTHING! GO BACK TO YOUR LITTER BOX, OLD MAN!
WHEN YOU'RE BILLY YOU'RE FINE, BUT NOT WHEN YOU'RE CAPTAIN MARVEL!
LISTEN, LITTLE GIRL, WHY DON'T YOU MAKE YOURSELF USEFUL AND GET ME ANOTHER SODA?
ENOUGH OF THIS!!

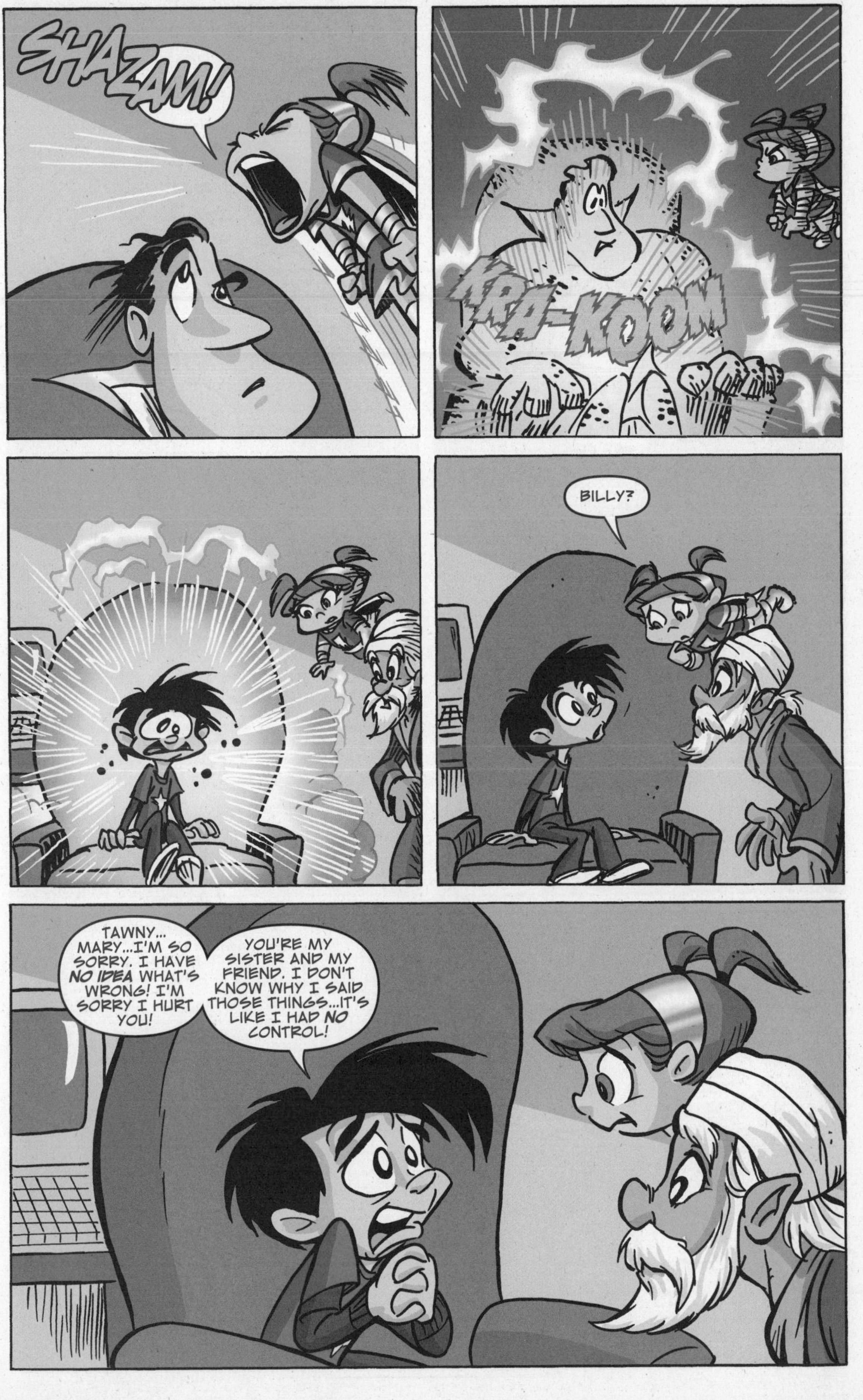
SHAZAM!
KRA-KOOM
BILLY?
TAWNY... MARY...I'M SO SORRY. I HAVE NO IDEA WHAT'S WRONG! I'M SORRY I HURT YOU!
YOU'RE MY SISTER AND MY FRIEND. I DON'T KNOW WHY I SAID THOSE THINGS...IT'S LIKE I HAD NO CONTROL!

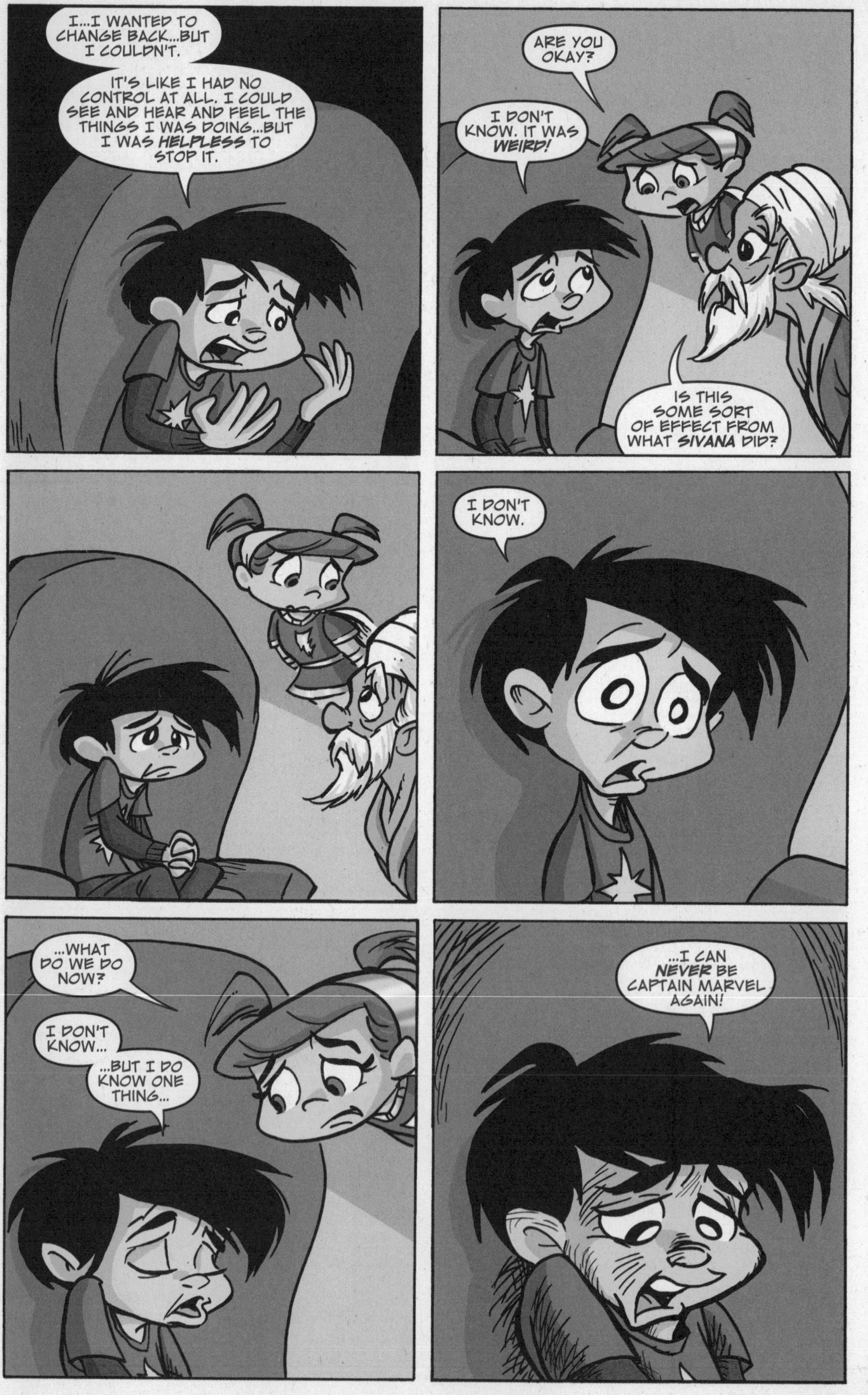
I...I WANTED TO CHANGE BACK...BUT I COULDN'T.
IT'S LIKE I HAD NO CONTROL AT ALL. I COULD SEE AND HEAR AND FEEL THE THINGS I WAS DOING...BUT I WAS HELPLESS TO STOP IT.
ARE YOU OKAY?
I DON'T KNOW. IT WAS WEIRD!
IS THIS SOME SORT OF EFFECT FROM WHAT SIVANA DID?
I DON'T KNOW.
...WHAT DO WE DO NOW?
I DON'T KNOW...
...BUT I DO KNOW ONE THING...
...I CAN NEVER BE CAPTAIN MARVEL AGAIN!

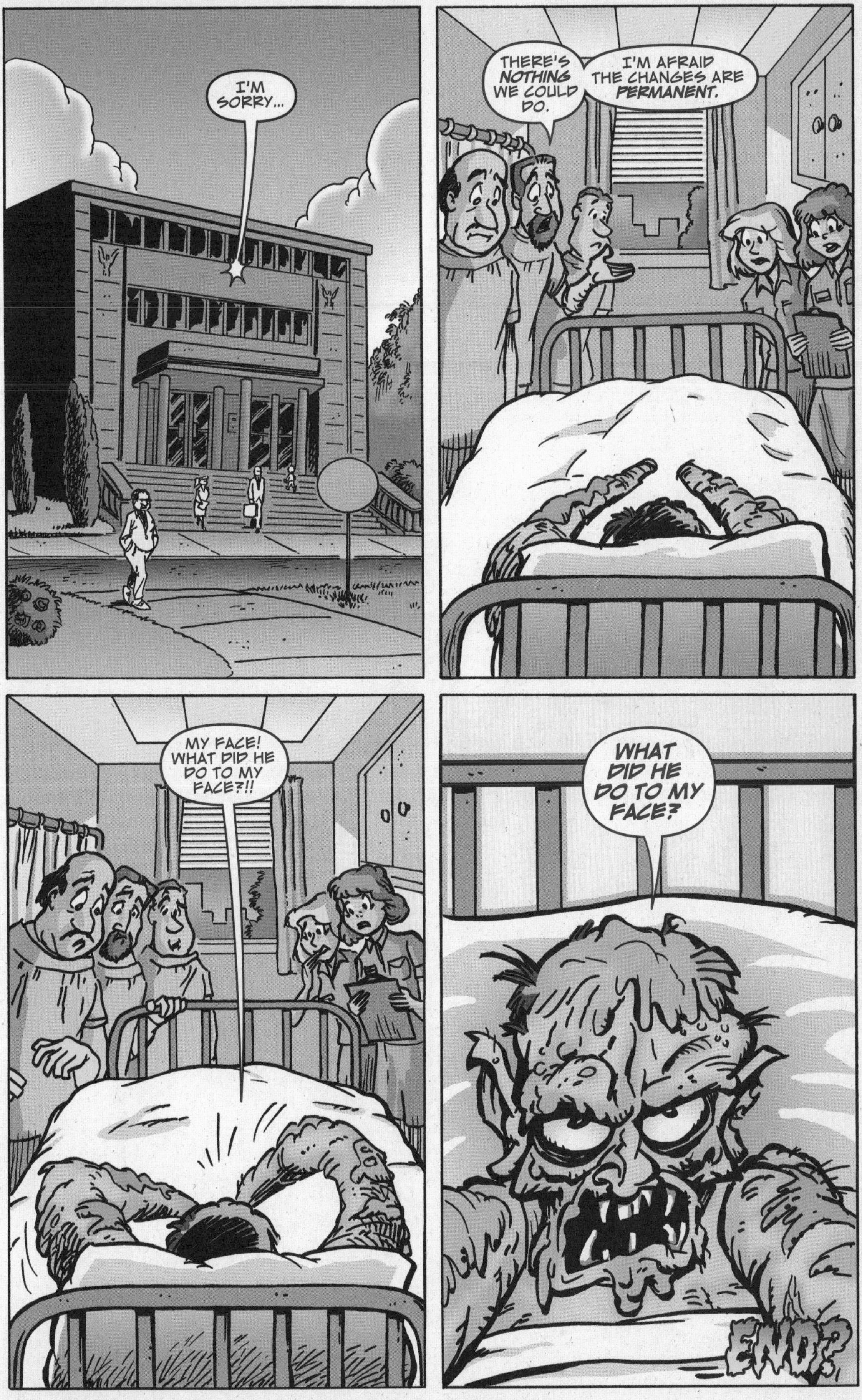
I'M SORRY...
THERE'S NOTHING WE COULD DO.
I'M AFRAID THE CHANGES ARE PERMANENT.
MY FACE! WHAT DID HE DO TO MY FACE?!!
WHAT DID HE DO TO MY FACE?
END?

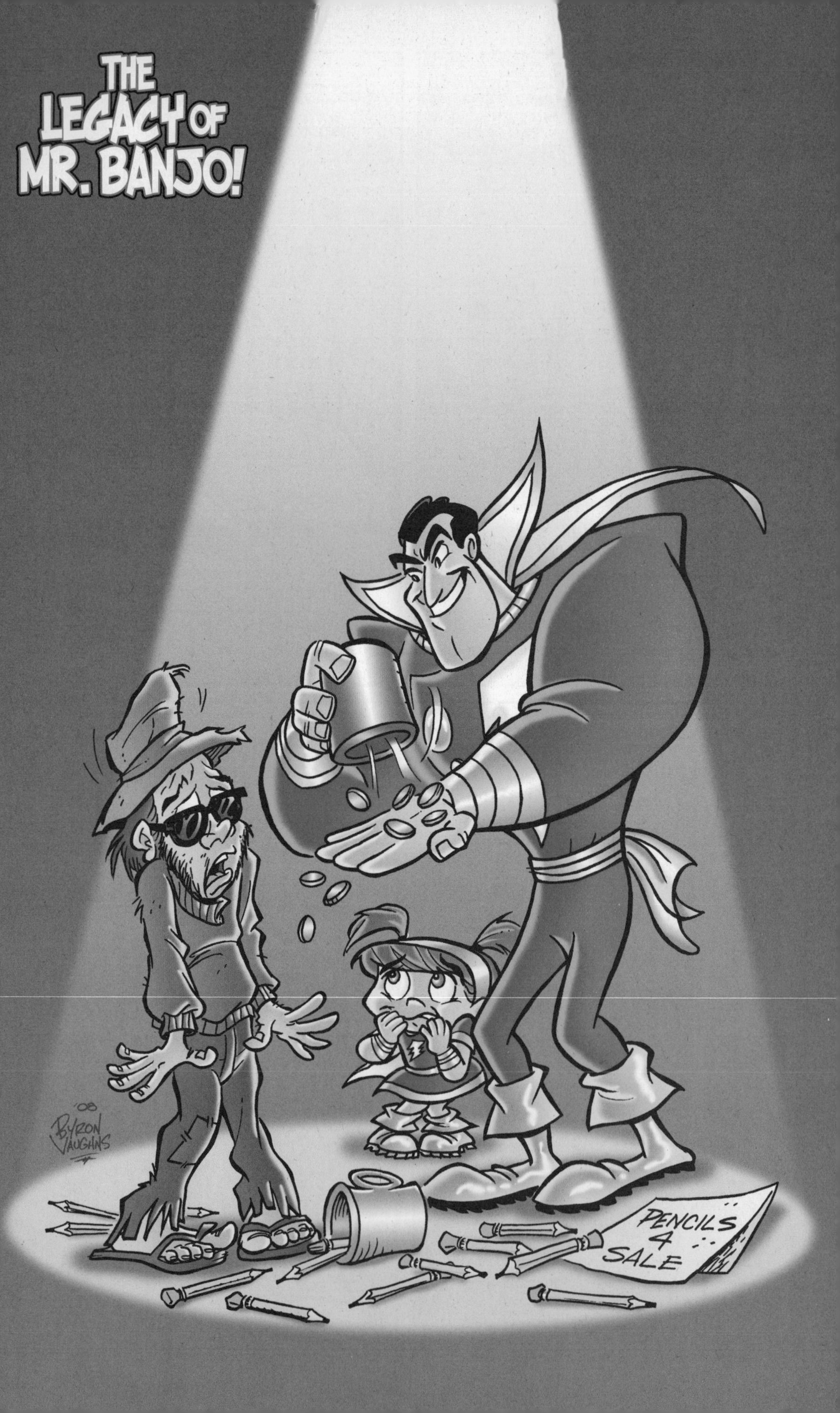
THE LEGACY OF MR. BANJO!
'08 BYRON VAUGHNS
PENCILS 4 SALE

A GUY **COULD** GET USED TO THIS!

BECK & PARKER APARTMENTS

I CAN LIVE ON THE STREETS... ACTUALLY HAVE FOR YEARS, BUT A GUY CAN GET USED TO A **SWEET** CUP OF STEAMING CHOCOLATE **ANYTIME** YOU WANT ONE TO SHAKE OFF THE CHILL IN YOUR BONES.

RECUPERATING HERE HAS BEEN A BLESSING. THE KIDS HAVE BEEN SO GOOD TO ME.

SIVANA REALLY BEAT ALL OF US UP BUT GOOD. I GUESS I GOT A LOT OF THE **PHYSICAL** BEATING UP BUT THE KIDS TOOK A LOT OF THE **EMOTIONAL STUFF.**

HE MANAGED TO FIND OUT WHERE THEY LIVE. HE STOLE THE MAGICAL LIGHTNING TO KICKSTART HIS **MECHANICAL MONSTROSITY** AND THEN USED ME AS A CONDUIT TO FUNNEL THAT ENERGY INTO IT.

SHE'S A SWEET KID.

SHE HAS TOO MUCH **HEART!** WEARS IT ON HER SLEEVE. SHE **CARES** ABOUT BILLY.

IF IT WASN'T FOR HER, BILLY WOULD BE IN A **HEAP** OF TROUBLES RIGHT NOW.

MARY IS THE ONE THAT CONVINCED CAPTAIN MARVEL TO TURN **BACK** INTO BILLY AND HELPED HIM REALIZE THERE WAS SOMETHING WRONG!

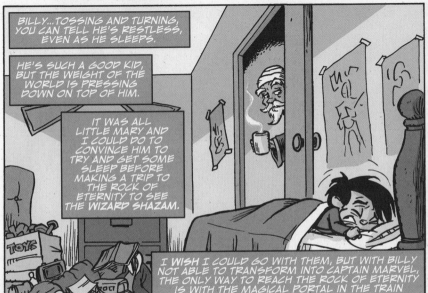

BILLY...TOSSING AND TURNING, YOU CAN TELL HE'S RESTLESS, EVEN AS HE SLEEPS.

HE'S SUCH A GOOD KID, BUT THE WEIGHT OF THE WORLD IS PRESSING DOWN ON TOP OF HIM.

IT WAS ALL LITTLE MARY AND I COULD DO TO CONVINCE HIM TO TRY AND GET SOME SLEEP BEFORE MAKING A TRIP TO THE ROCK OF ETERNITY TO SEE THE **WIZARD SHAZAM.**

I WISH I COULD GO WITH THEM, BUT WITH BILLY NOT ABLE TO TRANSFORM INTO CAPTAIN MARVEL, THE ONLY WAY TO REACH THE ROCK OF ETERNITY IS WITH THE MAGICAL PORTAL IN THE TRAIN STATION, BUT I'M IN NO SHAPE TO TRAVEL.

I HOPE THEY ARE ABLE TO GET SOME WELL DESERVED REST BEFORE THE LONG TRIP AHEAD OF THEM.

LET'S JUST HOPE IT'S AN **UNEVENTFUL** TRIP...

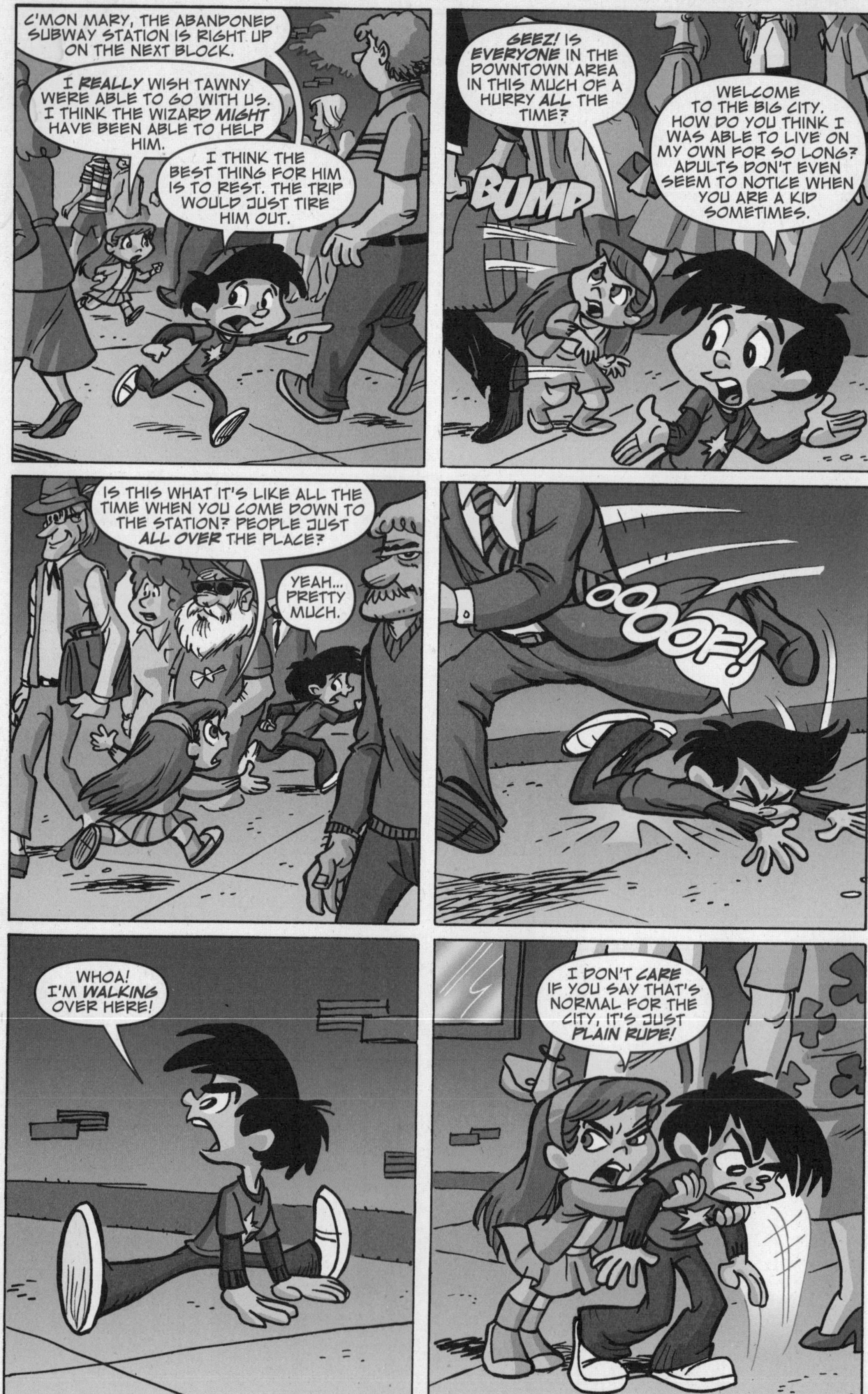
C'MON MARY, THE ABANDONED SUBWAY STATION IS RIGHT UP ON THE NEXT BLOCK.
I REALLY WISH TAWNY WERE ABLE TO GO WITH US. I THINK THE WIZARD MIGHT HAVE BEEN ABLE TO HELP HIM.
I THINK THE BEST THING FOR HIM IS TO REST. THE TRIP WOULD JUST TIRE HIM OUT.
GEEZ! IS EVERYONE IN THE DOWNTOWN AREA IN THIS MUCH OF A HURRY ALL THE TIME?
BUMP
WELCOME TO THE BIG CITY. HOW DO YOU THINK I WAS ABLE TO LIVE ON MY OWN FOR SO LONG? ADULTS DON'T EVEN SEEM TO NOTICE WHEN YOU ARE A KID SOMETIMES.
IS THIS WHAT IT'S LIKE ALL THE TIME WHEN YOU COME DOWN TO THE STATION? PEOPLE JUST ALL OVER THE PLACE?
YEAH... PRETTY MUCH.
OOOOF!
WHOA! I'M WALKING OVER HERE!
I DON'T CARE IF YOU SAY THAT'S NORMAL FOR THE CITY, IT'S JUST PLAIN RUDE!

WELL, *USUALLY* WHEN THEY RUN YOU OVER THEY'RE A BIT MORE *POLITE* THAN THAT.

HEY! DO YOU NOTICE SOMETHING *WEIRD?*

EVERY TIME I COME DOWN *HERE* I *NOTICE SOMETHING WEIRD.* GIANT ROBOTS, EVEN BIGGER, MORE GIANTER MONSTERS FROM ANOTHER DIMENSION...

WAIT...IS *"GIANTER"* EVEN A WORD?

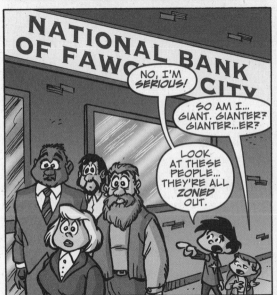

NATIONAL BANK OF FAWCETT CITY

NO, I'M SERIOUS!

SO AM I... GIANT. GIANTER? GIANTER...ER?

LOOK AT THESE PEOPLE... THEY'RE ALL *ZONED* OUT.

YEAH, YOU'RE RIGHT! IT'S LIKE THEY'RE ALL *ZOMBIFIED!* IS THIS WHAT YOU BECOME WHEN YOU'RE AN ADULT AND THEY SAY YOU BECOME A SLAVE TO YOUR JOB?

WHERE ARE THEY ALL GOING?

NATIONAL BANK OF FAWCETT CITY

THEY'RE ALL GOING INTO THE *BANK.*

SO WHAT? PEOPLE GO TO THE BANK ALL THE TIME! *WE* NEED TO GET TO THE SUBWAY STATION TO GET TO THE ROCK OF ETERNITY.

NO, THIS IS DIFFERENT! IT'S LIKE THEY'RE *UNDER* A SPELL OR SOMETHING... C'MON, WE SHOULD LOOK INTO THIS.

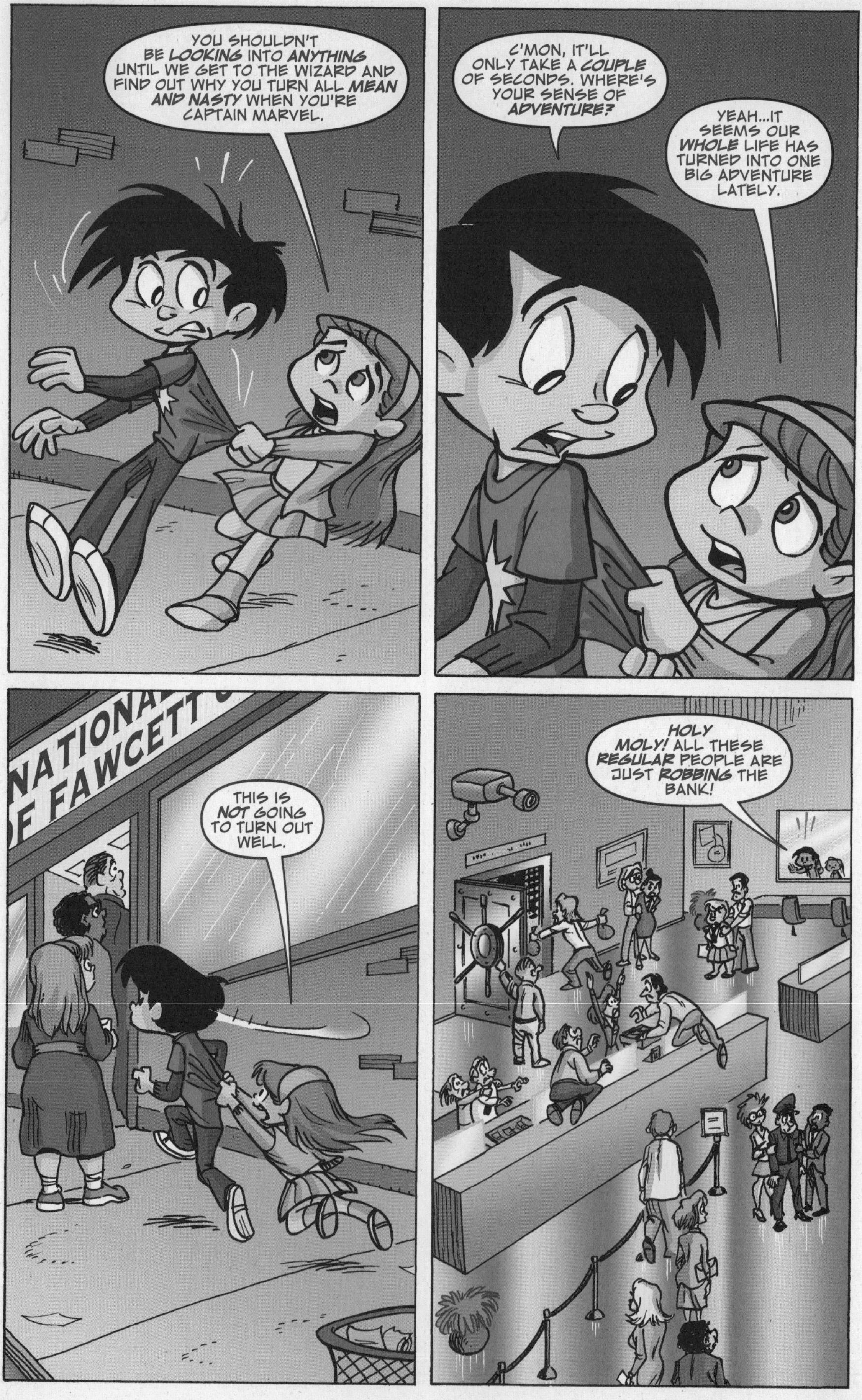
YOU SHOULDN'T BE LOOKING INTO ANYTHING UNTIL WE GET TO THE WIZARD AND FIND OUT WHY YOU TURN ALL MEAN AND NASTY WHEN YOU'RE CAPTAIN MARVEL.
C'MON, IT'LL ONLY TAKE A COUPLE OF SECONDS. WHERE'S YOUR SENSE OF ADVENTURE?
YEAH...IT SEEMS OUR WHOLE LIFE HAS TURNED INTO ONE BIG ADVENTURE LATELY.
NATIONA
OF FAWCETT
THIS IS NOT GOING TO TURN OUT WELL.
HOLY MOLY! ALL THESE REGULAR PEOPLE ARE JUST ROBBING THE BANK!

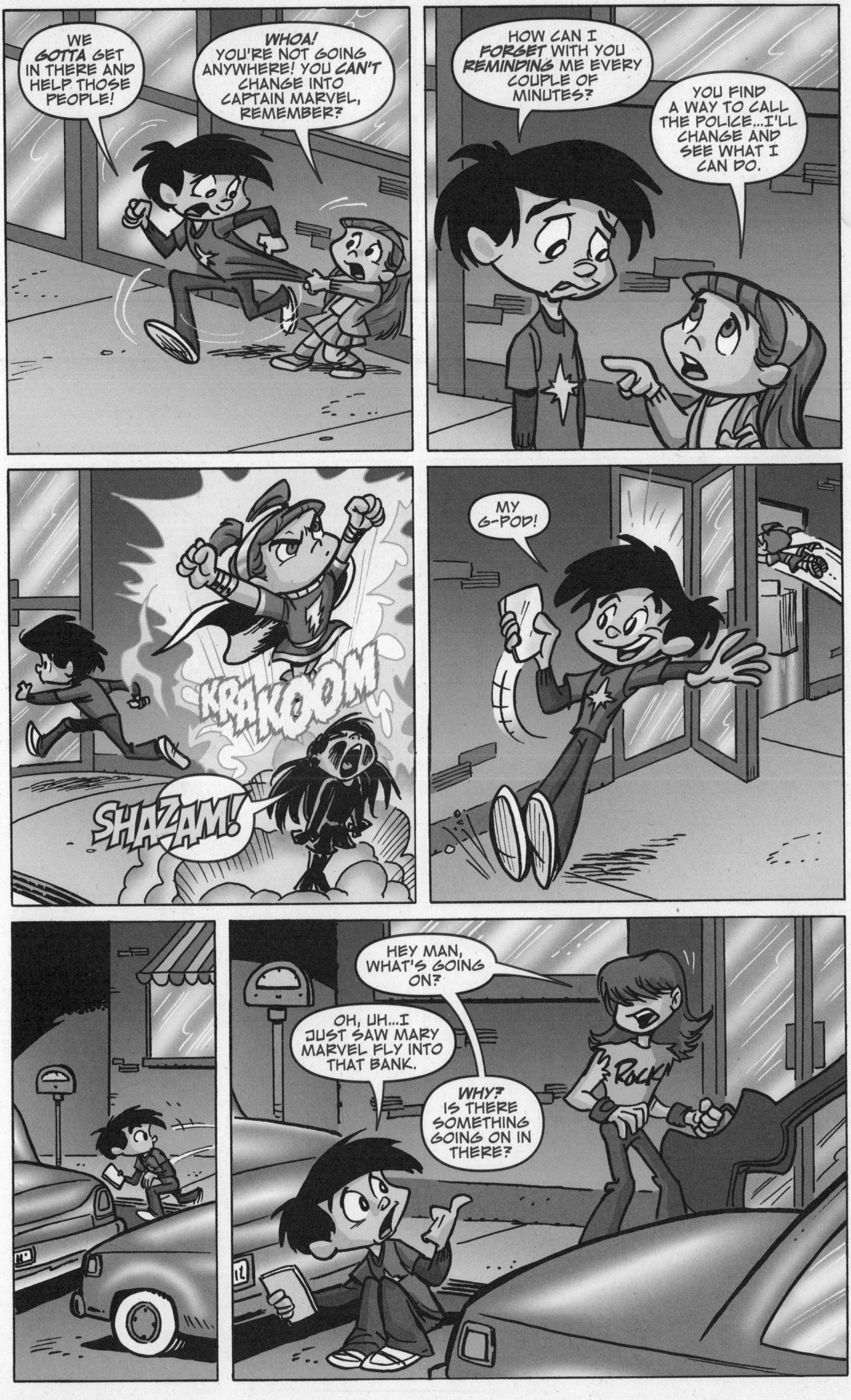
WE GOTTA GET IN THERE AND HELP THOSE PEOPLE!
WHOA! YOU'RE NOT GOING ANYWHERE! YOU CAN'T CHANGE INTO CAPTAIN MARVEL, REMEMBER?
HOW CAN I FORGET WITH YOU REMINDING ME EVERY COUPLE OF MINUTES?
YOU FIND A WAY TO CALL THE POLICE...I'LL CHANGE AND SEE WHAT I CAN DO.
KRAKOOM
SHAZAM!
MY G-POD!
HEY MAN, WHAT'S GOING ON?
OH, UH...I JUST SAW MARY MARVEL FLY INTO THAT BANK.
WHY? IS THERE SOMETHING GOING ON IN THERE?

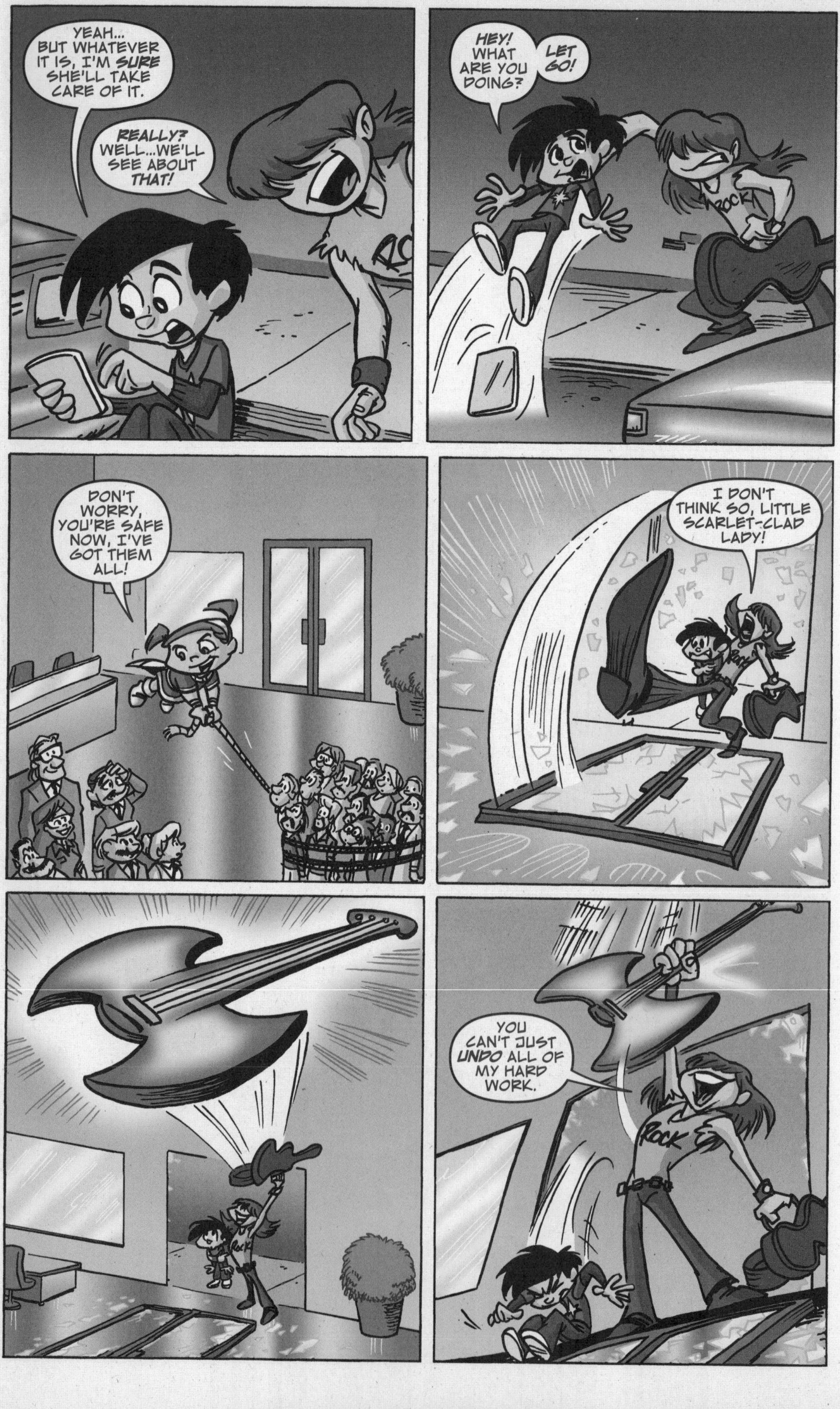
YEAH... BUT WHATEVER IT IS, I'M SURE SHE'LL TAKE CARE OF IT.
REALLY? WELL...WE'LL SEE ABOUT THAT!
HEY! WHAT ARE YOU DOING?
LET GO!
DON'T WORRY, YOU'RE SAFE NOW, I'VE GOT THEM ALL!
I DON'T THINK SO, LITTLE SCARLET-CLAD LADY!
YOU CAN'T JUST UNDO ALL OF MY HARD WORK.

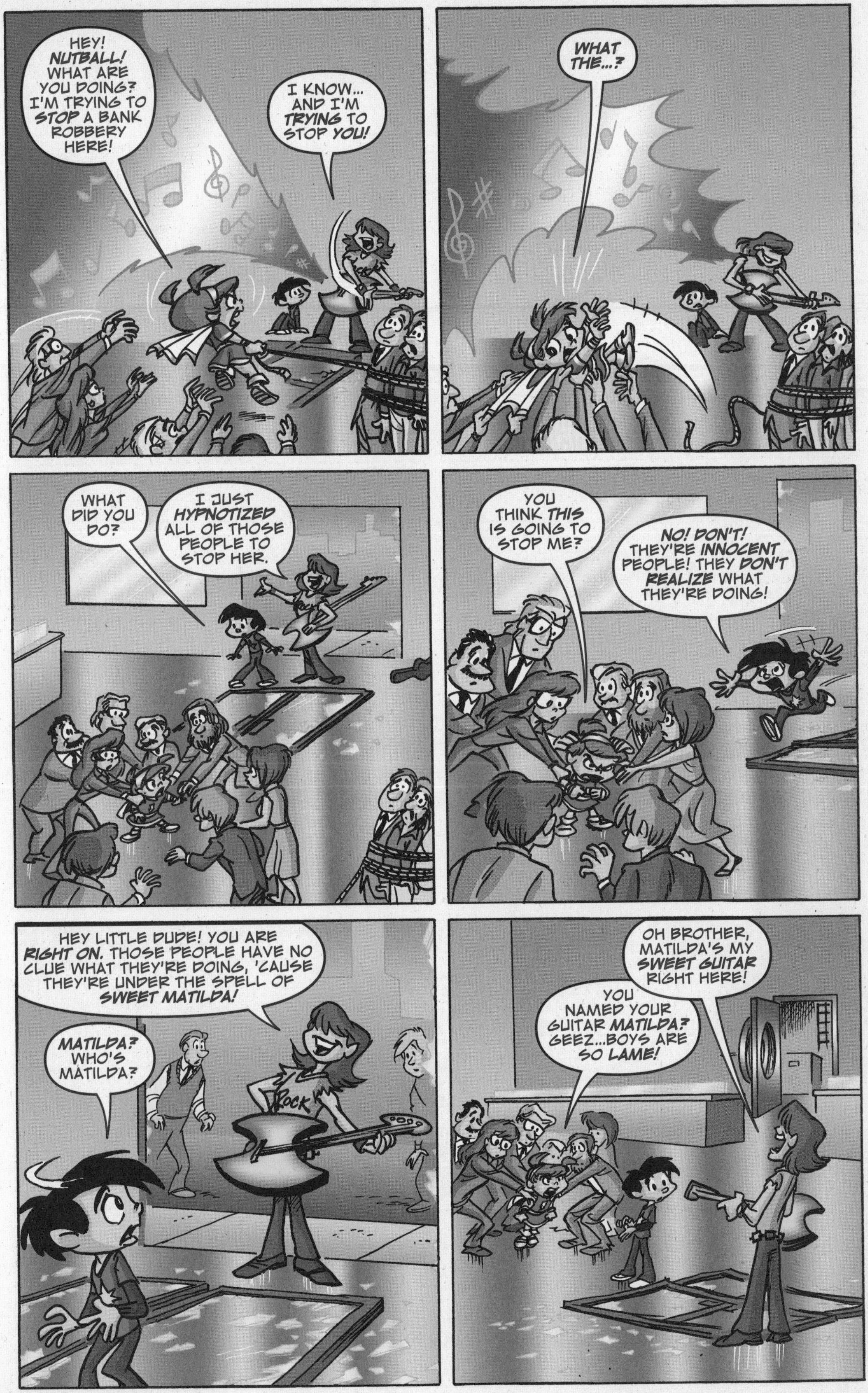
HEY! NUTBALL! WHAT ARE YOU DOING? I'M TRYING TO STOP A BANK ROBBERY HERE!
I KNOW... AND I'M TRYING TO STOP YOU!
WHAT THE...?
WHAT DID YOU DO?
I JUST HYPNOTIZED ALL OF THOSE PEOPLE TO STOP HER.
YOU THINK THIS IS GOING TO STOP ME?
NO! DON'T! THEY'RE INNOCENT PEOPLE! THEY DON'T REALIZE WHAT THEY'RE DOING!
HEY LITTLE DUDE! YOU ARE RIGHT ON. THOSE PEOPLE HAVE NO CLUE WHAT THEY'RE DOING, 'CAUSE THEY'RE UNDER THE SPELL OF SWEET MATILDA!
MATILDA? WHO'S MATILDA?
OH BROTHER, MATILDA'S MY SWEET GUITAR RIGHT HERE!
YOU NAMED YOUR GUITAR MATILDA? GEEZ...BOYS ARE SO LAME!

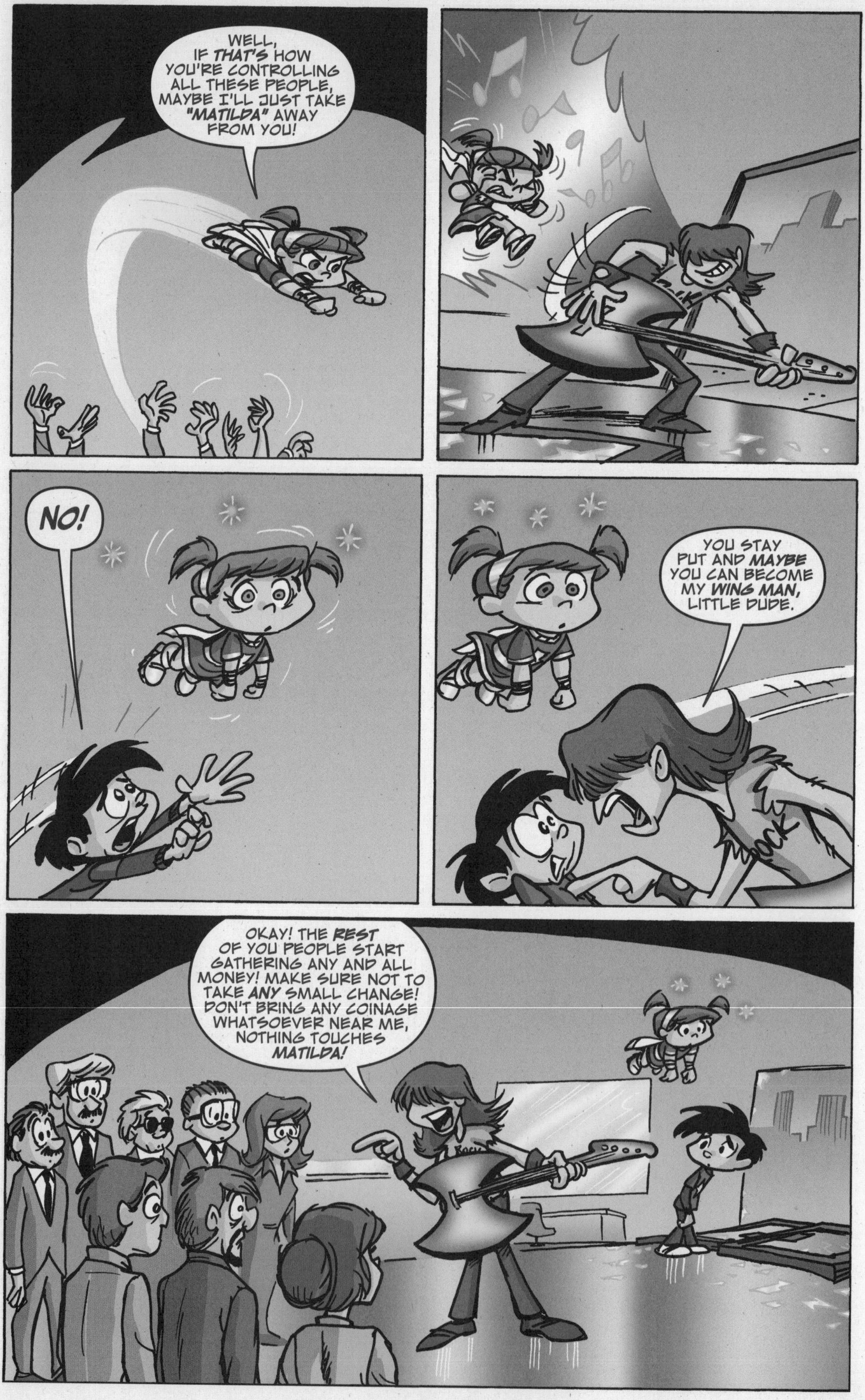
WELL, IF THAT'S HOW YOU'RE CONTROLLING ALL THESE PEOPLE, MAYBE I'LL JUST TAKE "MATILDA" AWAY FROM YOU!
NO!
YOU STAY PUT AND MAYBE YOU CAN BECOME MY WING MAN, LITTLE DUDE.
ROCK
OKAY! THE REST OF YOU PEOPLE START GATHERING ANY AND ALL MONEY! MAKE SURE NOT TO TAKE ANY SMALL CHANGE! DON'T BRING ANY COINAGE WHATSOEVER NEAR ME, NOTHING TOUCHES MATILDA!

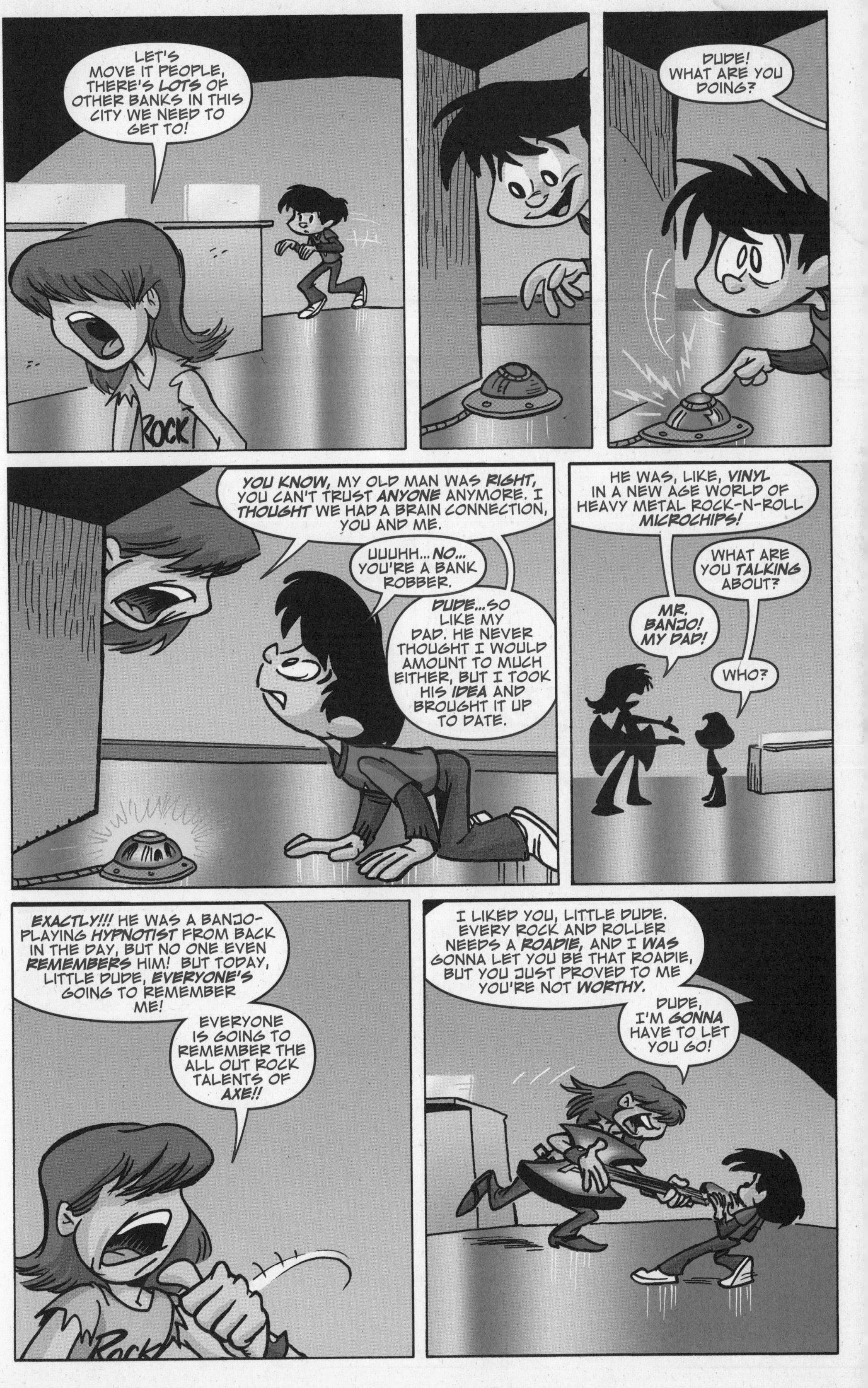
LET'S MOVE IT PEOPLE, THERE'S LOTS OF OTHER BANKS IN THIS CITY WE NEED TO GET TO!
DUDE! WHAT ARE YOU DOING?
YOU KNOW, MY OLD MAN WAS RIGHT, YOU CAN'T TRUST ANYONE ANYMORE. I THOUGHT WE HAD A BRAIN CONNECTION, YOU AND ME.
UUUHH... NO... YOU'RE A BANK ROBBER.
DUDE...SO LIKE MY DAD. HE NEVER THOUGHT I WOULD AMOUNT TO MUCH EITHER, BUT I TOOK HIS IDEA AND BROUGHT IT UP TO DATE.
HE WAS, LIKE, VINYL IN A NEW AGE WORLD OF HEAVY METAL ROCK-N-ROLL MICROCHIPS!
WHAT ARE YOU TALKING ABOUT?
MR. BANJO! MY DAD!
WHO?
EXACTLY!!! HE WAS A BANJO-PLAYING HYPNOTIST FROM BACK IN THE DAY, BUT NO ONE EVEN REMEMBERS HIM! BUT TODAY, LITTLE DUDE, EVERYONE'S GOING TO REMEMBER ME!
EVERYONE IS GOING TO REMEMBER THE ALL OUT ROCK TALENTS OF AXE!!
I LIKED YOU, LITTLE DUDE. EVERY ROCK AND ROLLER NEEDS A ROADIE, AND I WAS GONNA LET YOU BE THAT ROADIE, BUT YOU JUST PROVED TO ME YOU'RE NOT WORTHY.
DUDE, I'M GONNA HAVE TO LET YOU GO!

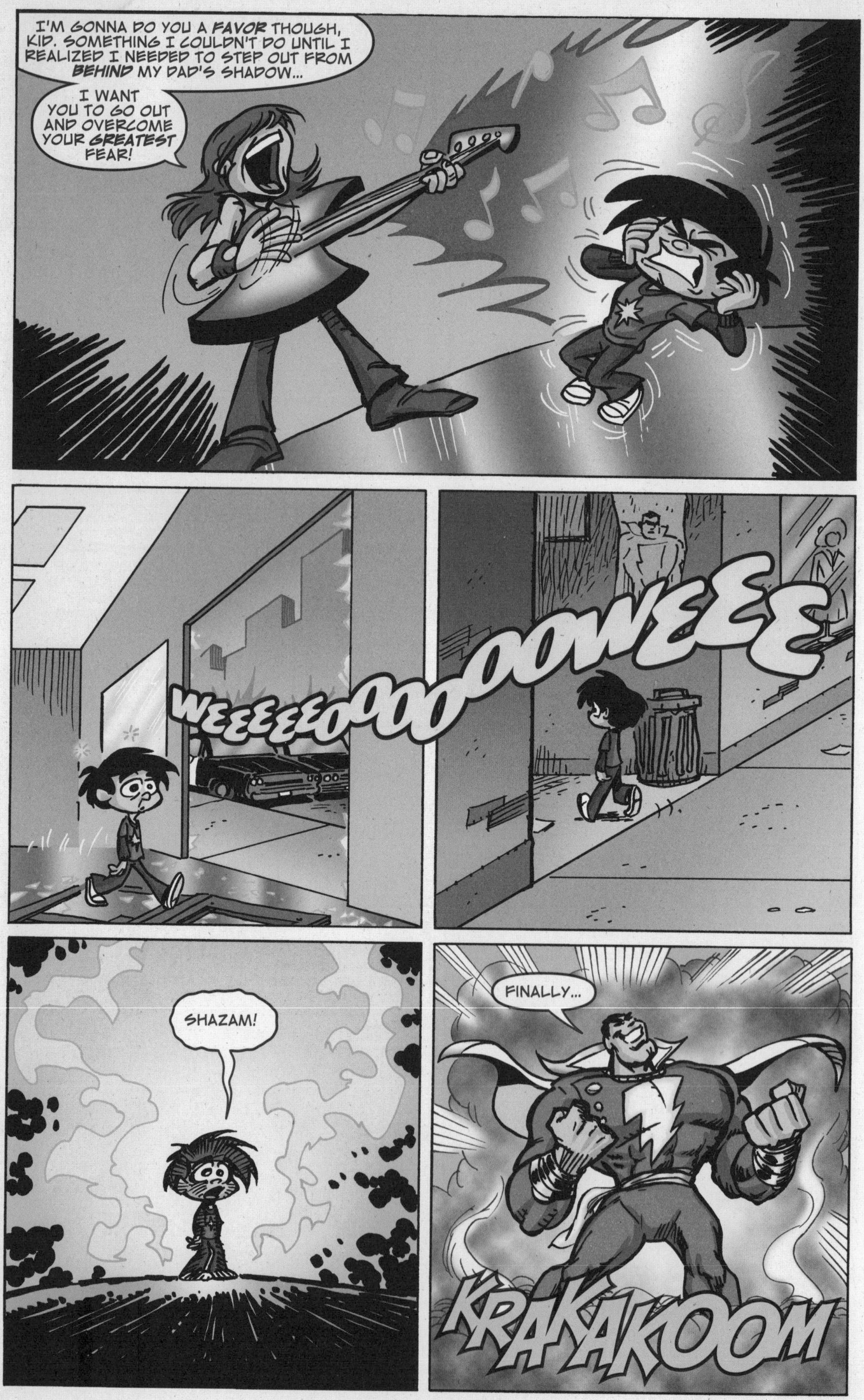
I'M GONNA DO YOU A FAVOR THOUGH, KID. SOMETHING I COULDN'T DO UNTIL I REALIZED I NEEDED TO STEP OUT FROM BEHIND MY DAD'S SHADOW...
I WANT YOU TO GO OUT AND OVERCOME YOUR GREATEST FEAR!
WEEEEOOOOOOOWEEE
SHAZAM!
FINALLY...
KRAKAKOOM

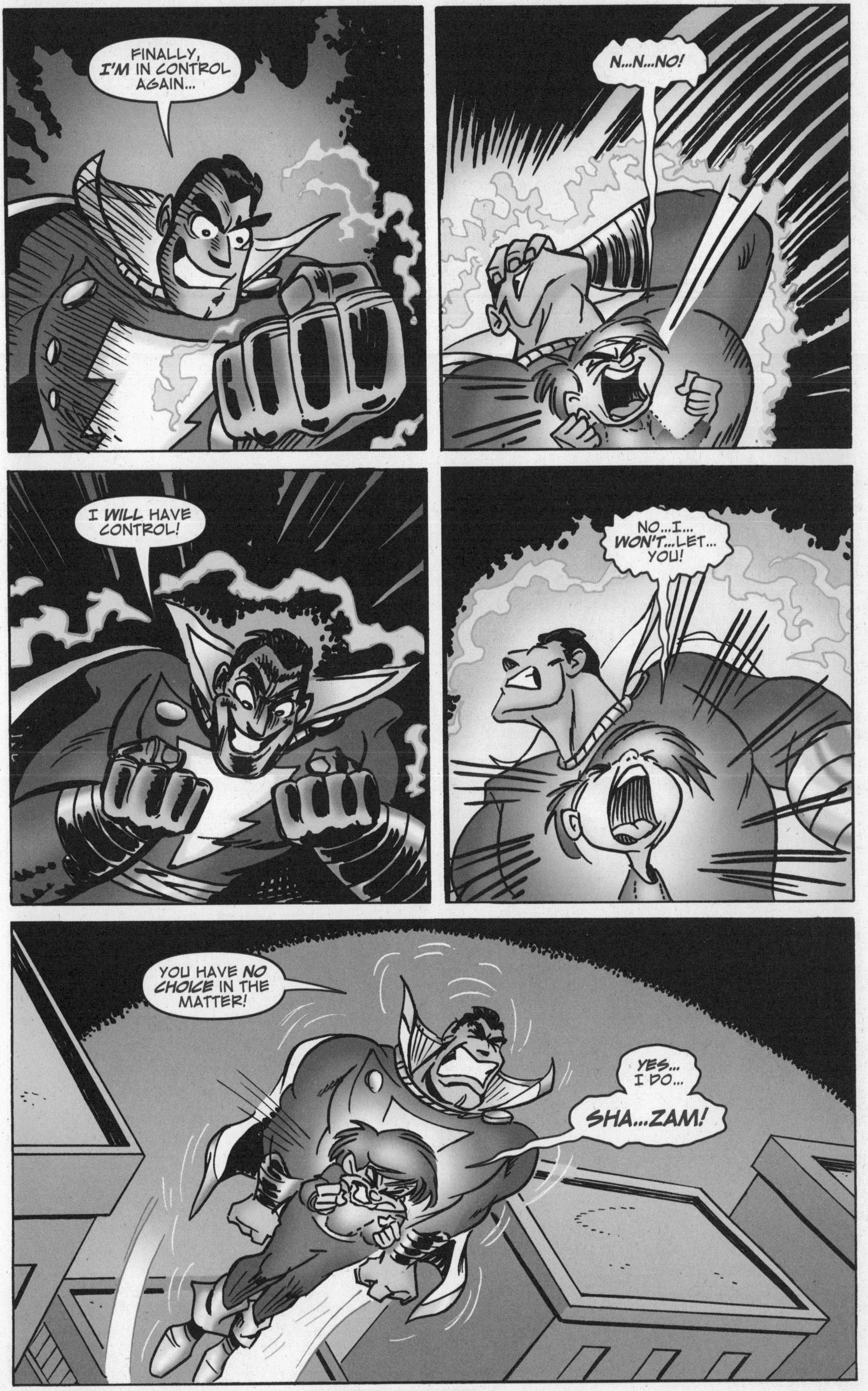
FINALLY, I'M IN CONTROL AGAIN...
N...N...NO!
I WILL HAVE CONTROL!
NO...I... WON'T...LET... YOU!
YOU HAVE NO CHOICE IN THE MATTER!
YES... I DO...
SHA...ZAM!

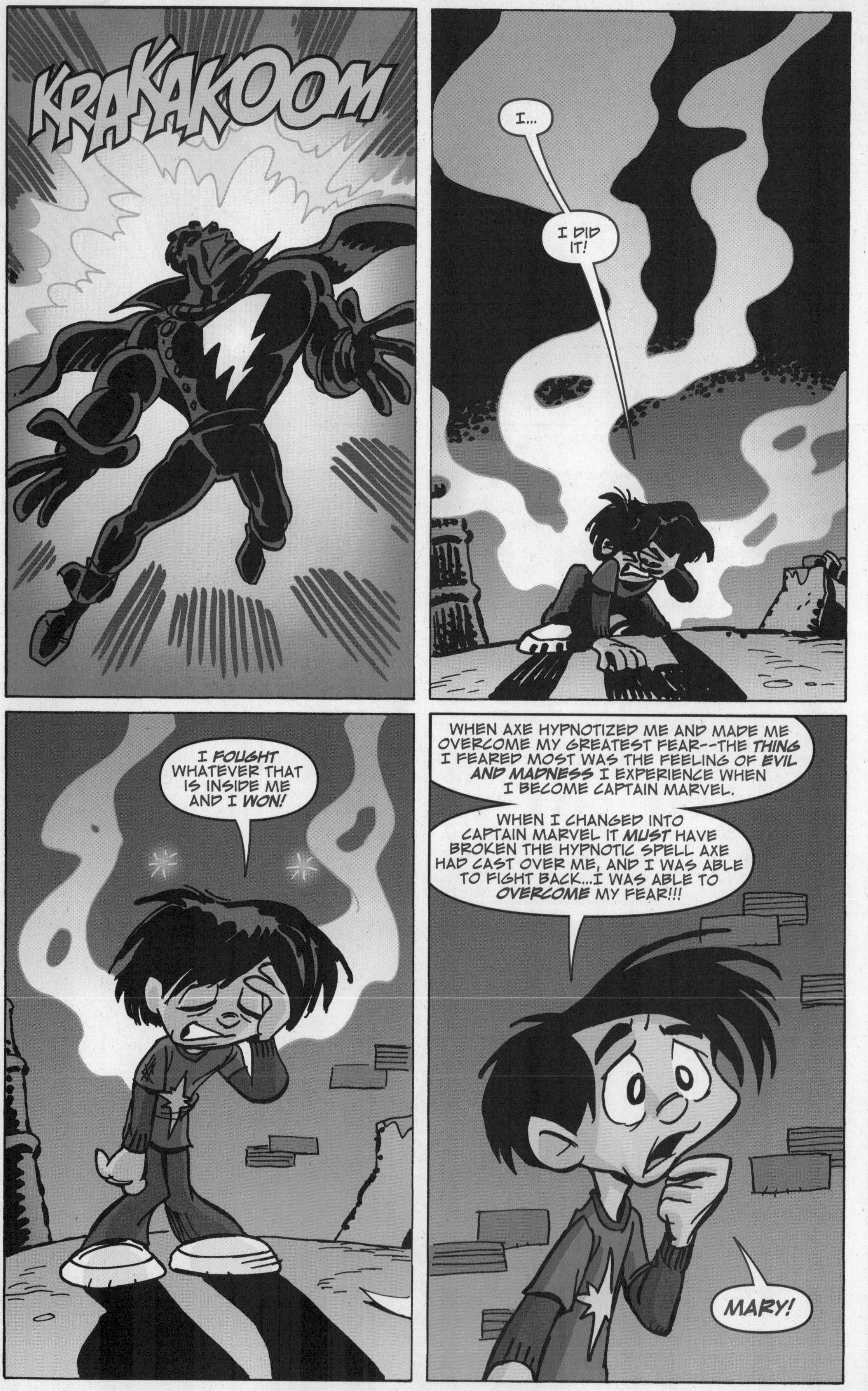
KRAKAKOOM
I...
I DID IT!
I FOUGHT WHATEVER THAT IS INSIDE ME AND I WON!
WHEN AXE HYPNOTIZED ME AND MADE ME OVERCOME MY GREATEST FEAR--THE THING I FEARED MOST WAS THE FEELING OF EVIL AND MADNESS I EXPERIENCE WHEN I BECOME CAPTAIN MARVEL.
WHEN I CHANGED INTO CAPTAIN MARVEL IT MUST HAVE BROKEN THE HYPNOTIC SPELL AXE HAD CAST OVER ME, AND I WAS ABLE TO FIGHT BACK...I WAS ABLE TO OVERCOME MY FEAR!!!
MARY!

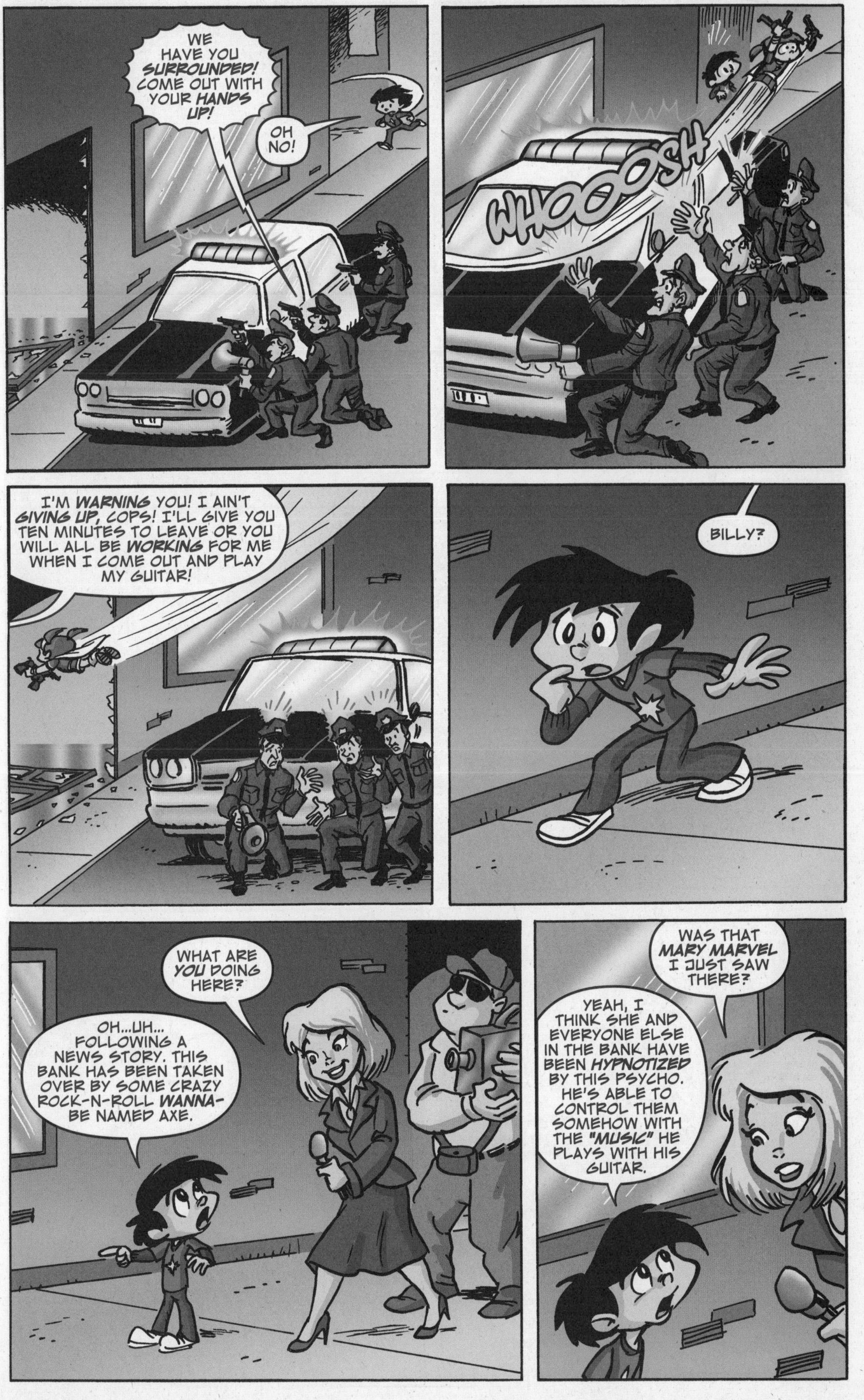
WE HAVE YOU SURROUNDED! COME OUT WITH YOUR HANDS UP!
OH NO!
WHOOOOSH
I'M WARNING YOU! I AIN'T GIVING UP, COPS! I'LL GIVE YOU TEN MINUTES TO LEAVE OR YOU WILL ALL BE WORKING FOR ME WHEN I COME OUT AND PLAY MY GUITAR!
BILLY?
WHAT ARE YOU DOING HERE?
OH...UH... FOLLOWING A NEWS STORY. THIS BANK HAS BEEN TAKEN OVER BY SOME CRAZY ROCK-N-ROLL WANNA-BE NAMED AXE.
WAS THAT MARY MARVEL I JUST SAW THERE?
YEAH, I THINK SHE AND EVERYONE ELSE IN THE BANK HAVE BEEN HYPNOTIZED BY THIS PSYCHO. HE'S ABLE TO CONTROL THEM SOMEHOW WITH THE "MUSIC" HE PLAYS WITH HIS GUITAR.

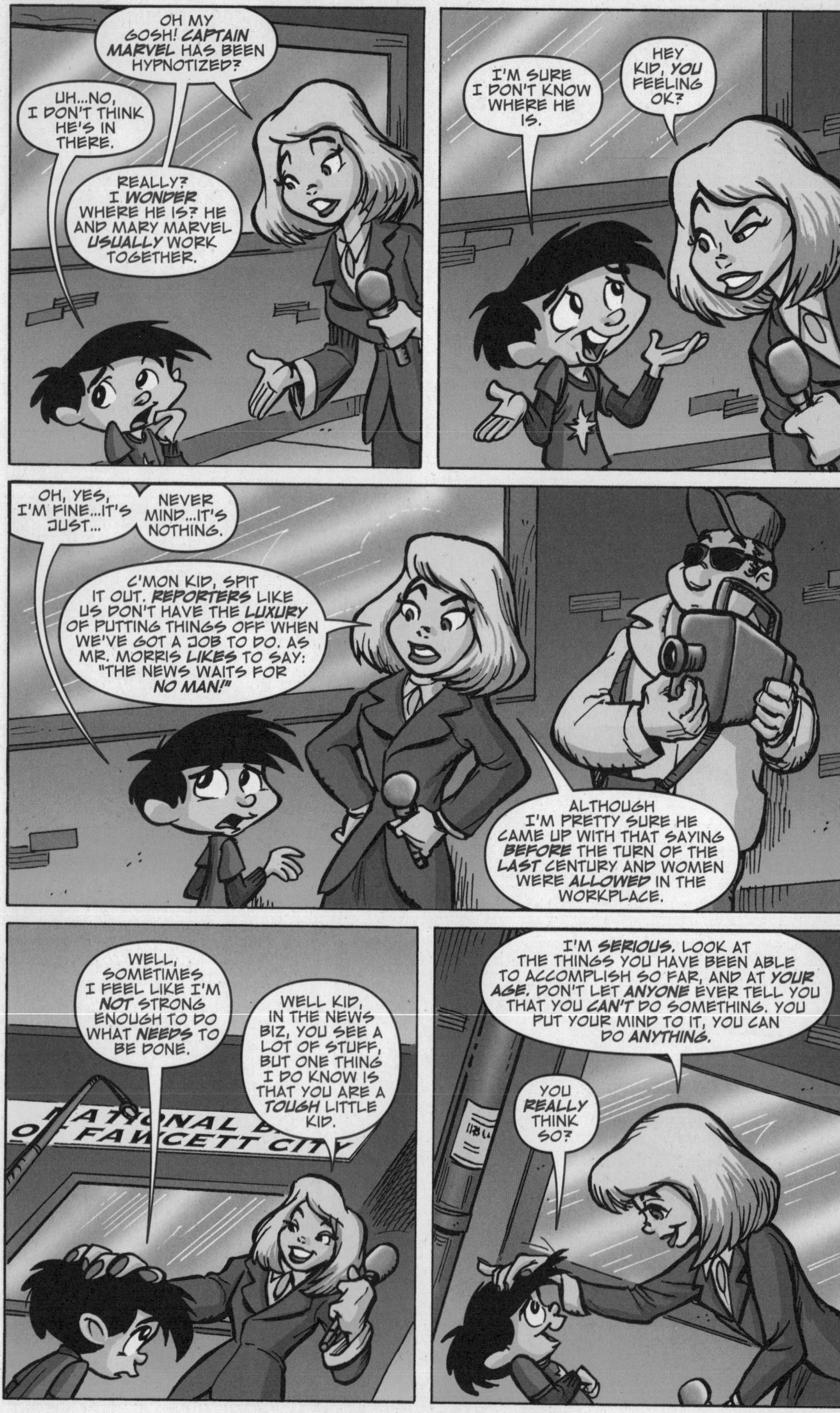
OH MY GOSH! CAPTAIN MARVEL HAS BEEN HYPNOTIZED?
UH...NO, I DON'T THINK HE'S IN THERE.
REALLY? I WONDER WHERE HE IS? HE AND MARY MARVEL USUALLY WORK TOGETHER.
I'M SURE I DON'T KNOW WHERE HE IS.
HEY KID, YOU FEELING OK?
OH, YES, I'M FINE...IT'S JUST...
NEVER MIND...IT'S NOTHING.
C'MON KID, SPIT IT OUT. REPORTERS LIKE US DON'T HAVE THE LUXURY OF PUTTING THINGS OFF WHEN WE'VE GOT A JOB TO DO. AS MR. MORRIS LIKES TO SAY: "THE NEWS WAITS FOR NO MAN!"
ALTHOUGH I'M PRETTY SURE HE CAME UP WITH THAT SAYING BEFORE THE TURN OF THE LAST CENTURY AND WOMEN WERE ALLOWED IN THE WORKPLACE.
WELL, SOMETIMES I FEEL LIKE I'M NOT STRONG ENOUGH TO DO WHAT NEEDS TO BE DONE.
WELL KID, IN THE NEWS BIZ, YOU SEE A LOT OF STUFF, BUT ONE THING I DO KNOW IS THAT YOU ARE A TOUGH LITTLE KID.
I'M SERIOUS. LOOK AT THE THINGS YOU HAVE BEEN ABLE TO ACCOMPLISH SO FAR, AND AT YOUR AGE. DON'T LET ANYONE EVER TELL YOU THAT YOU CAN'T DO SOMETHING. YOU PUT YOUR MIND TO IT, YOU CAN DO ANYTHING.
YOU REALLY THINK SO?

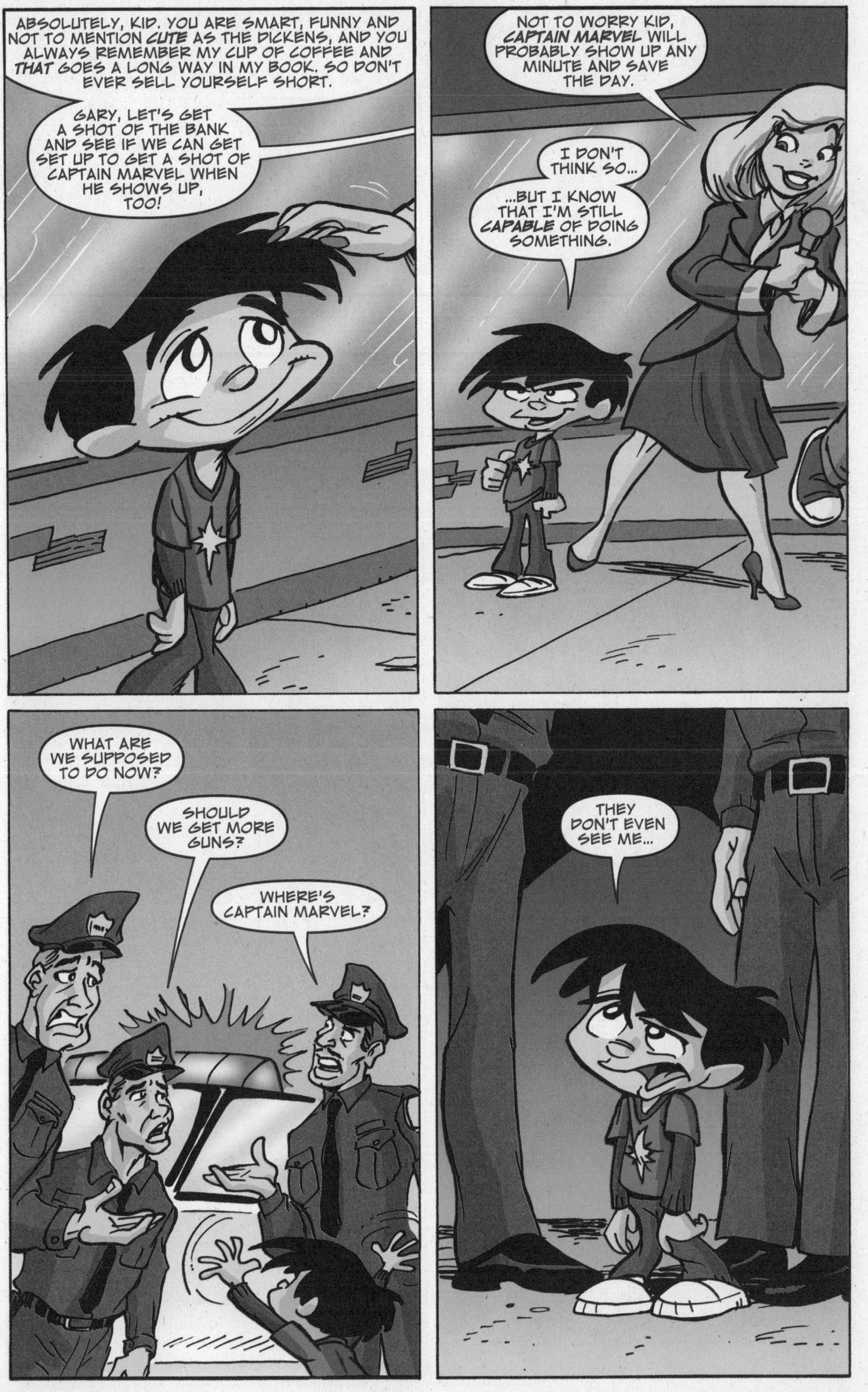
ABSOLUTELY, KID. YOU ARE SMART, FUNNY AND NOT TO MENTION CUTE AS THE DICKENS, AND YOU ALWAYS REMEMBER MY CUP OF COFFEE AND THAT GOES A LONG WAY IN MY BOOK. SO DON'T EVER SELL YOURSELF SHORT.
GARY, LET'S GET A SHOT OF THE BANK AND SEE IF WE CAN GET SET UP TO GET A SHOT OF CAPTAIN MARVEL WHEN HE SHOWS UP, TOO!
NOT TO WORRY KID, CAPTAIN MARVEL WILL PROBABLY SHOW UP ANY MINUTE AND SAVE THE DAY.
I DON'T THINK SO...
...BUT I KNOW THAT I'M STILL CAPABLE OF DOING SOMETHING.
WHAT ARE WE SUPPOSED TO DO NOW?
SHOULD WE GET MORE GUNS?
WHERE'S CAPTAIN MARVEL?
THEY DON'T EVEN SEE ME...

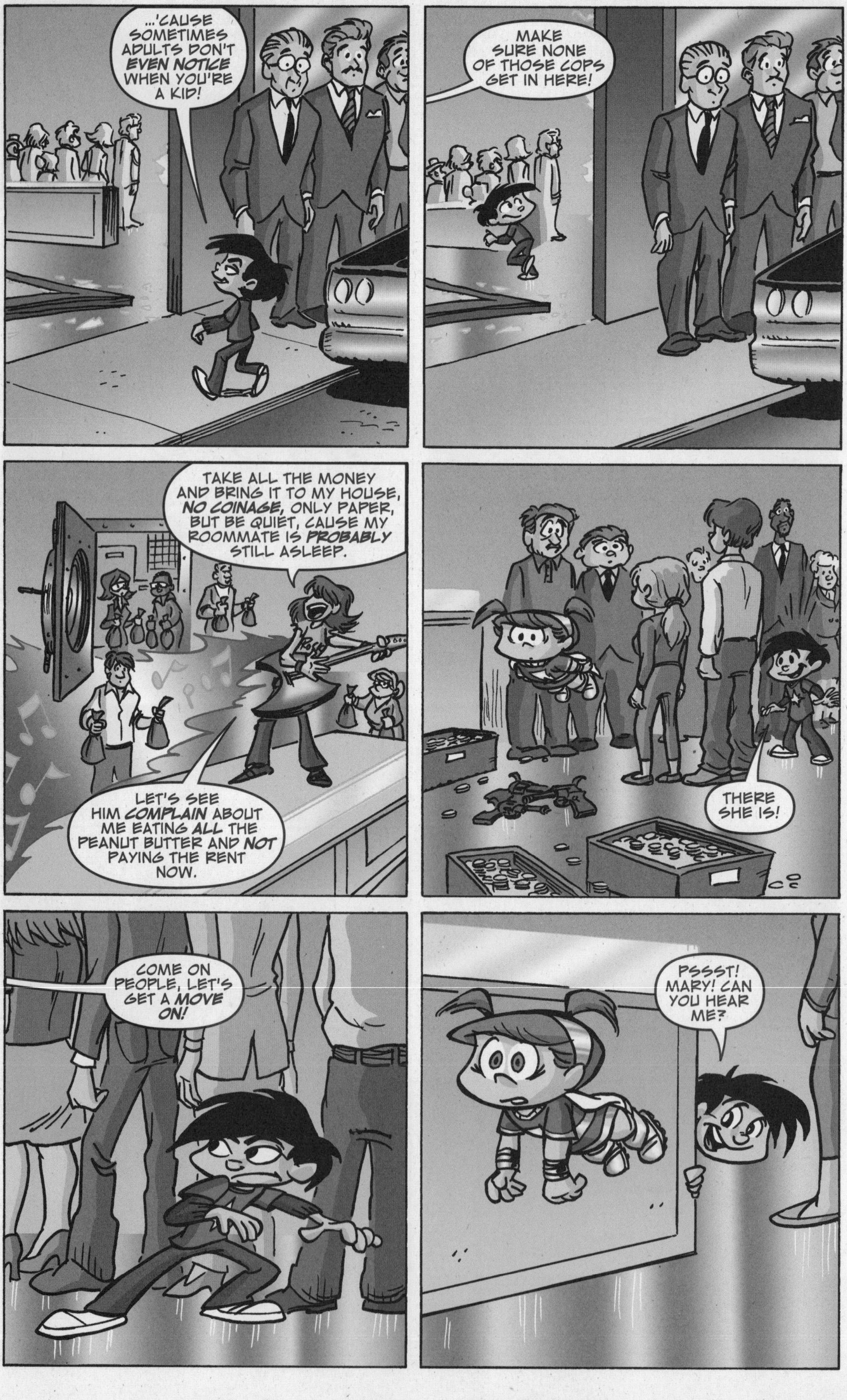
...'CAUSE SOMETIMES ADULTS DON'T *EVEN NOTICE* WHEN YOU'RE A KID!
MAKE SURE NONE OF THOSE COPS GET IN HERE!
TAKE ALL THE MONEY AND BRING IT TO MY HOUSE, *NO COINAGE,* ONLY PAPER, BUT BE QUIET, CAUSE MY ROOMMATE IS *PROBABLY* STILL ASLEEP.
LET'S SEE HIM *COMPLAIN* ABOUT ME EATING *ALL* THE PEANUT BUTTER AND *NOT* PAYING THE RENT NOW.
THERE SHE IS!
COME ON PEOPLE, LET'S GET A *MOVE ON!*
PSSST! MARY! CAN YOU HEAR ME?

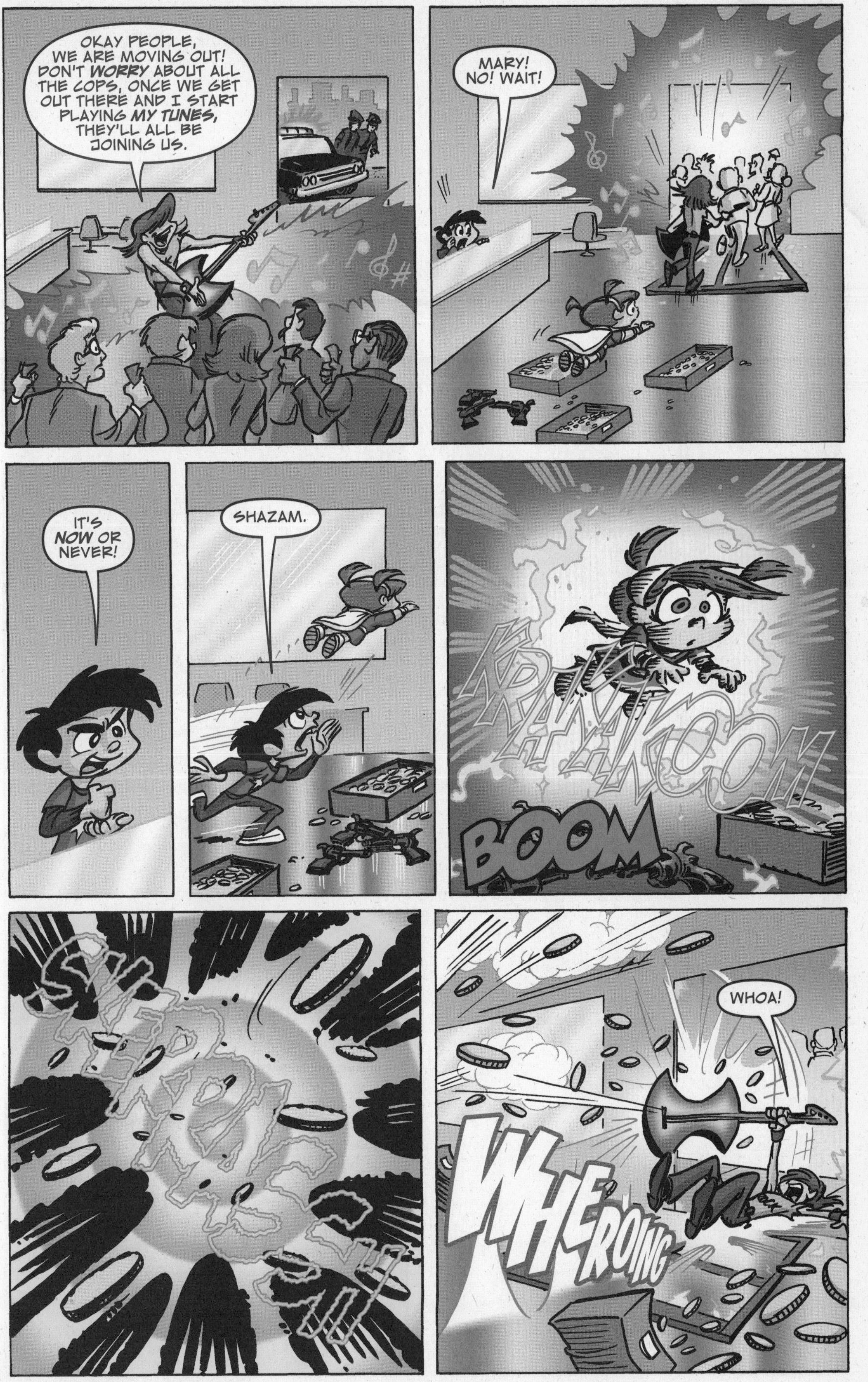
OKAY PEOPLE, WE ARE MOVING OUT! DON'T WORRY ABOUT ALL THE COPS, ONCE WE GET OUT THERE AND I START PLAYING MY TUNES, THEY'LL ALL BE JOINING US.
MARY! NO! WAIT!
IT'S NOW OR NEVER!
SHAZAM.
KRAKKOOM
BOOM
WHOA!
WHEROING

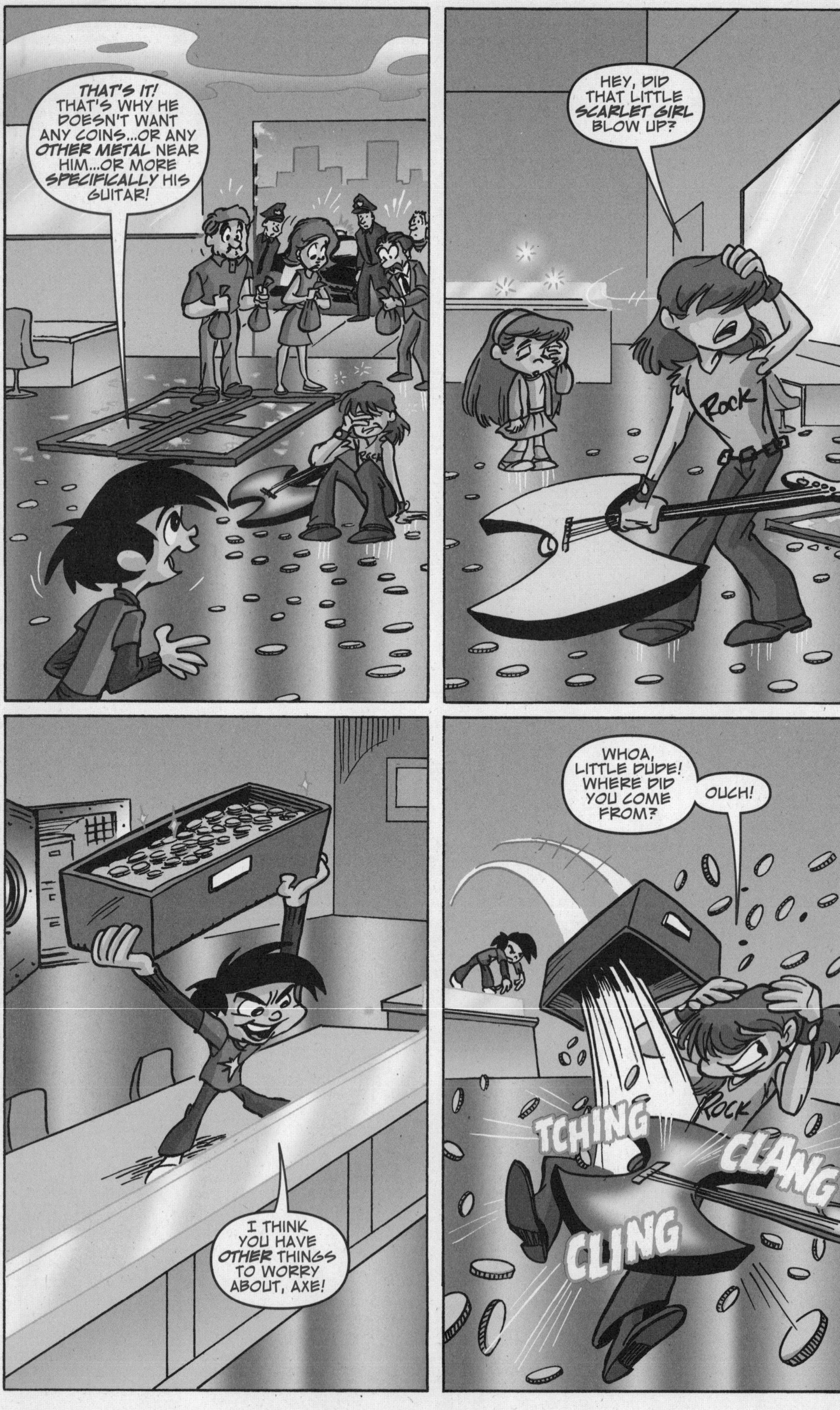
THAT'S IT! THAT'S WHY HE DOESN'T WANT ANY COINS...OR ANY OTHER METAL NEAR HIM...OR MORE SPECIFICALLY HIS GUITAR!
ROCK
HEY, DID THAT LITTLE SCARLET GIRL BLOW UP?
ROCK
I THINK YOU HAVE OTHER THINGS TO WORRY ABOUT, AXE!
WHOA, LITTLE DUDE! WHERE DID YOU COME FROM?
OUCH!
TCHING
CLANG
CLING
ROCK

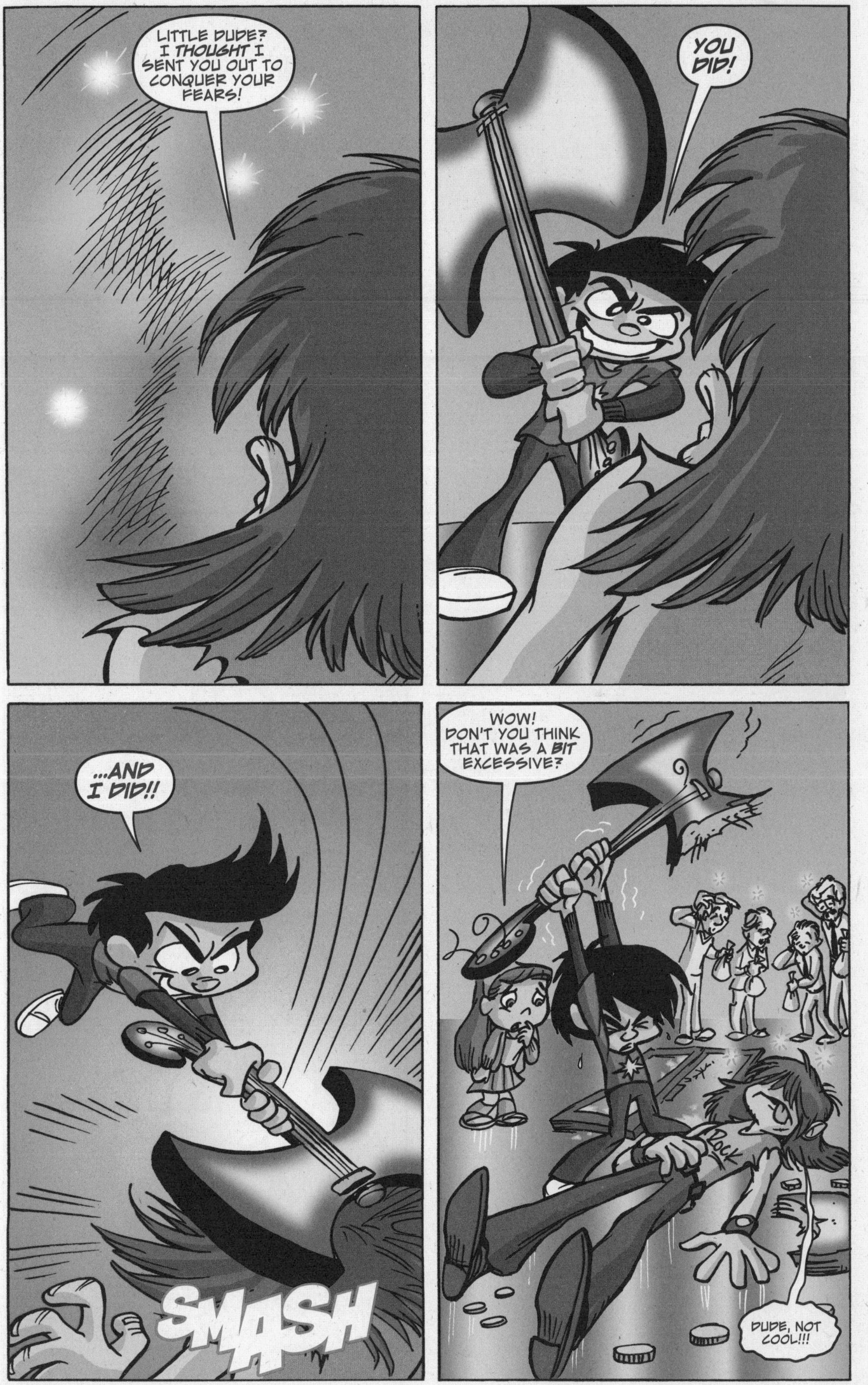
LITTLE DUDE? I THOUGHT I SENT YOU OUT TO CONQUER YOUR FEARS!
YOU DID!
...AND I DID!!
SMASH
WOW! DON'T YOU THINK THAT WAS A BIT EXCESSIVE?
ROCK
DUDE, NOT COOL!!!

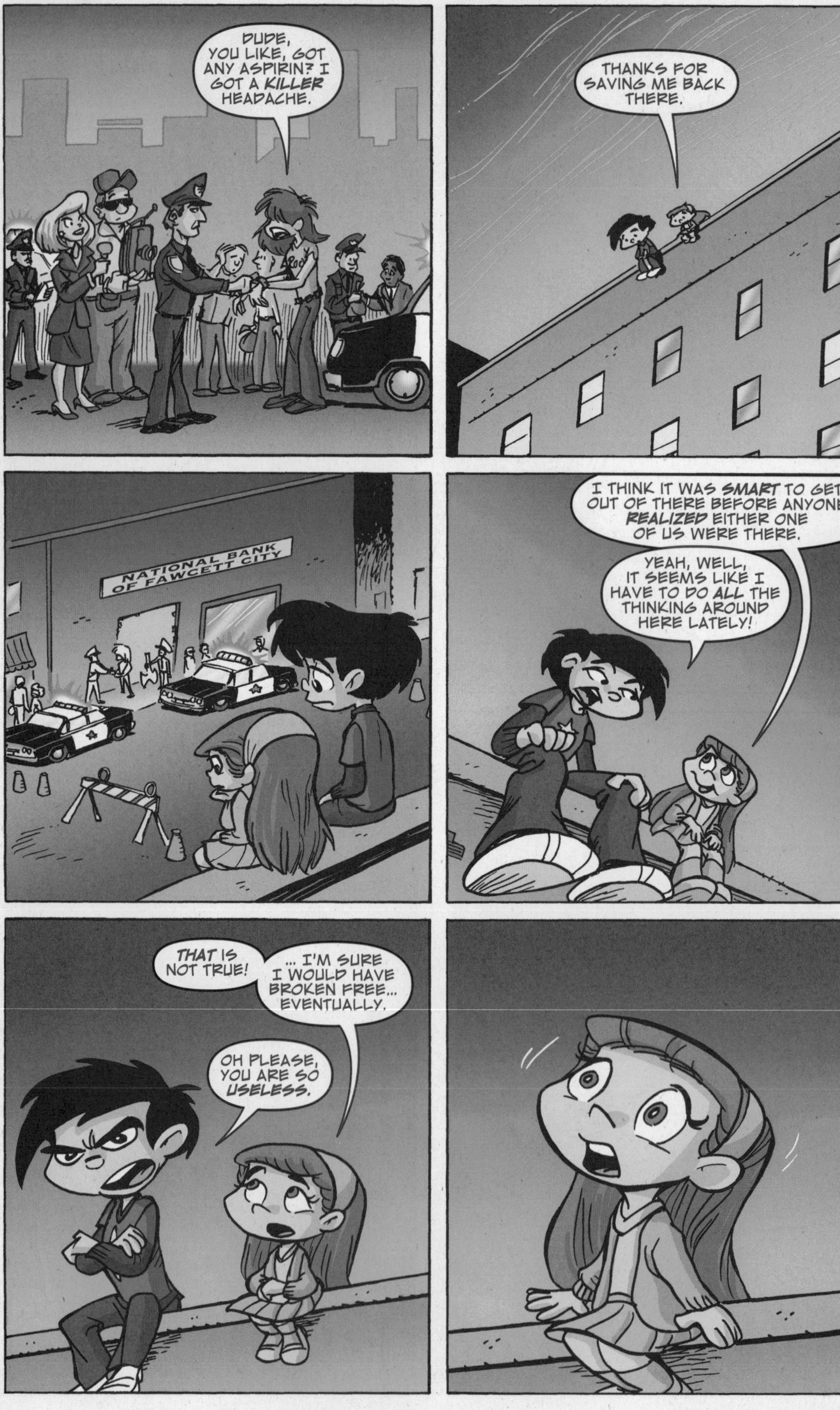
DUDE, YOU LIKE, GOT ANY ASPIRIN? I GOT A KILLER HEADACHE.
THANKS FOR SAVING ME BACK THERE.
NATIONAL BANK OF FAWCETT CITY
I THINK IT WAS SMART TO GET OUT OF THERE BEFORE ANYONE REALIZED EITHER ONE OF US WERE THERE.
YEAH, WELL, IT SEEMS LIKE I HAVE TO DO ALL THE THINKING AROUND HERE LATELY!
THAT IS NOT TRUE!
... I'M SURE I WOULD HAVE BROKEN FREE... EVENTUALLY.
OH PLEASE, YOU ARE SO USELESS.

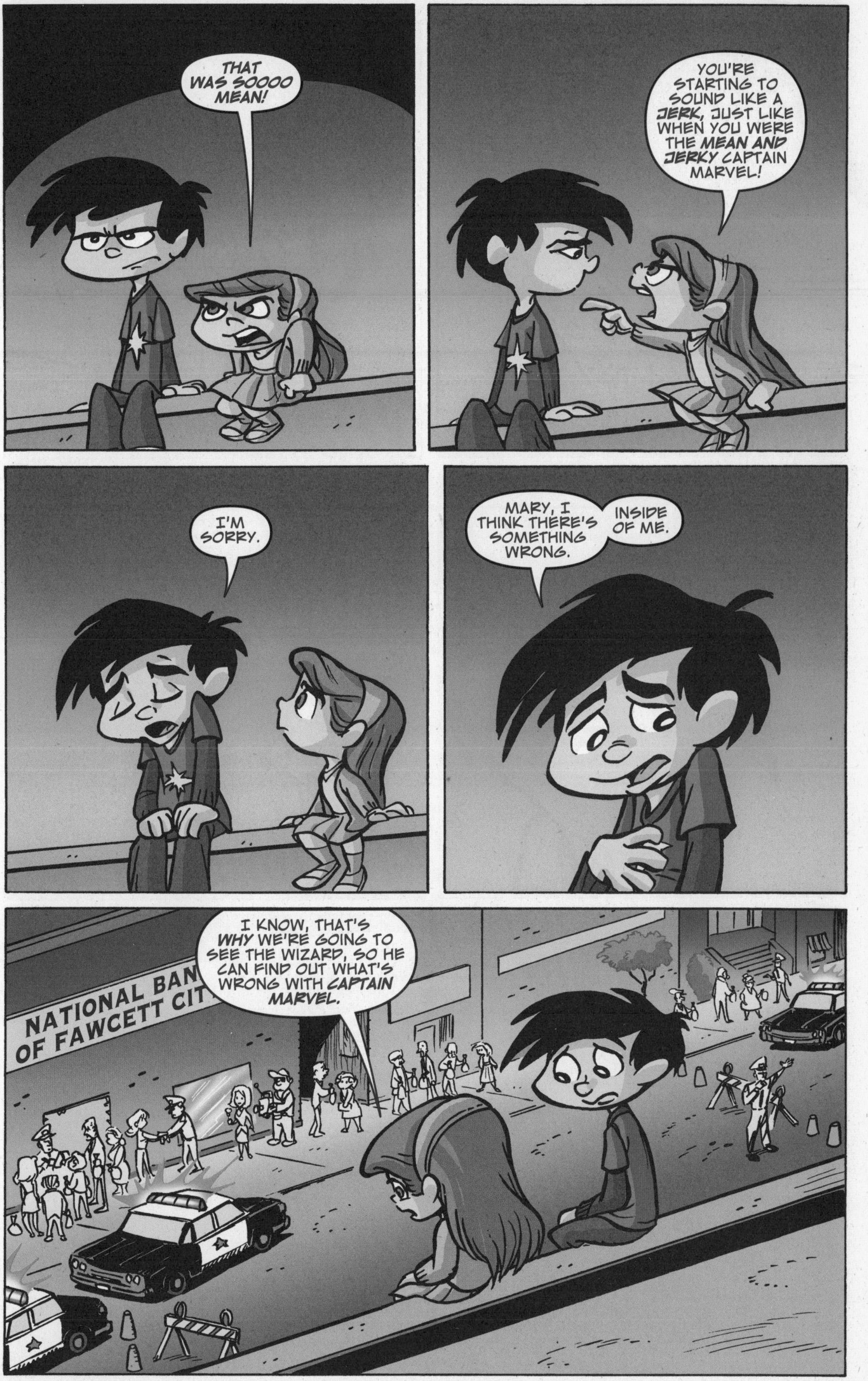
THAT WAS SOOOO MEAN!
YOU'RE STARTING TO SOUND LIKE A JERK, JUST LIKE WHEN YOU WERE THE MEAN AND JERKY CAPTAIN MARVEL!
I'M SORRY.
MARY, I THINK THERE'S SOMETHING WRONG.
INSIDE OF ME.
I KNOW, THAT'S WHY WE'RE GOING TO SEE THE WIZARD, SO HE CAN FIND OUT WHAT'S WRONG WITH CAPTAIN MARVEL.
NATIONAL BAN
OF FAWCETT CIT

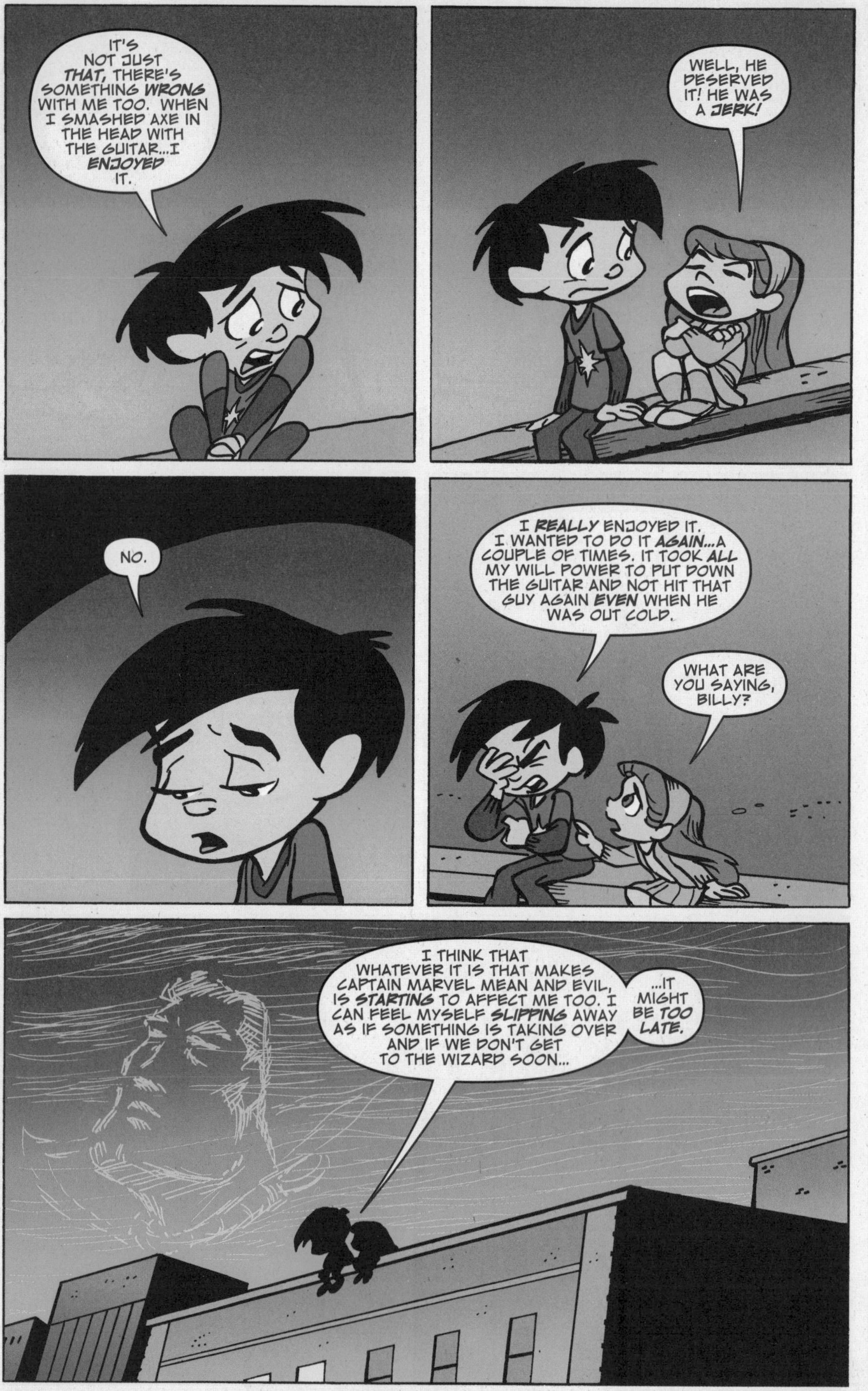
IT'S NOT JUST THAT, THERE'S SOMETHING WRONG WITH ME TOO. WHEN I SMASHED AXE IN THE HEAD WITH THE GUITAR...I ENJOYED IT.
WELL, HE DESERVED IT! HE WAS A JERK!
NO.
I REALLY ENJOYED IT. I WANTED TO DO IT AGAIN...A COUPLE OF TIMES. IT TOOK ALL MY WILL POWER TO PUT DOWN THE GUITAR AND NOT HIT THAT GUY AGAIN EVEN WHEN HE WAS OUT COLD.
WHAT ARE YOU SAYING, BILLY?
I THINK THAT WHATEVER IT IS THAT MAKES CAPTAIN MARVEL MEAN AND EVIL, IS STARTING TO AFFECT ME TOO. I CAN FEEL MYSELF SLIPPING AWAY AS IF SOMETHING IS TAKING OVER AND IF WE DON'T GET TO THE WIZARD SOON...
...IT MIGHT BE TOO LATE.

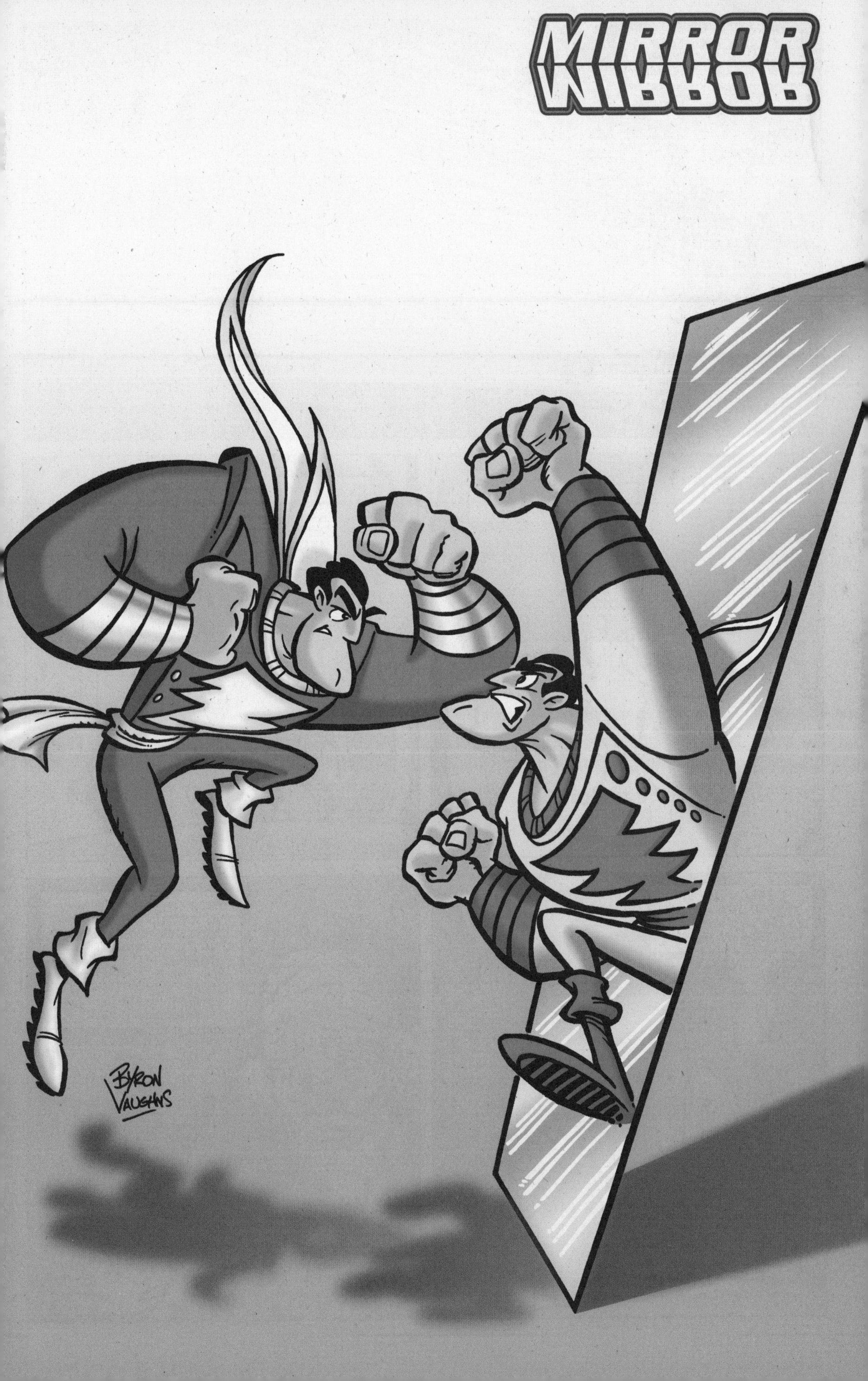
MIRROR
MIRROR
BYRON VAUGHNS

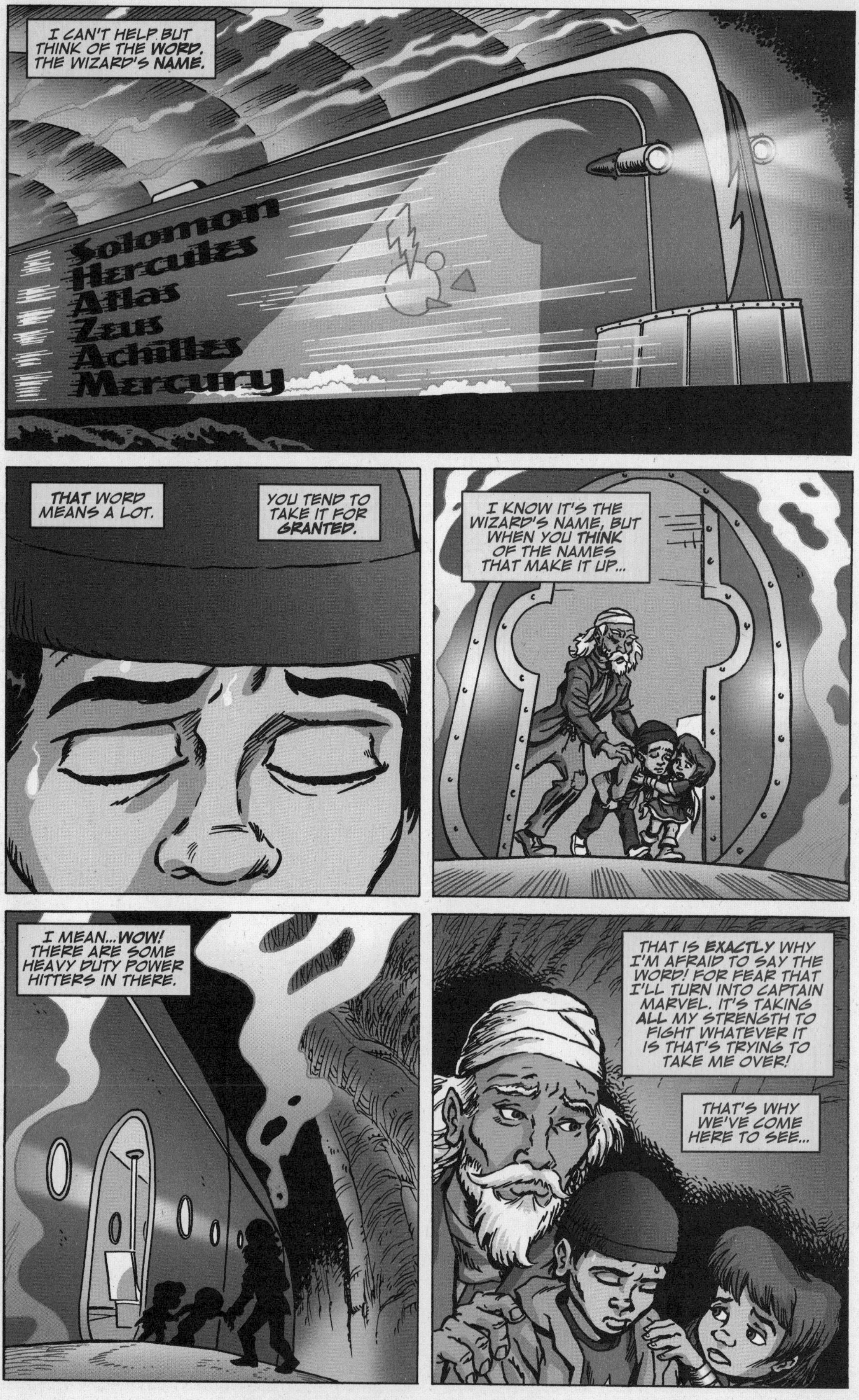
I CAN'T HELP BUT THINK OF THE WORD. THE WIZARD'S NAME.
Solomon
Hercules
Atlas
Zeus
Achilles
Mercury
THAT WORD MEANS A LOT.
YOU TEND TO TAKE IT FOR GRANTED.
I KNOW IT'S THE WIZARD'S NAME, BUT WHEN YOU THINK OF THE NAMES THAT MAKE IT UP...
I MEAN...WOW! THERE ARE SOME HEAVY DUTY POWER HITTERS IN THERE.
THAT IS EXACTLY WHY I'M AFRAID TO SAY THE WORD! FOR FEAR THAT I'LL TURN INTO CAPTAIN MARVEL. IT'S TAKING ALL MY STRENGTH TO FIGHT WHATEVER IT IS THAT'S TRYING TO TAKE ME OVER!
THAT'S WHY WE'VE COME HERE TO SEE...

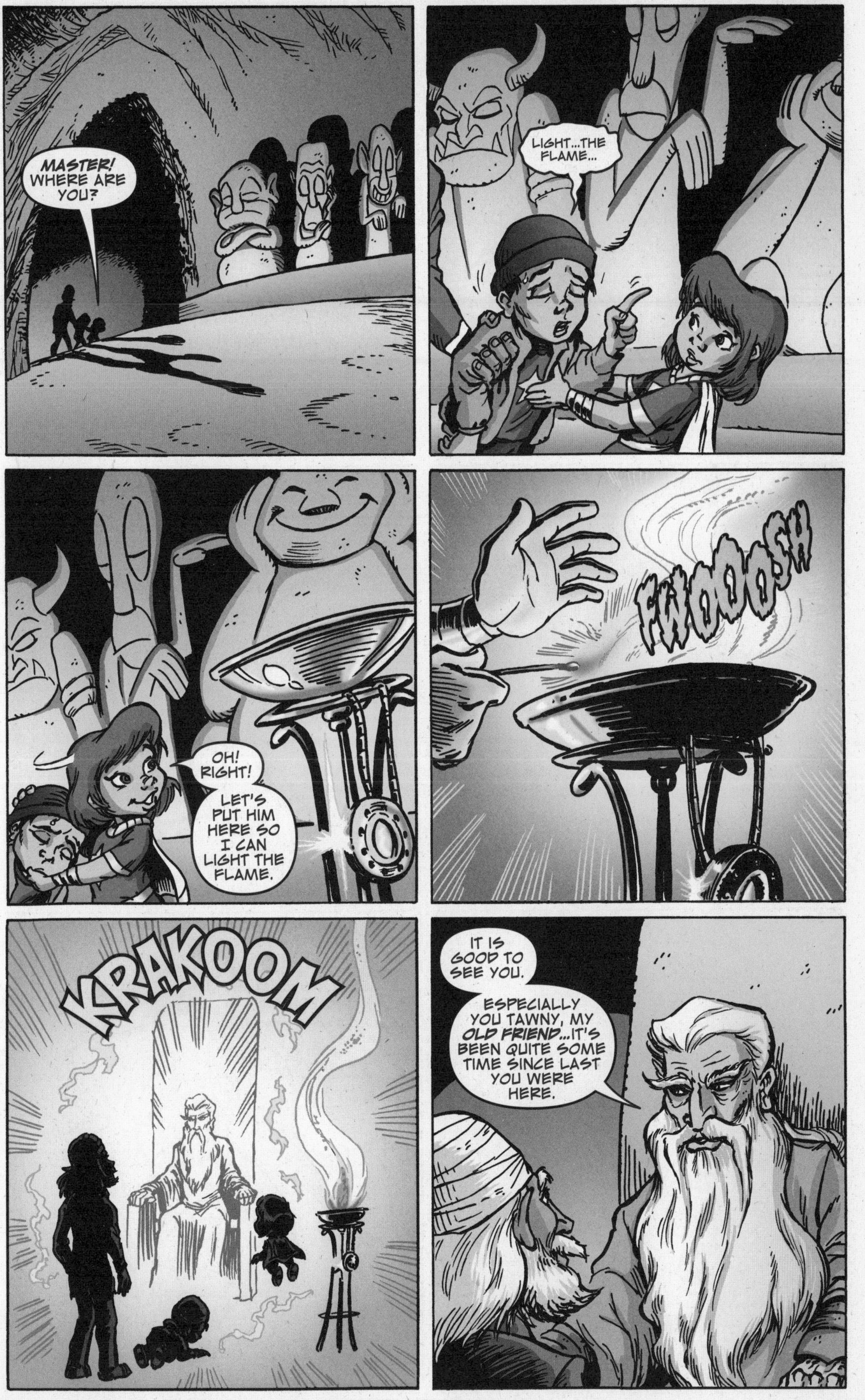
MASTER! WHERE ARE YOU?
LIGHT...THE FLAME...
OH! RIGHT!
LET'S PUT HIM HERE SO I CAN LIGHT THE FLAME.
FWOOOSH
KRAKOOM
IT IS GOOD TO SEE YOU.
ESPECIALLY YOU TAWNY, MY OLD FRIEND...IT'S BEEN QUITE SOME TIME SINCE LAST YOU WERE HERE.

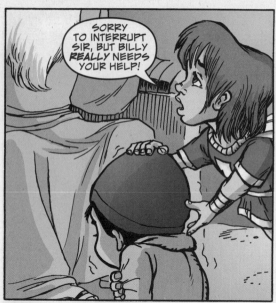

SORRY TO INTERRUPT SIR, BUT BILLY *REALLY* NEEDS YOUR HELP!

MY WORD, BILLY. WHAT HAS HAPPENED?

WE DON'T KNOW EXACTLY, ALL WE KNOW IS FIRST CAPTAIN MARVEL WAS TURNING ALL *MEAN* AND *EVIL* AND NOW THE *SAME THING* IS HAPPENING TO BILLY!

BILLY?

PLEASE SIR, HE'S JUST *BARELY* HOLDING IT TOGETHER! YOU *NEED* TO HELP HIM!

IT'S... DIFFICULT...TO CONCENTRATE...

THIS IS *MOST* DISTRESSING.

YOU KNOW WHAT IT IS? WHAT'S *DOING* THIS TO HIM?

NO.

THE *MOST* DISTRESSING THING ABOUT THIS IS THAT I DID NOT FORESEE IT! THERE IS *SOMETHING* WRONG WITH HIM AND WE MUST DRAW IT OUT.

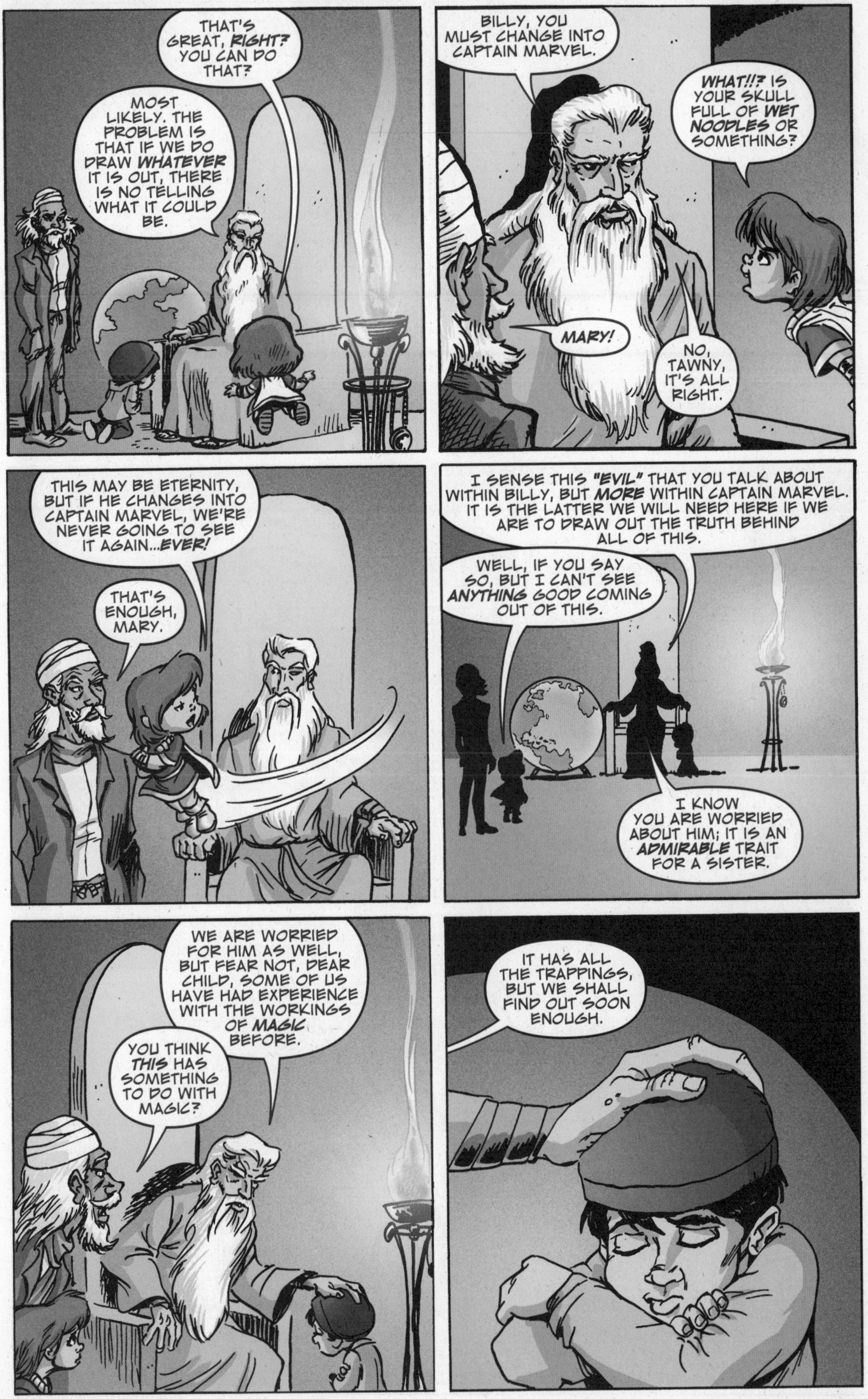
THAT'S GREAT, RIGHT? YOU CAN DO THAT?
MOST LIKELY. THE PROBLEM IS THAT IF WE DO DRAW WHATEVER IT IS OUT, THERE IS NO TELLING WHAT IT COULD BE.
BILLY, YOU MUST CHANGE INTO CAPTAIN MARVEL.
WHAT!!? IS YOUR SKULL FULL OF WET NOODLES OR SOMETHING?
MARY!
NO, TAWNY, IT'S ALL RIGHT.
THIS MAY BE ETERNITY, BUT IF HE CHANGES INTO CAPTAIN MARVEL, WE'RE NEVER GOING TO SEE IT AGAIN...EVER!
THAT'S ENOUGH, MARY.
I SENSE THIS "EVIL" THAT YOU TALK ABOUT WITHIN BILLY, BUT MORE WITHIN CAPTAIN MARVEL. IT IS THE LATTER WE WILL NEED HERE IF WE ARE TO DRAW OUT THE TRUTH BEHIND ALL OF THIS.
WELL, IF YOU SAY SO, BUT I CAN'T SEE ANYTHING GOOD COMING OUT OF THIS.
I KNOW YOU ARE WORRIED ABOUT HIM; IT IS AN ADMIRABLE TRAIT FOR A SISTER.
WE ARE WORRIED FOR HIM AS WELL, BUT FEAR NOT, DEAR CHILD, SOME OF US HAVE HAD EXPERIENCE WITH THE WORKINGS OF MAGIC BEFORE.
YOU THINK THIS HAS SOMETHING TO DO WITH MAGIC?
IT HAS ALL THE TRAPPINGS, BUT WE SHALL FIND OUT SOON ENOUGH.

BILLY, YOU MUST TRANSFORM INTO CAPTAIN MARVEL IF WE ARE TO SOLVE THIS MYSTERY.

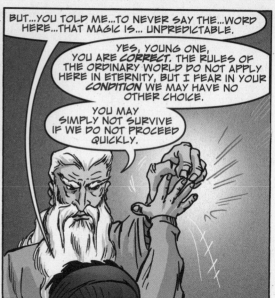

BUT...YOU TOLD ME...TO NEVER SAY THE...WORD HERE...THAT MAGIC IS... UNPREDICTABLE.

YES, YOUNG ONE, YOU ARE *CORRECT.* THE RULES OF THE ORDINARY WORLD DO NOT APPLY HERE IN ETERNITY, BUT I FEAR IN YOUR *CONDITION* WE MAY HAVE NO OTHER CHOICE.

YOU MAY SIMPLY NOT SURVIVE IF WE DO NOT PROCEED QUICKLY.

WELL... IF YOU SAY SO...

I KNOW IT WILL BE DIFFICULT, BUT ONCE YOU TRANSFORM, TRY TO STAY IN CONTROL AS MUCH AS POSSIBLE.

HE CAN DO IT! HE HAS HIS *FAMILY* HERE TO HELP HIM!

SHAZAM...

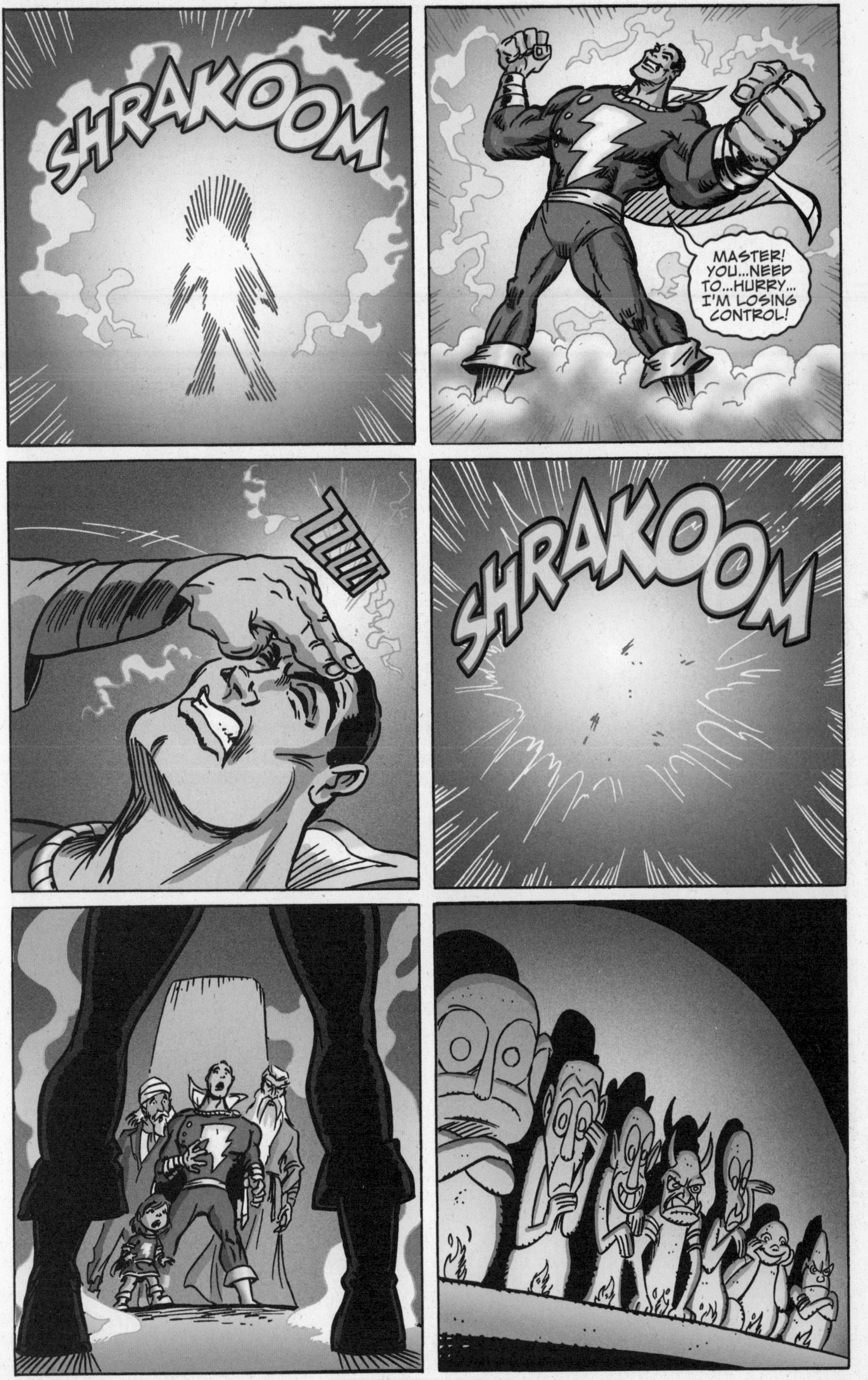
SHRAKOOM
MASTER! YOU...NEED TO...HURRY... I'M LOSING CONTROL!
ZZZZT
SHRAKOOM

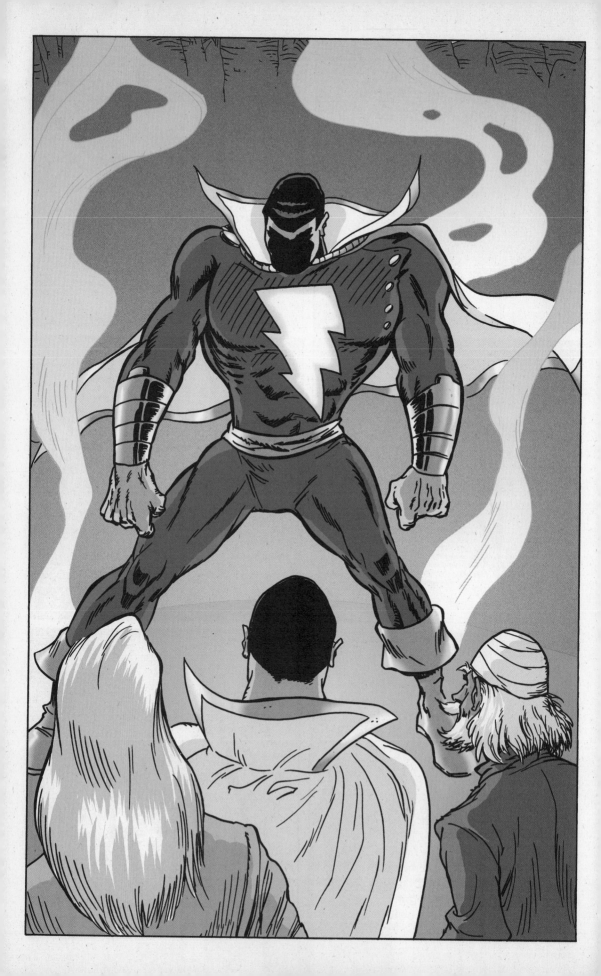

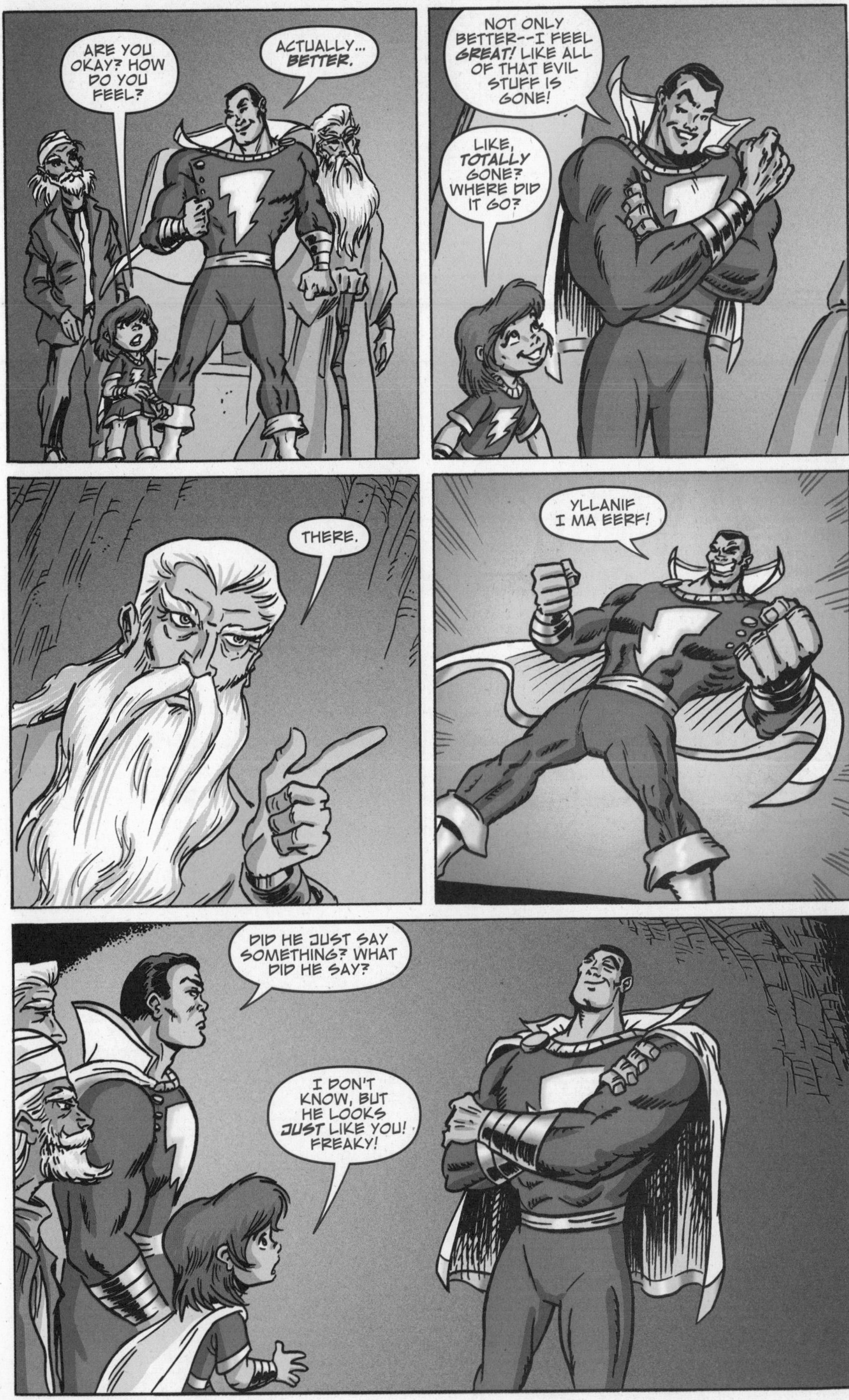
ARE YOU OKAY? HOW DO YOU FEEL?
ACTUALLY... BETTER.
NOT ONLY BETTER--I FEEL GREAT! LIKE ALL OF THAT EVIL STUFF IS GONE!
LIKE, TOTALLY GONE? WHERE DID IT GO?
THERE.
YLLANIF I MA EERF!
DID HE JUST SAY SOMETHING? WHAT DID HE SAY?
I DON'T KNOW, BUT HE LOOKS JUST LIKE YOU! FREAKY!

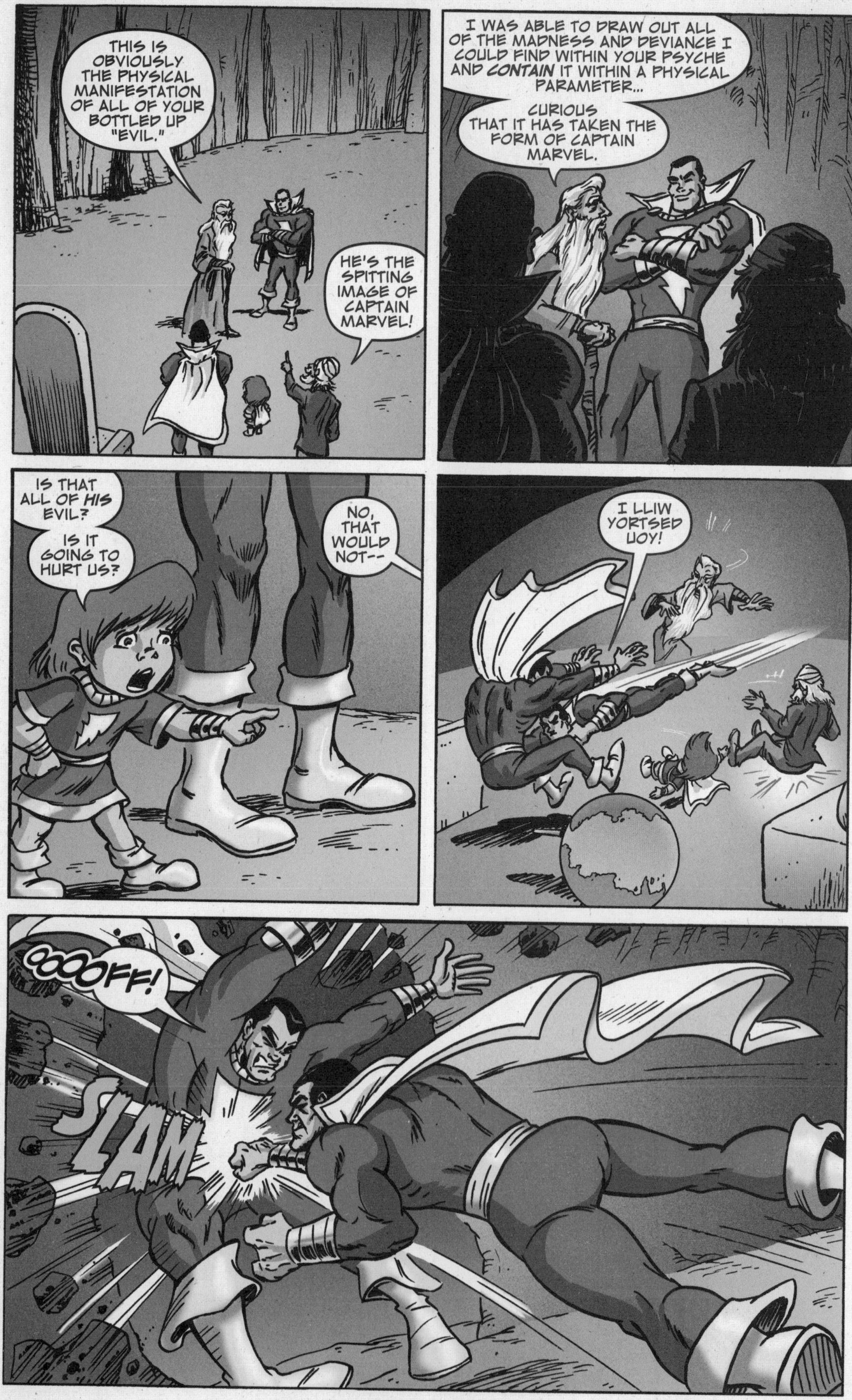
THIS IS OBVIOUSLY THE PHYSICAL MANIFESTATION OF ALL OF YOUR BOTTLED UP "EVIL."
HE'S THE SPITTING IMAGE OF CAPTAIN MARVEL!
I WAS ABLE TO DRAW OUT ALL OF THE MADNESS AND DEVIANCE I COULD FIND WITHIN YOUR PSYCHE AND CONTAIN IT WITHIN A PHYSICAL PARAMETER...
CURIOUS THAT IT HAS TAKEN THE FORM OF CAPTAIN MARVEL.
IS THAT ALL OF HIS EVIL?
IS IT GOING TO HURT US?
NO, THAT WOULD NOT--
I LLIW YORTSED UOY!
OOOOFF!
SLAM

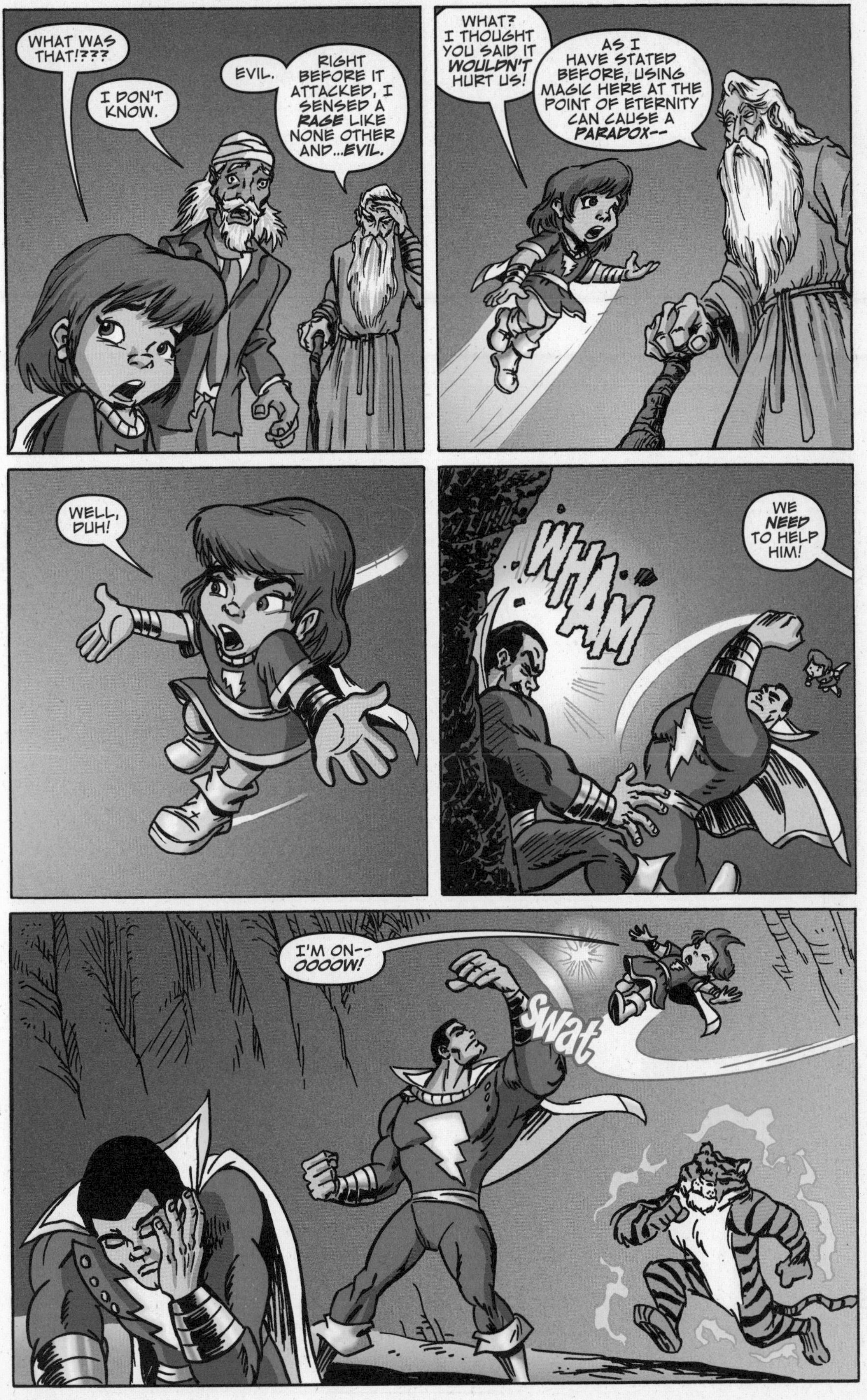
WHAT WAS THAT!???
I DON'T KNOW.
EVIL.
RIGHT BEFORE IT ATTACKED, I SENSED A RAGE LIKE NONE OTHER AND...EVIL.
WHAT? I THOUGHT YOU SAID IT WOULDN'T HURT US!
AS I HAVE STATED BEFORE, USING MAGIC HERE AT THE POINT OF ETERNITY CAN CAUSE A PARADOX--
WELL, DUH!
WHAM
WE NEED TO HELP HIM!
I'M ON-- OOOOW!
SWAT

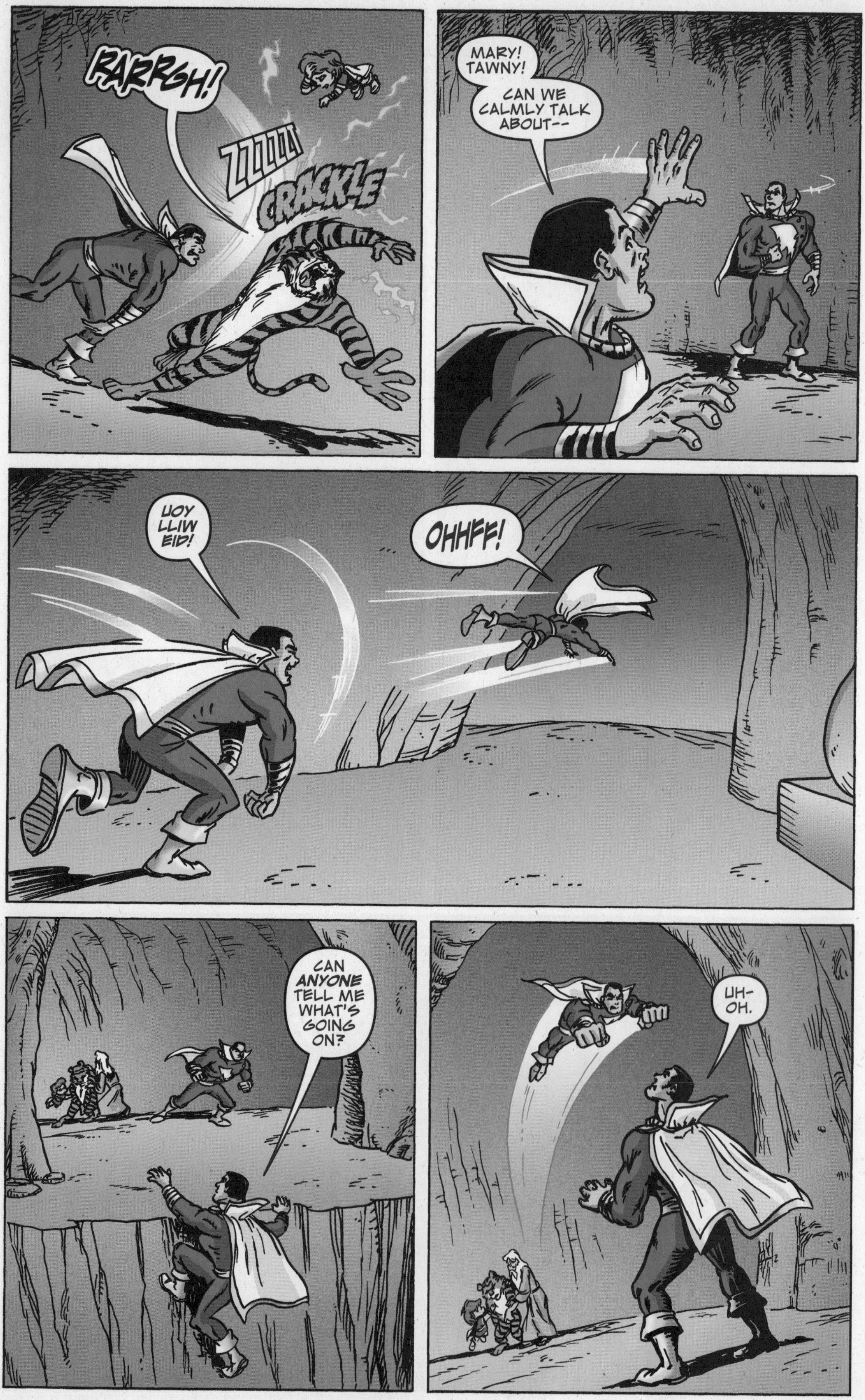
RARRGH!
ZZZZZZ
CRACKLE
MARY! TAWNY!
CAN WE CALMLY TALK ABOUT--
UOY LLIW EID!
OHHFF!
CAN ANYONE TELL ME WHAT'S GOING ON?
UH-OH.

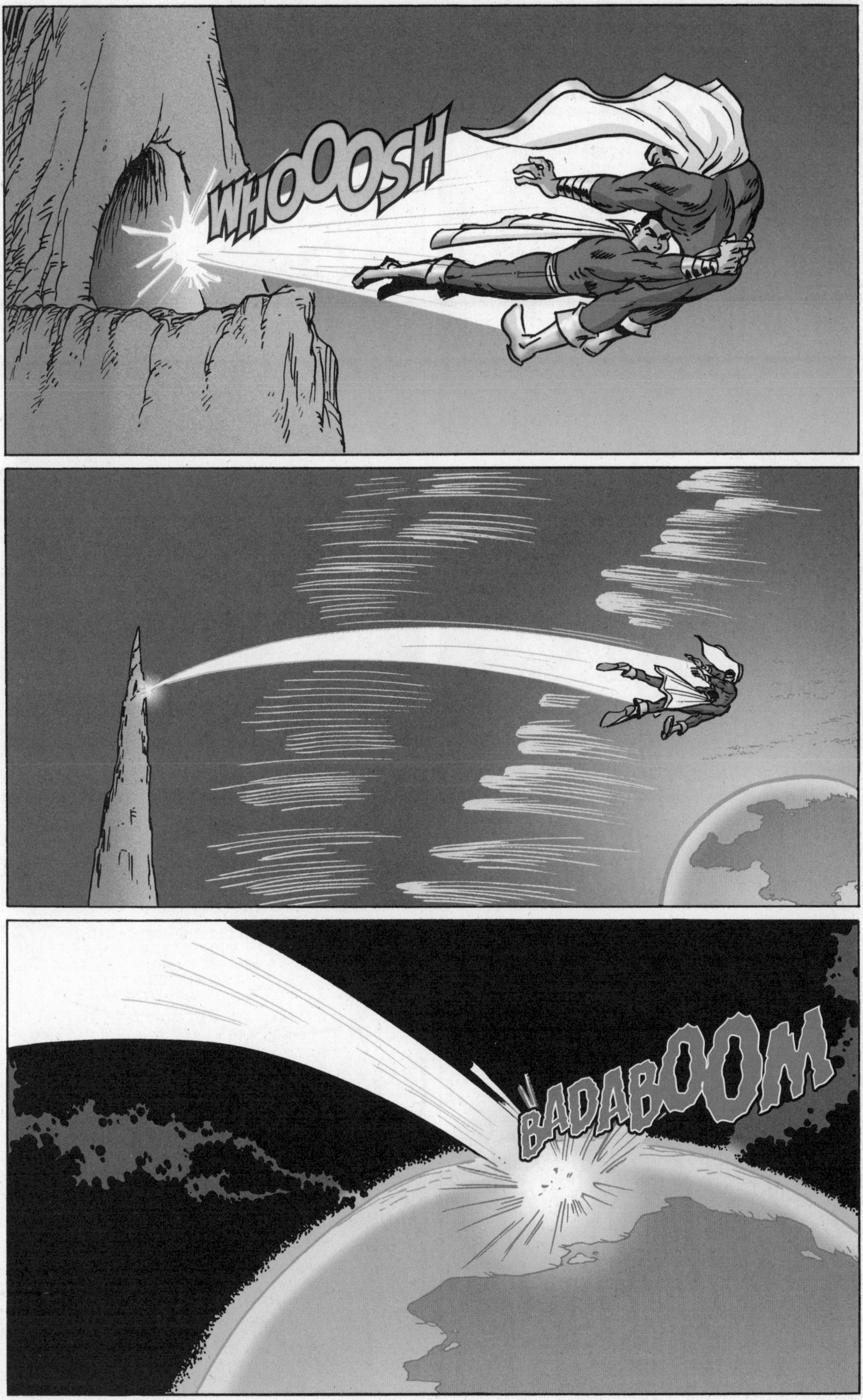
WHOOOOSH
BADABOOM

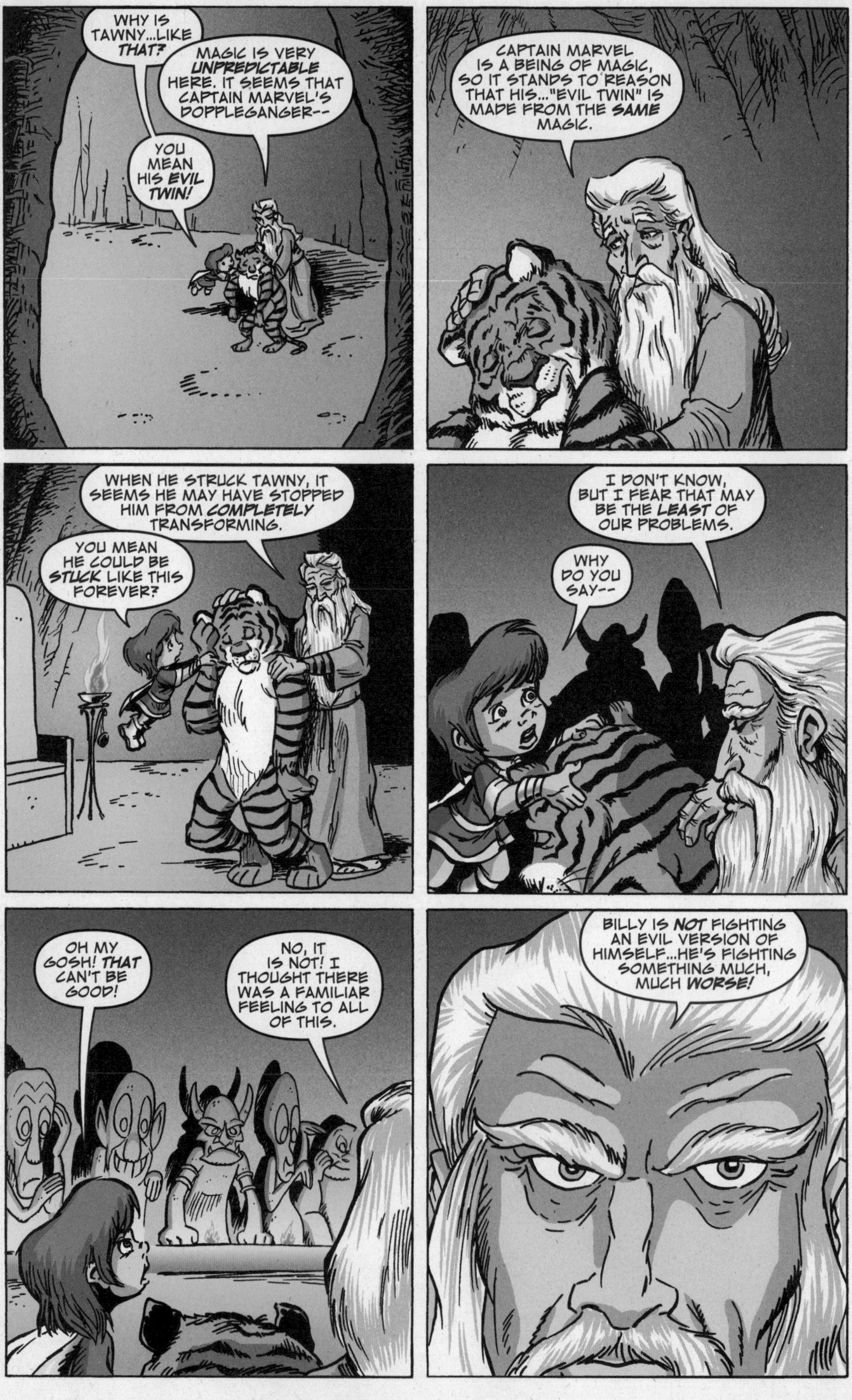
WHY IS TAWNY...LIKE THAT?
MAGIC IS VERY UNPREDICTABLE HERE. IT SEEMS THAT CAPTAIN MARVEL'S DOPPLEGANGER--
YOU MEAN HIS EVIL TWIN!
CAPTAIN MARVEL IS A BEING OF MAGIC, SO IT STANDS TO REASON THAT HIS..."EVIL TWIN" IS MADE FROM THE SAME MAGIC.
WHEN HE STRUCK TAWNY, IT SEEMS HE MAY HAVE STOPPED HIM FROM COMPLETELY TRANSFORMING.
YOU MEAN HE COULD BE STUCK LIKE THIS FOREVER?
I DON'T KNOW, BUT I FEAR THAT MAY BE THE LEAST OF OUR PROBLEMS.
WHY DO YOU SAY--
OH MY GOSH! THAT CAN'T BE GOOD!
NO, IT IS NOT! I THOUGHT THERE WAS A FAMILIAR FEELING TO ALL OF THIS.
BILLY IS NOT FIGHTING AN EVIL VERSION OF HIMSELF...HE'S FIGHTING SOMETHING MUCH, MUCH WORSE!

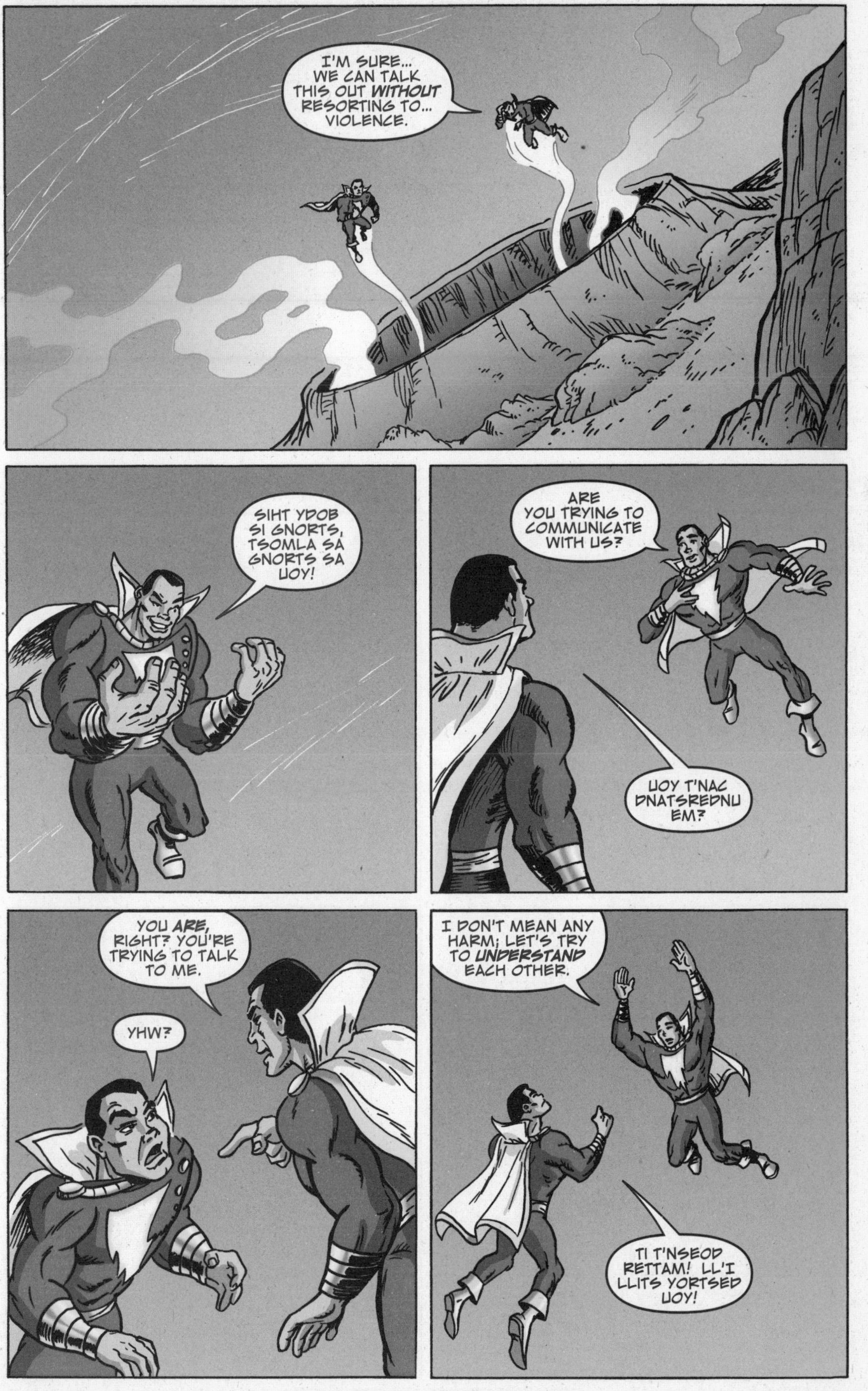
I'M SURE... WE CAN TALK THIS OUT WITHOUT RESORTING TO... VIOLENCE.
SIHT YDOB SI GNORTS, TSOMLA SA GNORTS SA UOY!
ARE YOU TRYING TO COMMUNICATE WITH US?
UOY T'NAC DNATSREDNU EM?
YOU ARE, RIGHT? YOU'RE TRYING TO TALK TO ME.
YHW?
I DON'T MEAN ANY HARM; LET'S TRY TO UNDERSTAND EACH OTHER.
TI T'NSEOD RETTAM! LL'I LLITS YORTSED UOY!

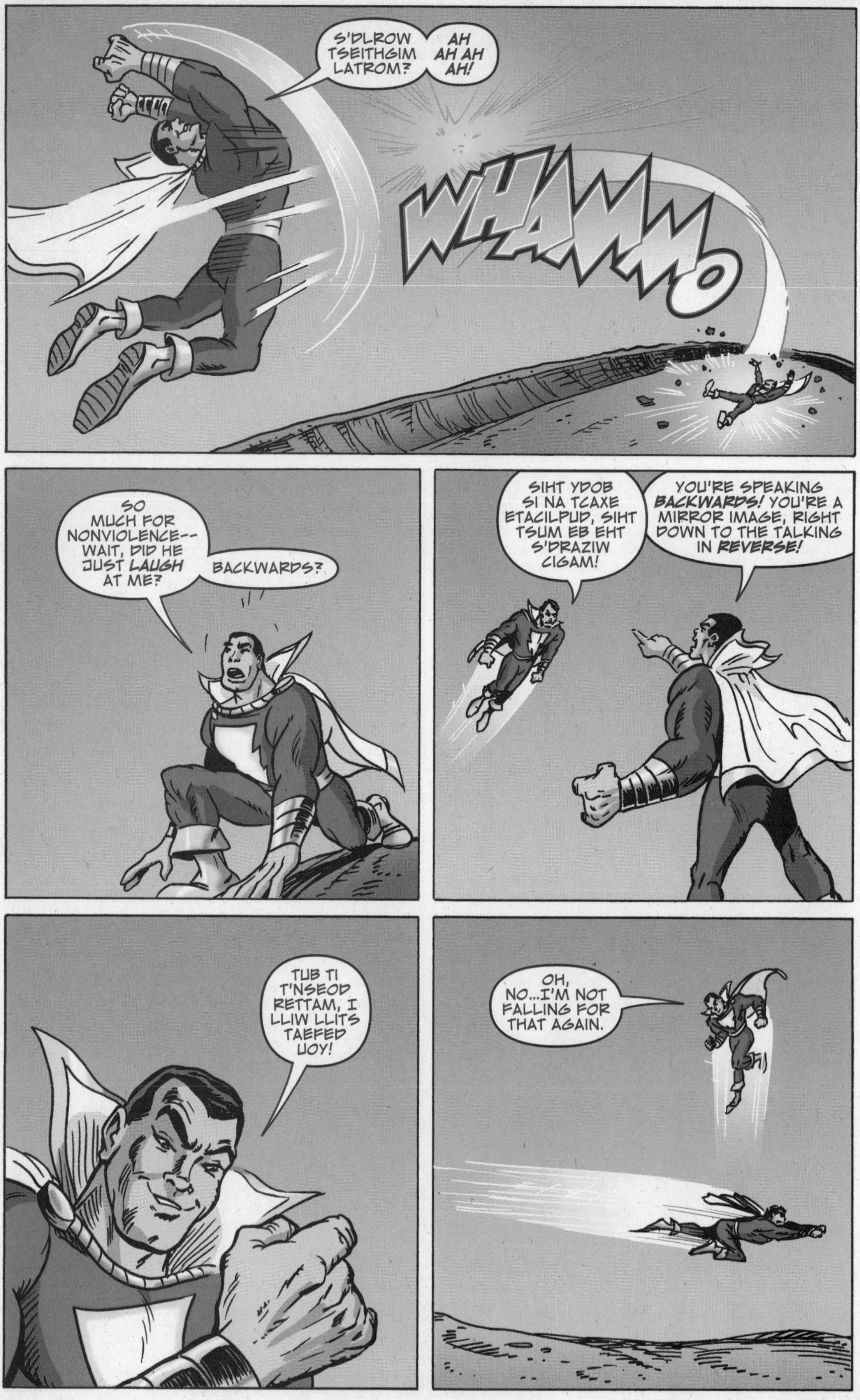
S'DLROW TSEITHGIM LATROM?
AH AH AH AH AH!
WHAMMO
SO MUCH FOR NONVIOLENCE--WAIT, DID HE JUST LAUGH AT ME?
BACKWARDS?
SIHT YDOB SI NA TCAXE ETACILPUD, SIHT TSUM EB EHT S'DRAZIW CIGAM!
YOU'RE SPEAKING BACKWARDS! YOU'RE A MIRROR IMAGE, RIGHT DOWN TO THE TALKING IN REVERSE!
TUB TI T'NSEOD RETTAM, I LLIW LLITS TAEFED UOY!
OH, NO...I'M NOT FALLING FOR THAT AGAIN.

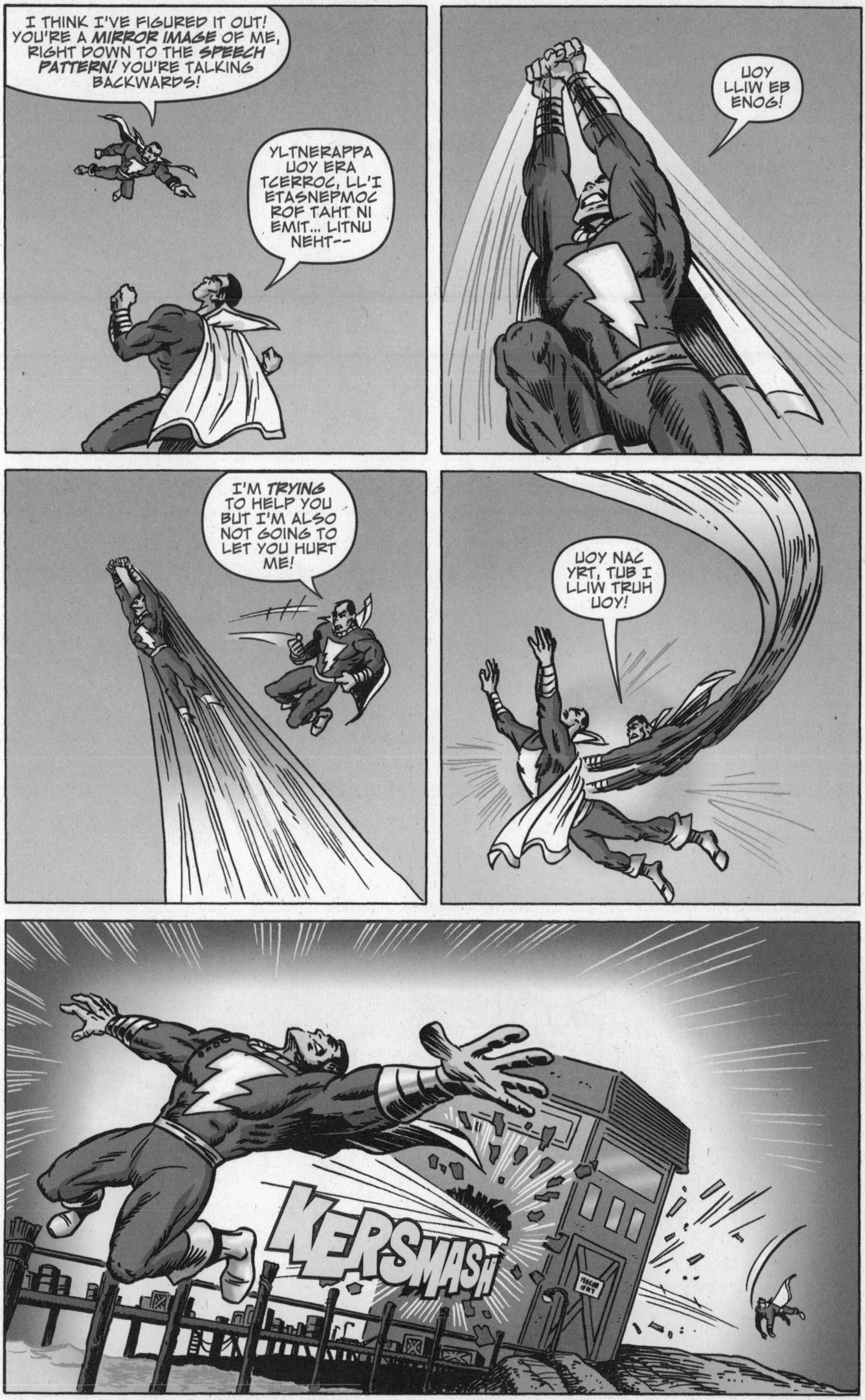
I THINK I'VE FIGURED IT OUT! YOU'RE A MIRROR IMAGE OF ME, RIGHT DOWN TO THE SPEECH PATTERN! YOU'RE TALKING BACKWARDS!
YLTNERAPPA UOY ERA TCERROC, LL'I ETASNEPMOC ROF TAHT NI EMIT... LITNU NEHT--
UOY LLIW EB ENOG!
I'M TRYING TO HELP YOU BUT I'M ALSO NOT GOING TO LET YOU HURT ME!
UOY NAC YRT, TUB I LLIW TRUH UOY!
KERSMASH

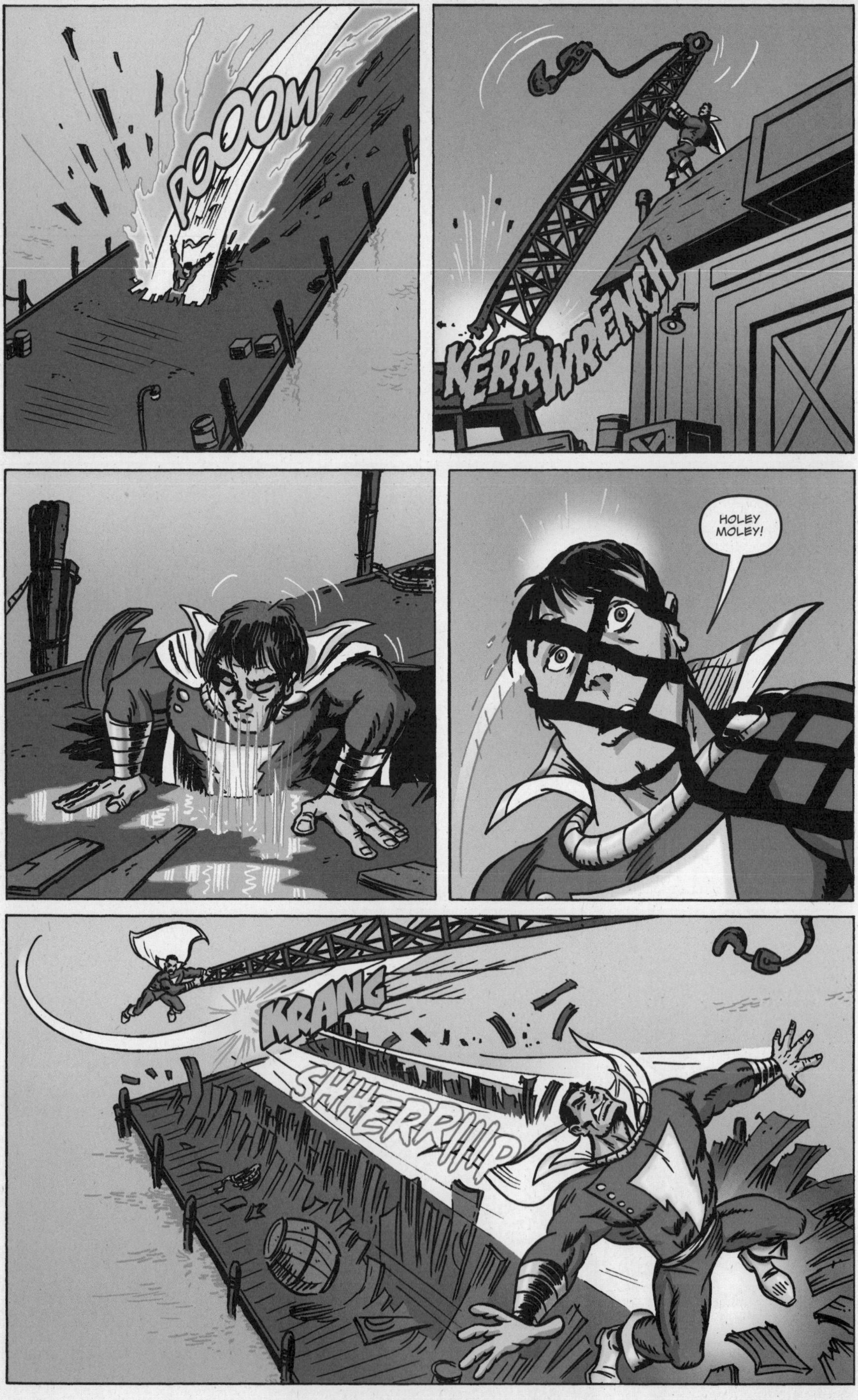
POOOM
KERRWRENCH
HOLEY MOLEY!
KRANG
SHHERRHHP

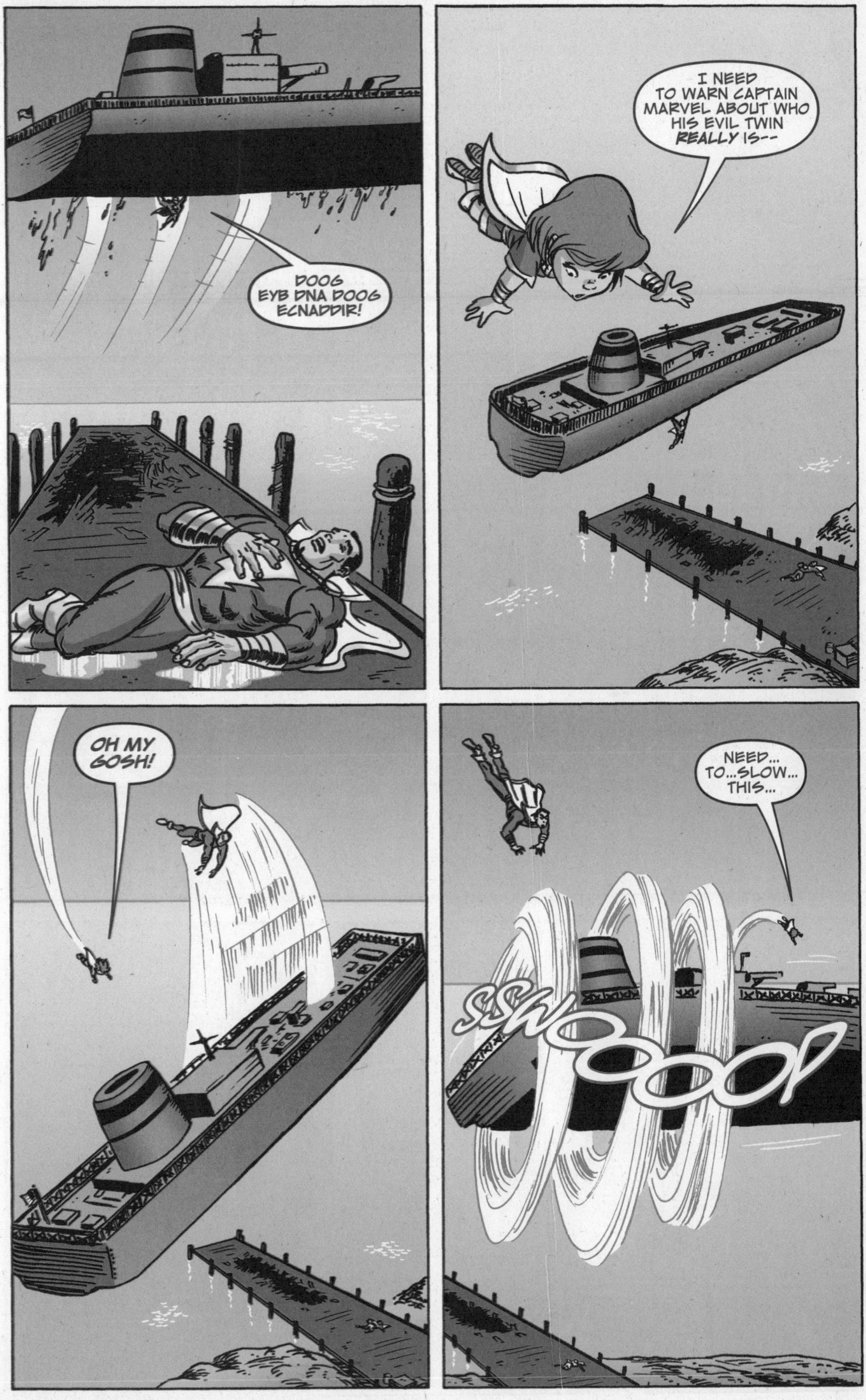
DOOG EYB DNA DOOG ECNADDIR!
I NEED TO WARN CAPTAIN MARVEL ABOUT WHO HIS EVIL TWIN REALLY IS--
OH MY GOSH!
NEED... TO...SLOW... THIS...
SSWOOOOP!

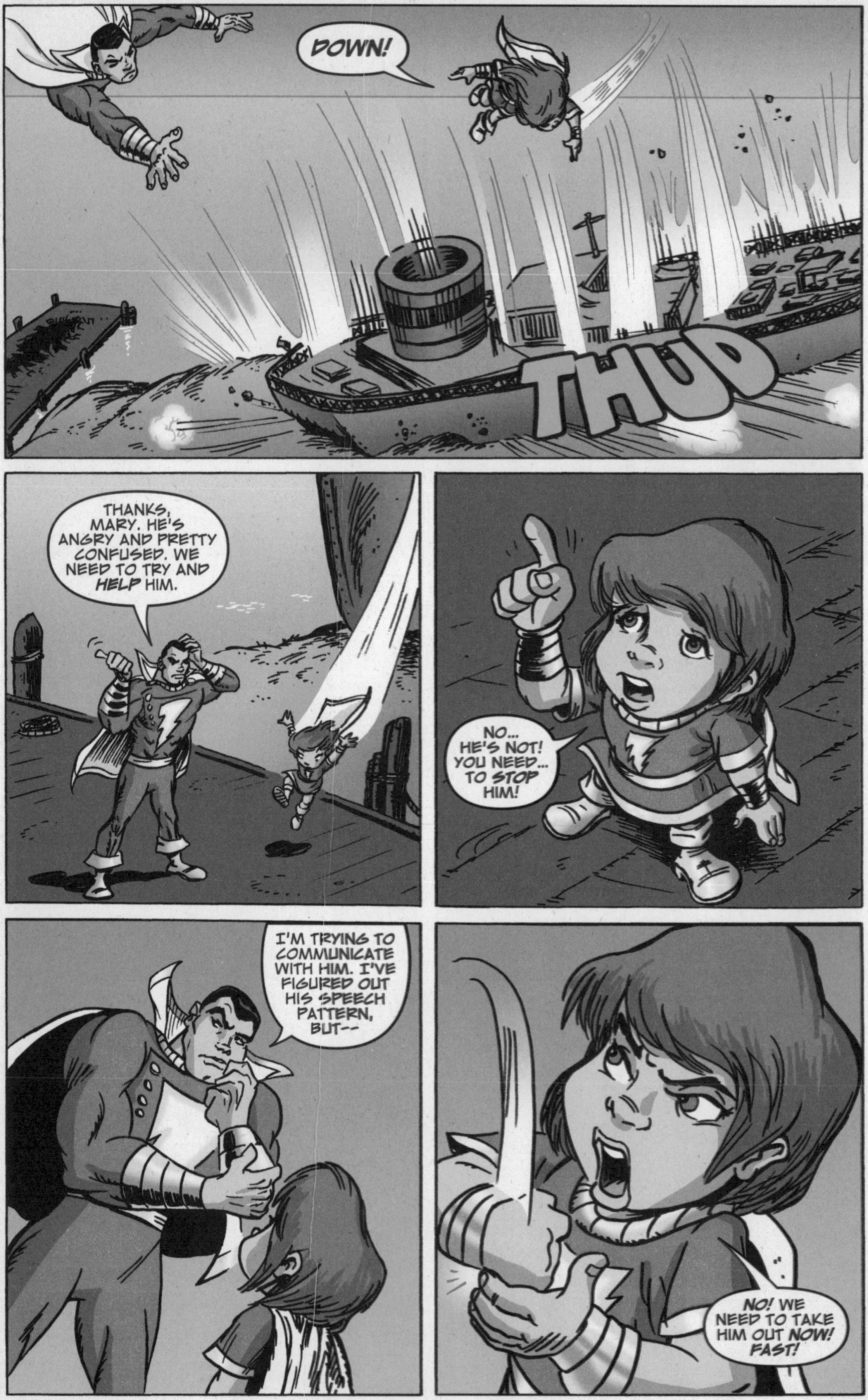
DOWN!
THUD
THANKS, MARY. HE'S ANGRY AND PRETTY CONFUSED. WE NEED TO TRY AND HELP HIM.
NO... HE'S NOT! YOU NEED... TO STOP HIM!
I'M TRYING TO COMMUNICATE WITH HIM. I'VE FIGURED OUT HIS SPEECH PATTERN, BUT--
NO! WE NEED TO TAKE HIM OUT NOW! FAST!

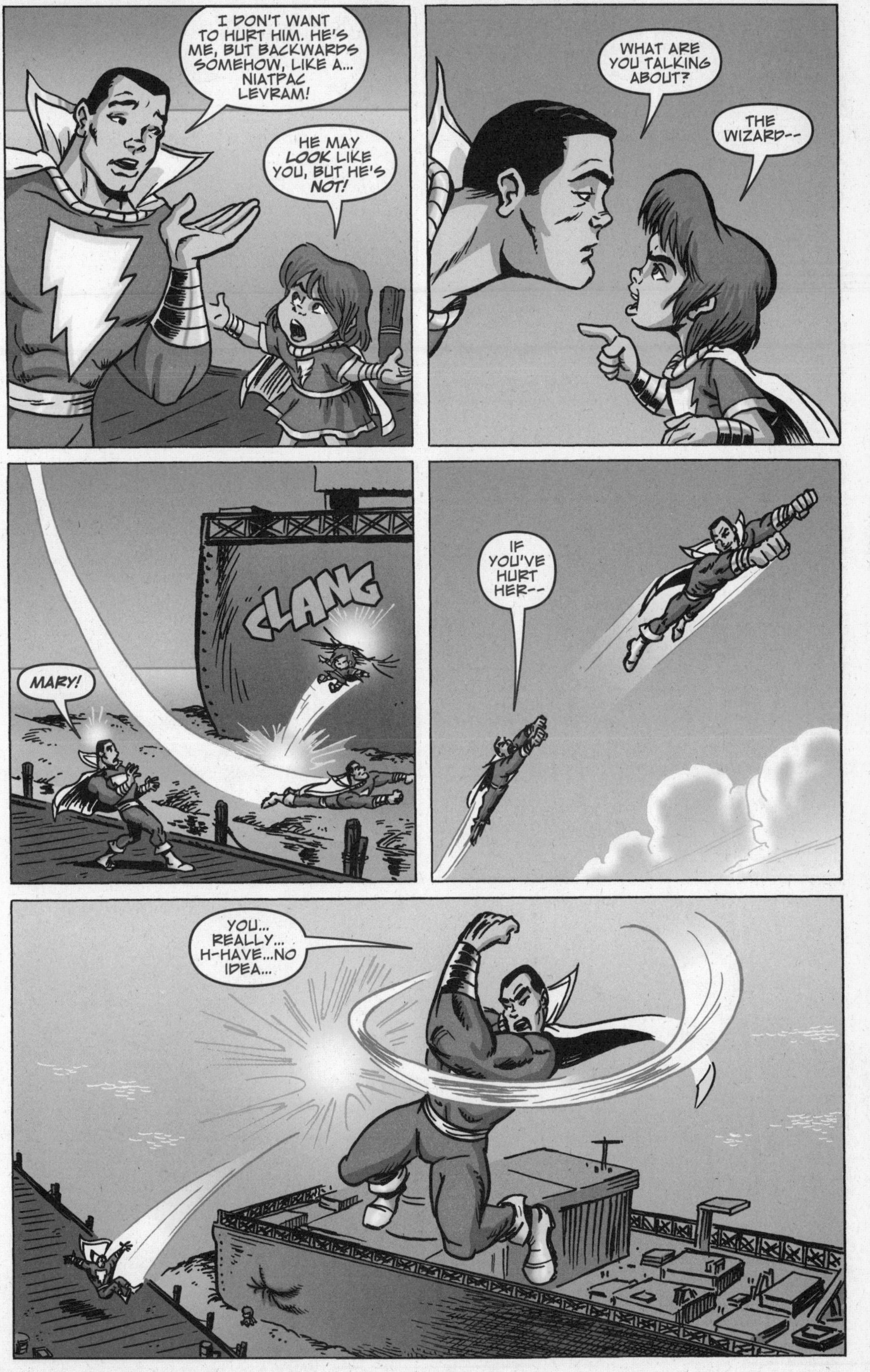
I DON'T WANT TO HURT HIM. HE'S ME, BUT BACKWARDS SOMEHOW, LIKE A... NIATPAC LEVRAM!
HE MAY *LOOK* LIKE YOU, BUT HE'S *NOT*!
WHAT ARE YOU TALKING ABOUT?
THE WIZARD--
CLANG
MARY!
IF YOU'VE HURT HER--
YOU... REALLY... H-HAVE...NO IDEA...

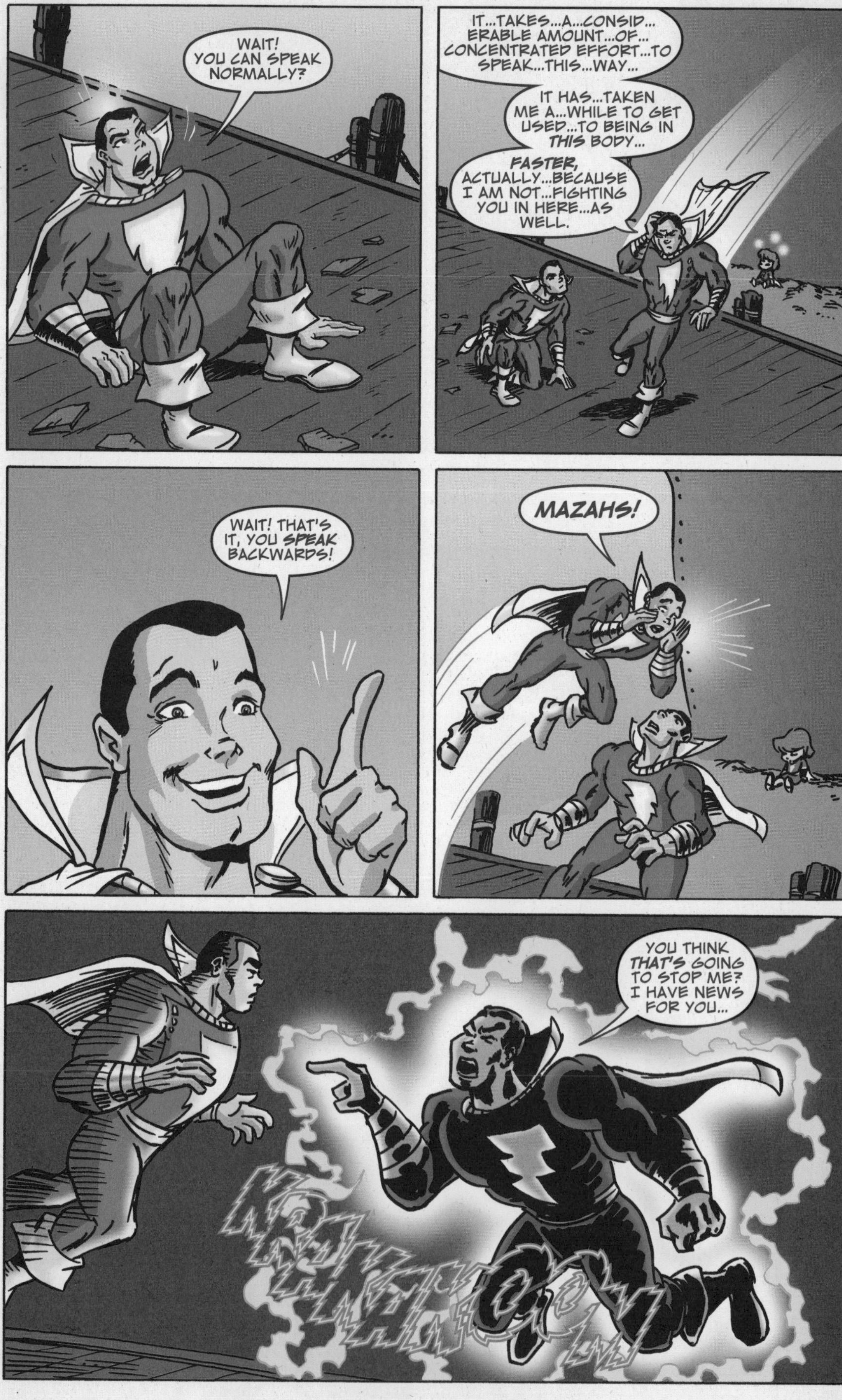
WAIT! YOU CAN SPEAK NORMALLY?
IT...TAKES...A...CONSID... ERABLE AMOUNT...OF... CONCENTRATED EFFORT...TO SPEAK...THIS...WAY...
IT HAS...TAKEN ME A...WHILE TO GET USED...TO BEING IN THIS BODY...
FASTER, ACTUALLY...BECAUSE I AM NOT...FIGHTING YOU IN HERE...AS WELL.
WAIT! THAT'S IT, YOU SPEAK BACKWARDS!
MAZAHS!
YOU THINK THAT'S GOING TO STOP ME? I HAVE NEWS FOR YOU...

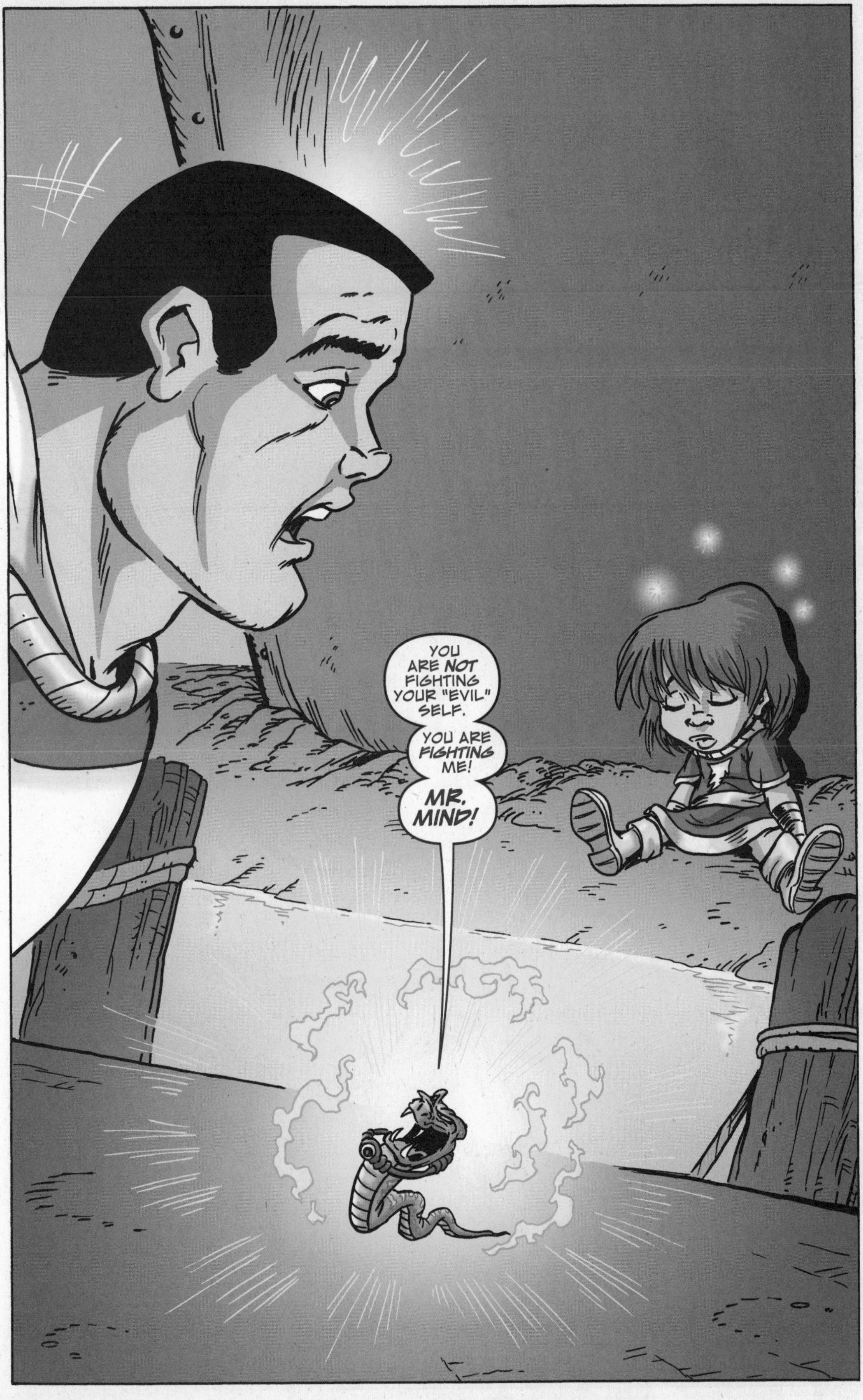
YOU ARE NOT FIGHTING YOUR "EVIL" SELF.
YOU ARE FIGHTING ME!
MR. MIND!

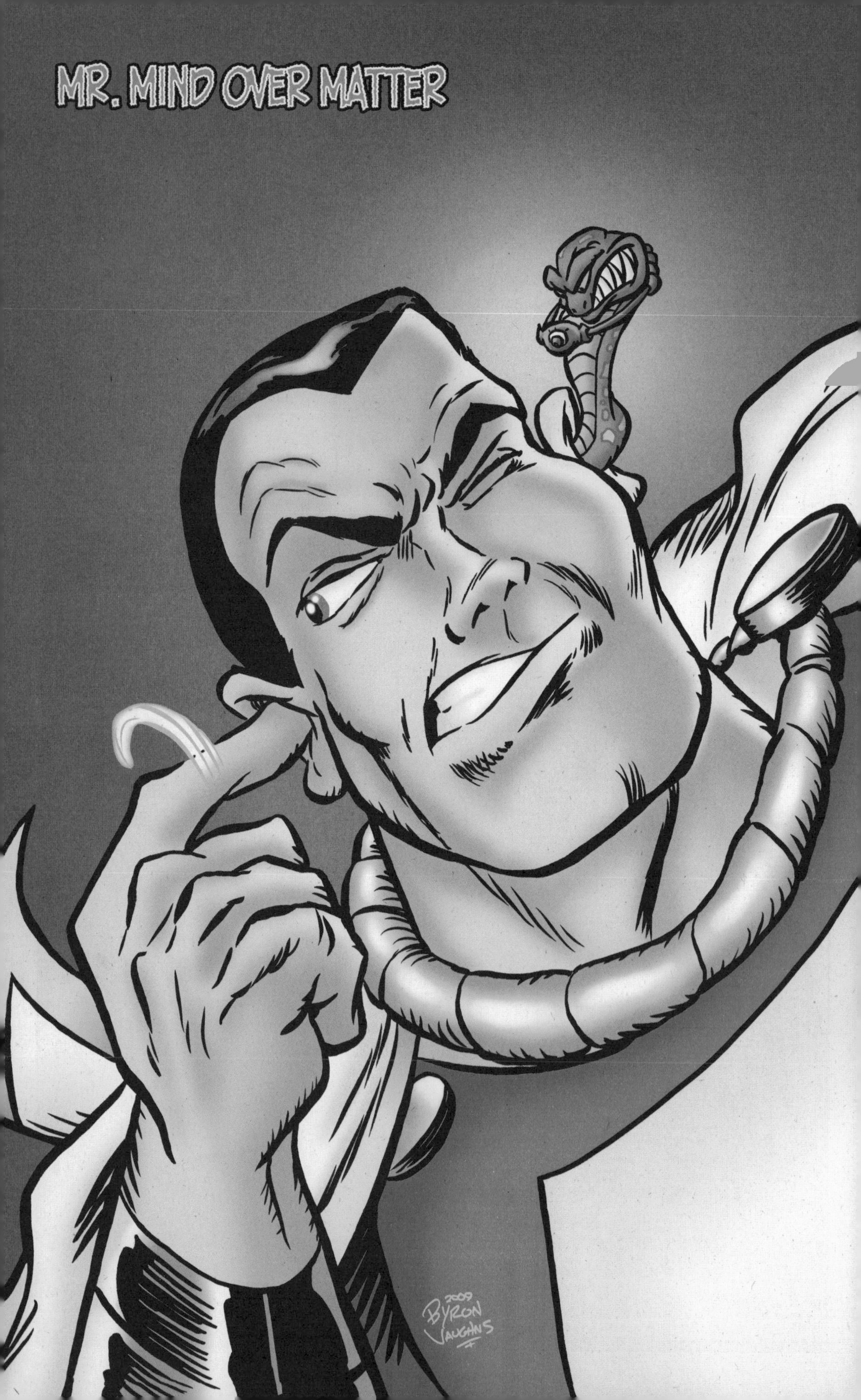
MR. MIND OVER MATTER
2009
BYRON VAUGHNS

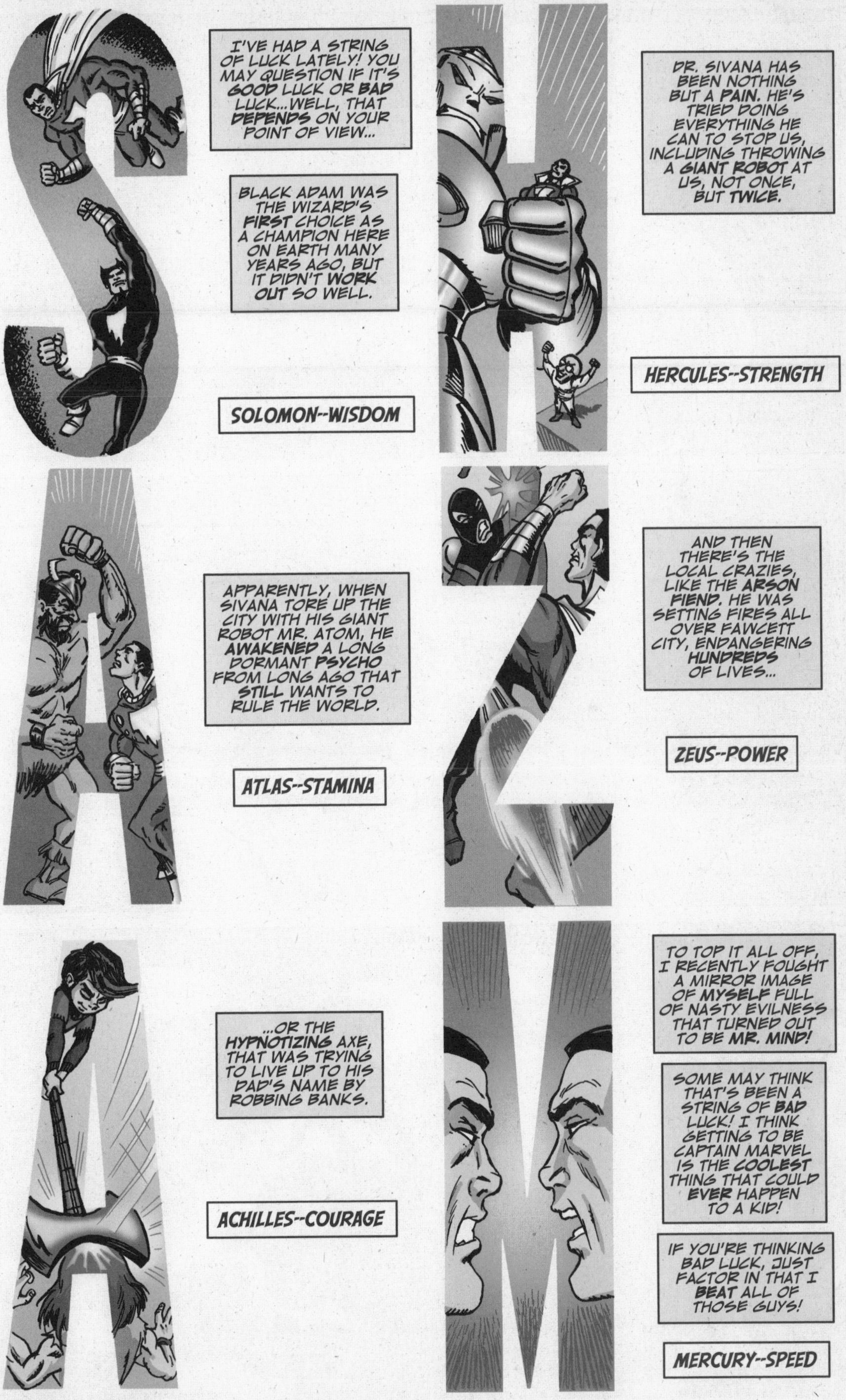

I'VE HAD A STRING OF LUCK LATELY! YOU MAY QUESTION IF IT'S GOOD LUCK OR BAD LUCK...WELL, THAT DEPENDS ON YOUR POINT OF VIEW...

BLACK ADAM WAS THE WIZARD'S FIRST CHOICE AS A CHAMPION HERE ON EARTH MANY YEARS AGO, BUT IT DIDN'T WORK OUT SO WELL.

SOLOMON--WISDOM

DR. SIVANA HAS BEEN NOTHING BUT A PAIN. HE'S TRIED DOING EVERYTHING HE CAN TO STOP US, INCLUDING THROWING A GIANT ROBOT AT US, NOT ONCE, BUT TWICE.

HERCULES--STRENGTH

APPARENTLY, WHEN SIVANA TORE UP THE CITY WITH HIS GIANT ROBOT MR. ATOM, HE AWAKENED A LONG DORMANT PSYCHO FROM LONG AGO THAT STILL WANTS TO RULE THE WORLD.

ATLAS--STAMINA

AND THEN THERE'S THE LOCAL CRAZIES, LIKE THE ARSON FIEND. HE WAS SETTING FIRES ALL OVER FAWCETT CITY, ENDANGERING HUNDREDS OF LIVES...

ZEUS--POWER

...OR THE HYPNOTIZING AXE, THAT WAS TRYING TO LIVE UP TO HIS DAD'S NAME BY ROBBING BANKS.

ACHILLES--COURAGE

TO TOP IT ALL OFF, I RECENTLY FOUGHT A MIRROR IMAGE OF MYSELF FULL OF NASTY EVILNESS THAT TURNED OUT TO BE MR. MIND!

SOME MAY THINK THAT'S BEEN A STRING OF BAD LUCK! I THINK GETTING TO BE CAPTAIN MARVEL IS THE COOLEST THING THAT COULD EVER HAPPEN TO A KID!

IF YOU'RE THINKING BAD LUCK, JUST FACTOR IN THAT I BEAT ALL OF THOSE GUYS!

MERCURY--SPEED

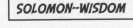

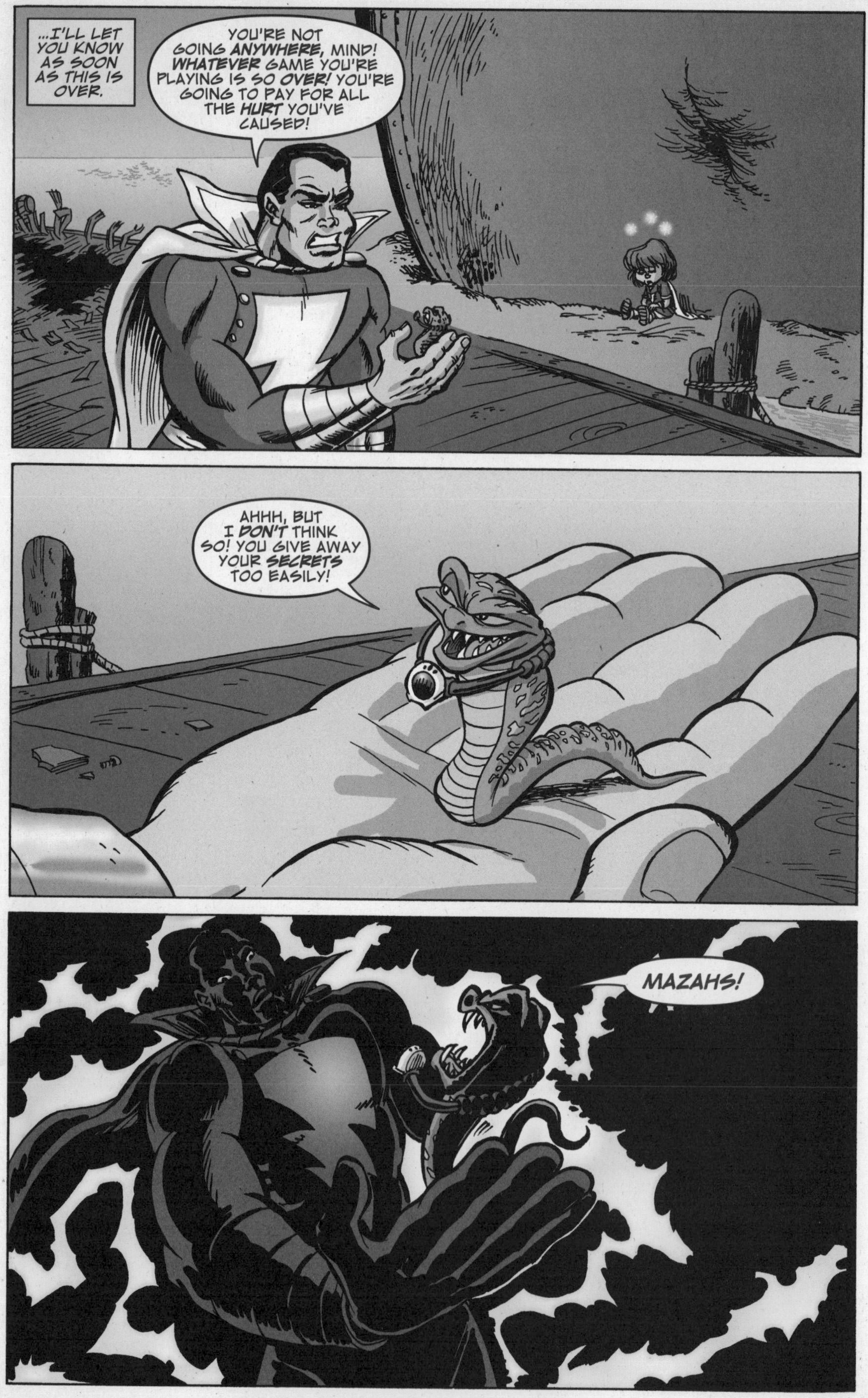
...I'LL LET YOU KNOW AS SOON AS THIS IS OVER.
YOU'RE NOT GOING ANYWHERE, MIND! WHATEVER GAME YOU'RE PLAYING IS SO OVER! YOU'RE GOING TO PAY FOR ALL THE HURT YOU'VE CAUSED!
AHHH, BUT I DON'T THINK SO! YOU GIVE AWAY YOUR SECRETS TOO EASILY!
MAZAHS!

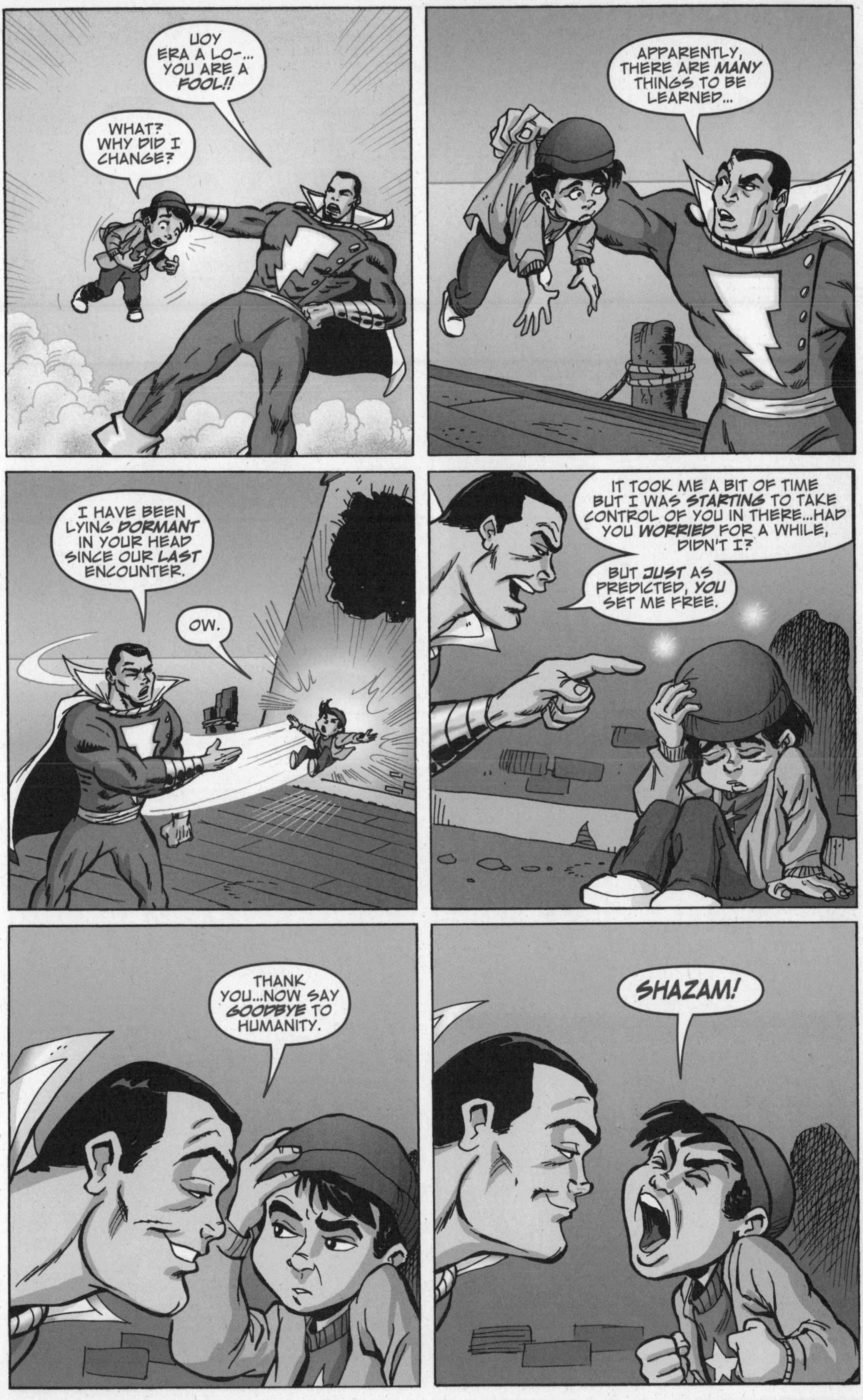

UOY ERA A LO-... YOU ARE A FOOL!!
WHAT? WHY DID I CHANGE?
APPARENTLY, THERE ARE MANY THINGS TO BE LEARNED...
I HAVE BEEN LYING DORMANT IN YOUR HEAD SINCE OUR LAST ENCOUNTER.
OW.
IT TOOK ME A BIT OF TIME BUT I WAS STARTING TO TAKE CONTROL OF YOU IN THERE...HAD YOU WORRIED FOR A WHILE, DIDN'T I?
BUT JUST AS PREDICTED, YOU SET ME FREE.
THANK YOU...NOW SAY GOODBYE TO HUMANITY.
SHAZAM!

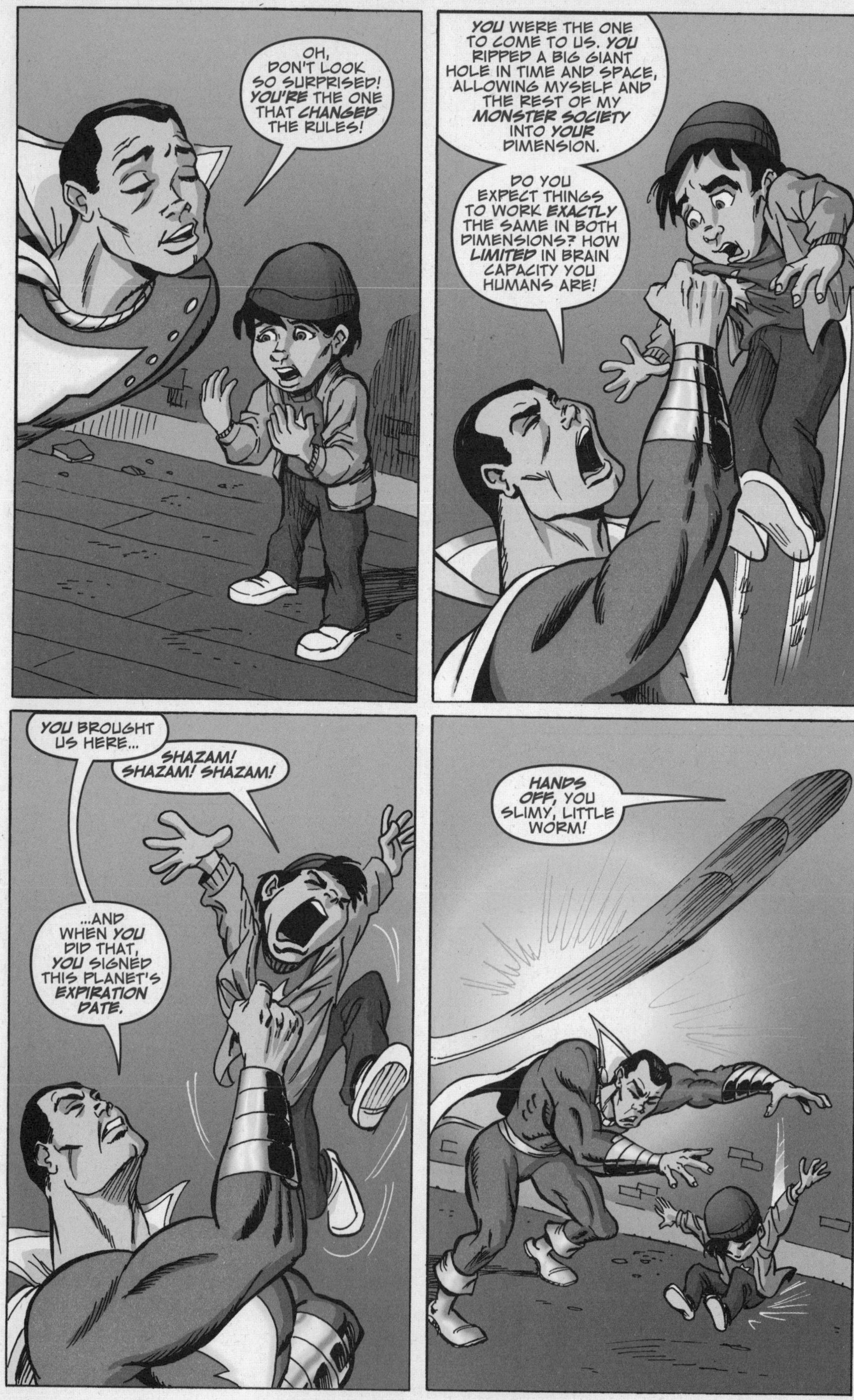
OH, DON'T LOOK SO SURPRISED! YOU'RE THE ONE THAT CHANGED THE RULES!
YOU WERE THE ONE TO COME TO US. YOU RIPPED A BIG GIANT HOLE IN TIME AND SPACE, ALLOWING MYSELF AND THE REST OF MY MONSTER SOCIETY INTO YOUR DIMENSION.
DO YOU EXPECT THINGS TO WORK EXACTLY THE SAME IN BOTH DIMENSIONS? HOW LIMITED IN BRAIN CAPACITY YOU HUMANS ARE!
YOU BROUGHT US HERE...
SHAZAM! SHAZAM! SHAZAM!
...AND WHEN YOU DID THAT, YOU SIGNED THIS PLANET'S EXPIRATION DATE.
HANDS OFF, YOU SLIMY, LITTLE WORM!

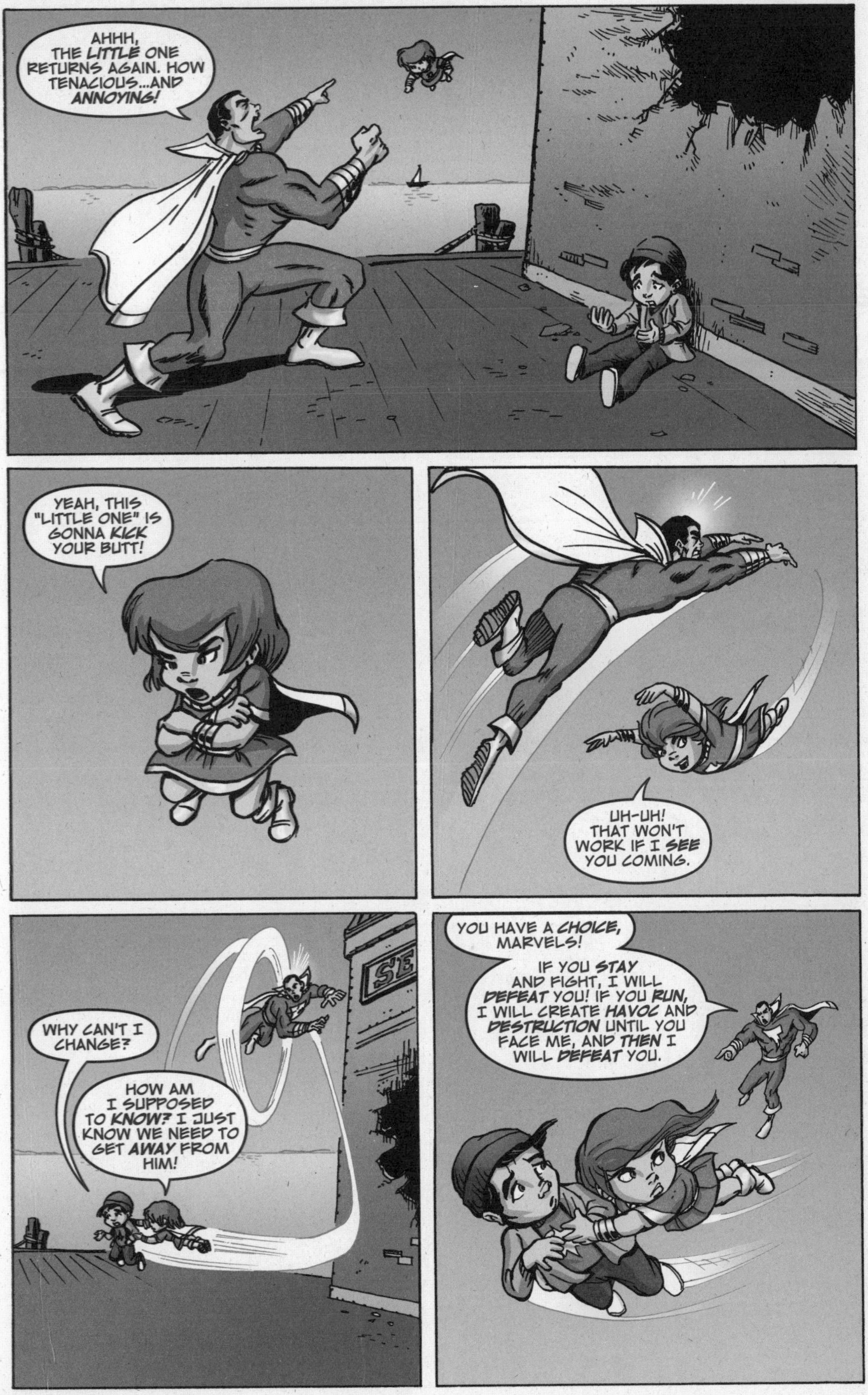
AHHH, THE LITTLE ONE RETURNS AGAIN. HOW TENACIOUS...AND ANNOYING!
YEAH, THIS "LITTLE ONE" IS GONNA KICK YOUR BUTT!
UH-UH! THAT WON'T WORK IF I SEE YOU COMING.
WHY CAN'T I CHANGE?
HOW AM I SUPPOSED TO KNOW? I JUST KNOW WE NEED TO GET AWAY FROM HIM!
YOU HAVE A CHOICE, MARVELS!
IF YOU STAY AND FIGHT, I WILL DEFEAT YOU! IF YOU RUN, I WILL CREATE HAVOC AND DESTRUCTION UNTIL YOU FACE ME, AND THEN I WILL DEFEAT YOU.

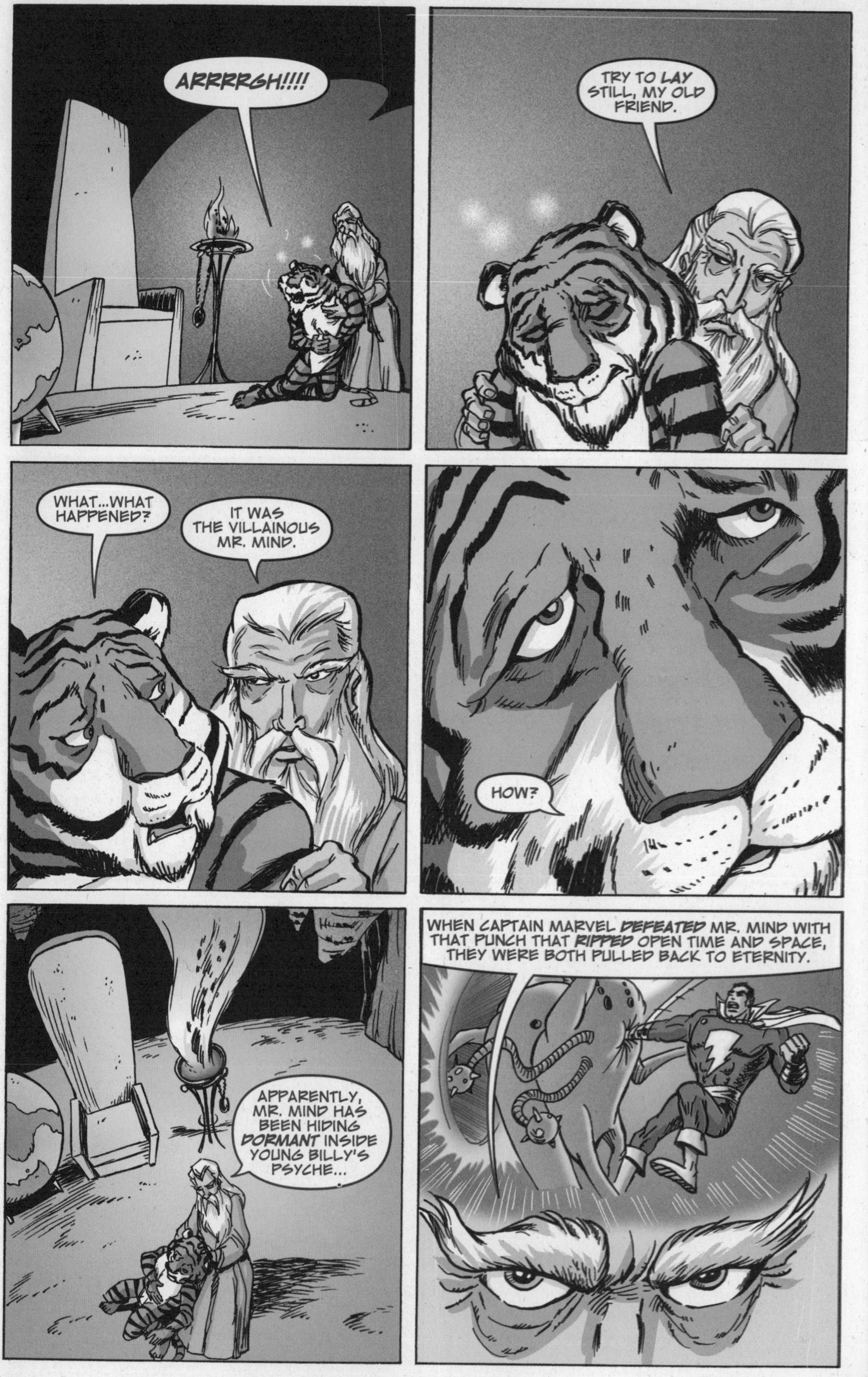
ARRRRGH!!!!
TRY TO LAY STILL, MY OLD FRIEND.
WHAT...WHAT HAPPENED?
IT WAS THE VILLAINOUS MR. MIND.
HOW?
APPARENTLY, MR. MIND HAS BEEN HIDING DORMANT INSIDE YOUNG BILLY'S PSYCHE...
WHEN CAPTAIN MARVEL DEFEATED MR. MIND WITH THAT PUNCH THAT RIPPED OPEN TIME AND SPACE, THEY WERE BOTH PULLED BACK TO ETERNITY.

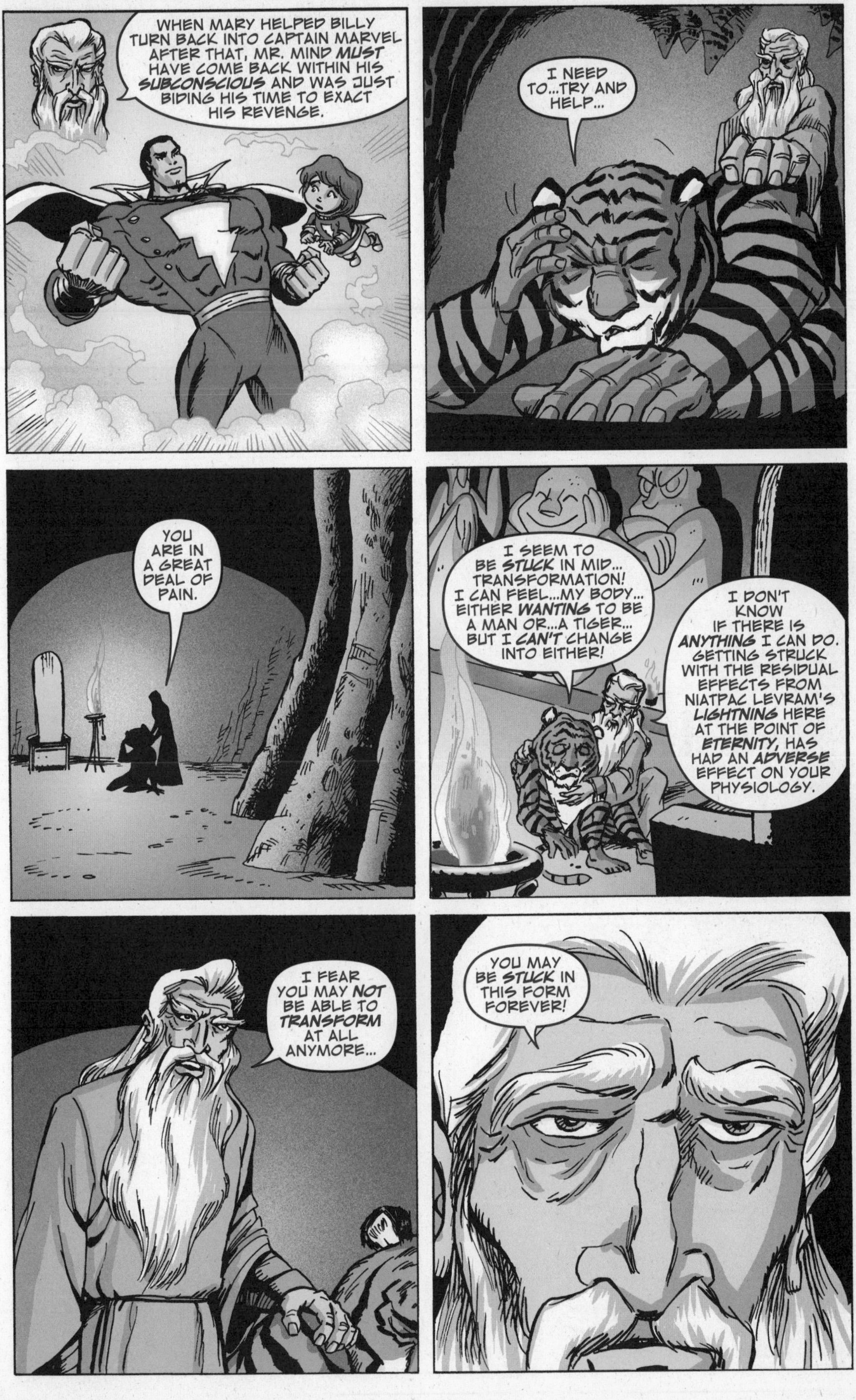
WHEN MARY HELPED BILLY TURN BACK INTO CAPTAIN MARVEL AFTER THAT, MR. MIND MUST HAVE COME BACK WITHIN HIS SUBCONSCIOUS AND WAS JUST BIDING HIS TIME TO EXACT HIS REVENGE.
I NEED TO...TRY AND HELP...
YOU ARE IN A GREAT DEAL OF PAIN.
I SEEM TO BE STUCK IN MID... TRANSFORMATION! I CAN FEEL...MY BODY... EITHER WANTING TO BE A MAN OR...A TIGER... BUT I CAN'T CHANGE INTO EITHER!
I DON'T KNOW IF THERE IS ANYTHING I CAN DO. GETTING STRUCK WITH THE RESIDUAL EFFECTS FROM NIATPAC LEVRAM'S LIGHTNING HERE AT THE POINT OF ETERNITY, HAS HAD AN ADVERSE EFFECT ON YOUR PHYSIOLOGY.
I FEAR YOU MAY NOT BE ABLE TO TRANSFORM AT ALL ANYMORE...
YOU MAY BE STUCK IN THIS FORM FOREVER!

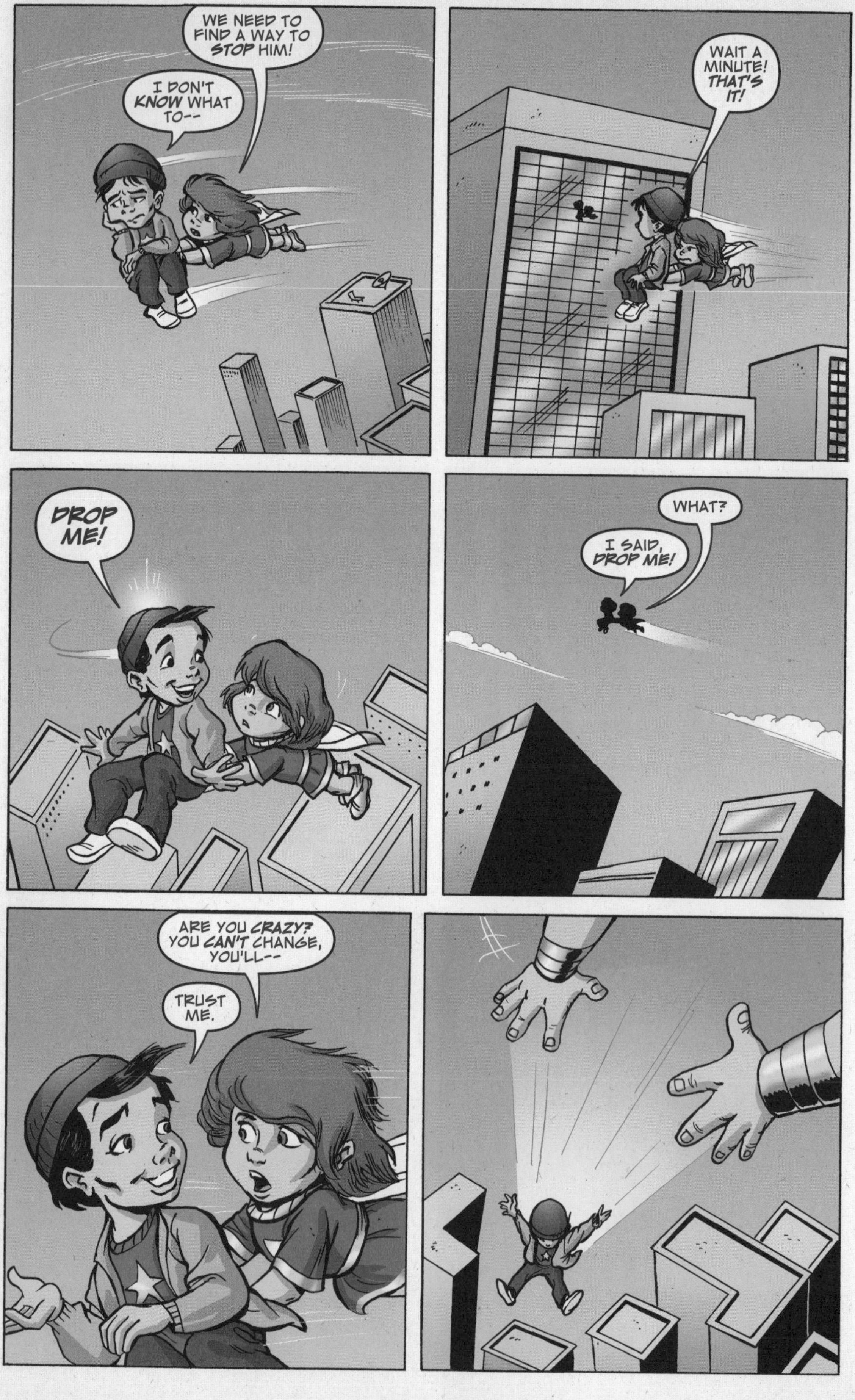
WE NEED TO FIND A WAY TO STOP HIM!
I DON'T KNOW WHAT TO--
WAIT A MINUTE! THAT'S IT!
DROP ME!
WHAT?
I SAID, DROP ME!
ARE YOU CRAZY? YOU CAN'T CHANGE, YOU'LL--
TRUST ME.

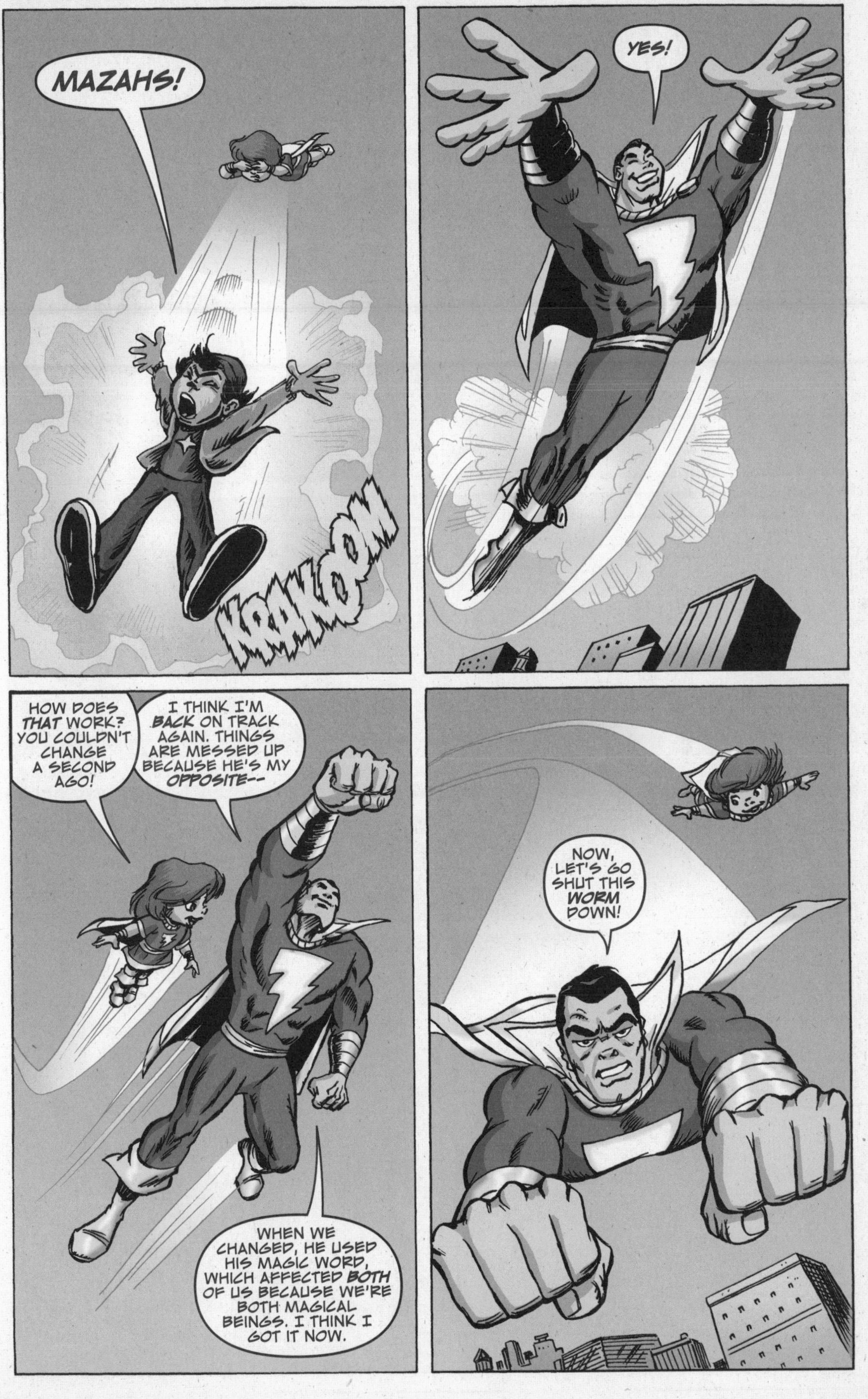
MAZAHS!
KRAKOOM
YES!
HOW DOES THAT WORK? YOU COULDN'T CHANGE A SECOND AGO!
I THINK I'M BACK ON TRACK AGAIN. THINGS ARE MESSED UP BECAUSE HE'S MY OPPOSITE--
WHEN WE CHANGED, HE USED HIS MAGIC WORD, WHICH AFFECTED BOTH OF US BECAUSE WE'RE BOTH MAGICAL BEINGS. I THINK I GOT IT NOW.
NOW, LET'S GO SHUT THIS WORM DOWN!

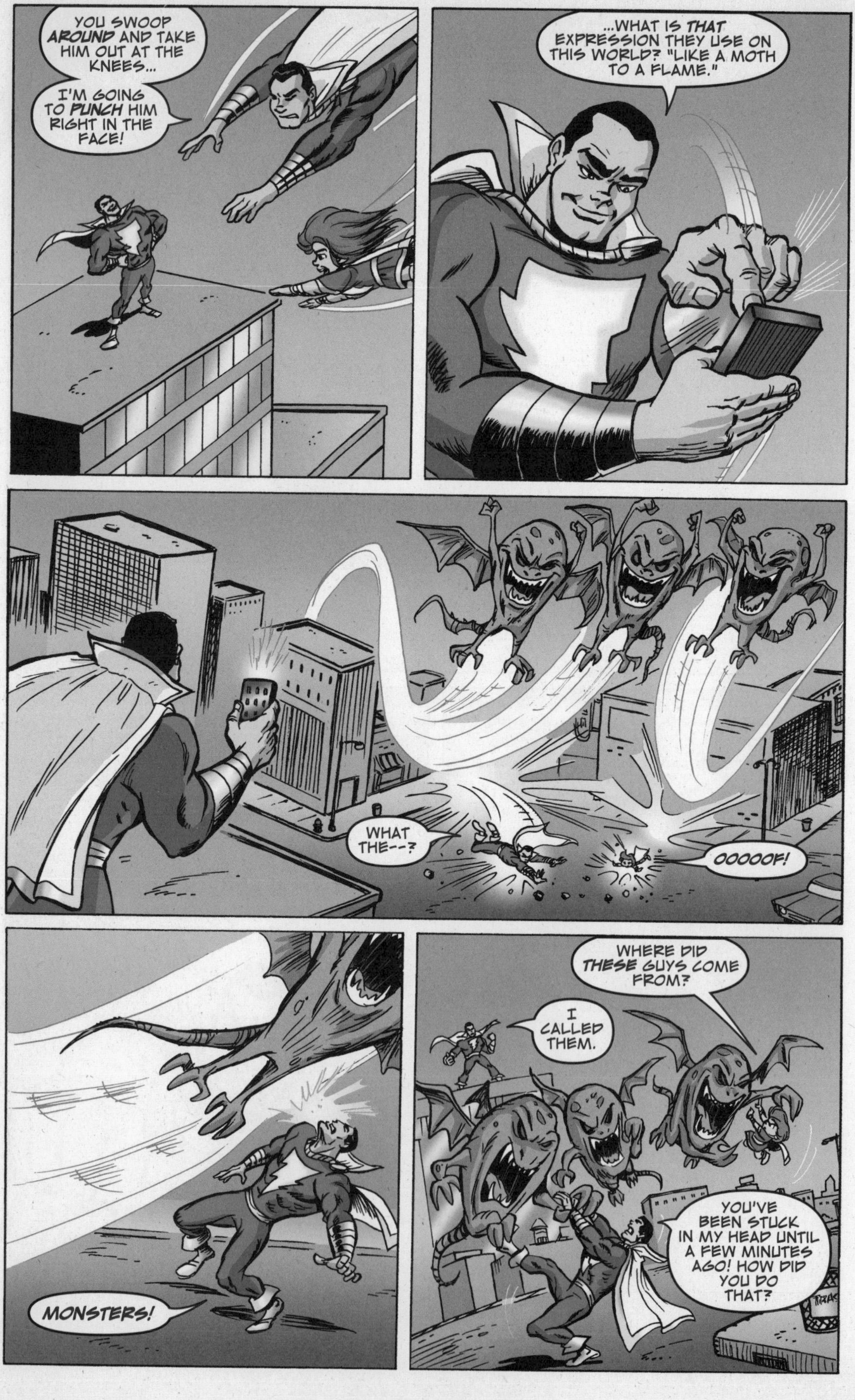
YOU SWOOP AROUND AND TAKE HIM OUT AT THE KNEES...
I'M GOING TO PUNCH HIM RIGHT IN THE FACE!
...WHAT IS THAT EXPRESSION THEY USE ON THIS WORLD? "LIKE A MOTH TO A FLAME."
WHAT THE--?
OOOOOF!
MONSTERS!
WHERE DID THESE GUYS COME FROM?
I CALLED THEM.
YOU'VE BEEN STUCK IN MY HEAD UNTIL A FEW MINUTES AGO! HOW DID YOU DO THAT?

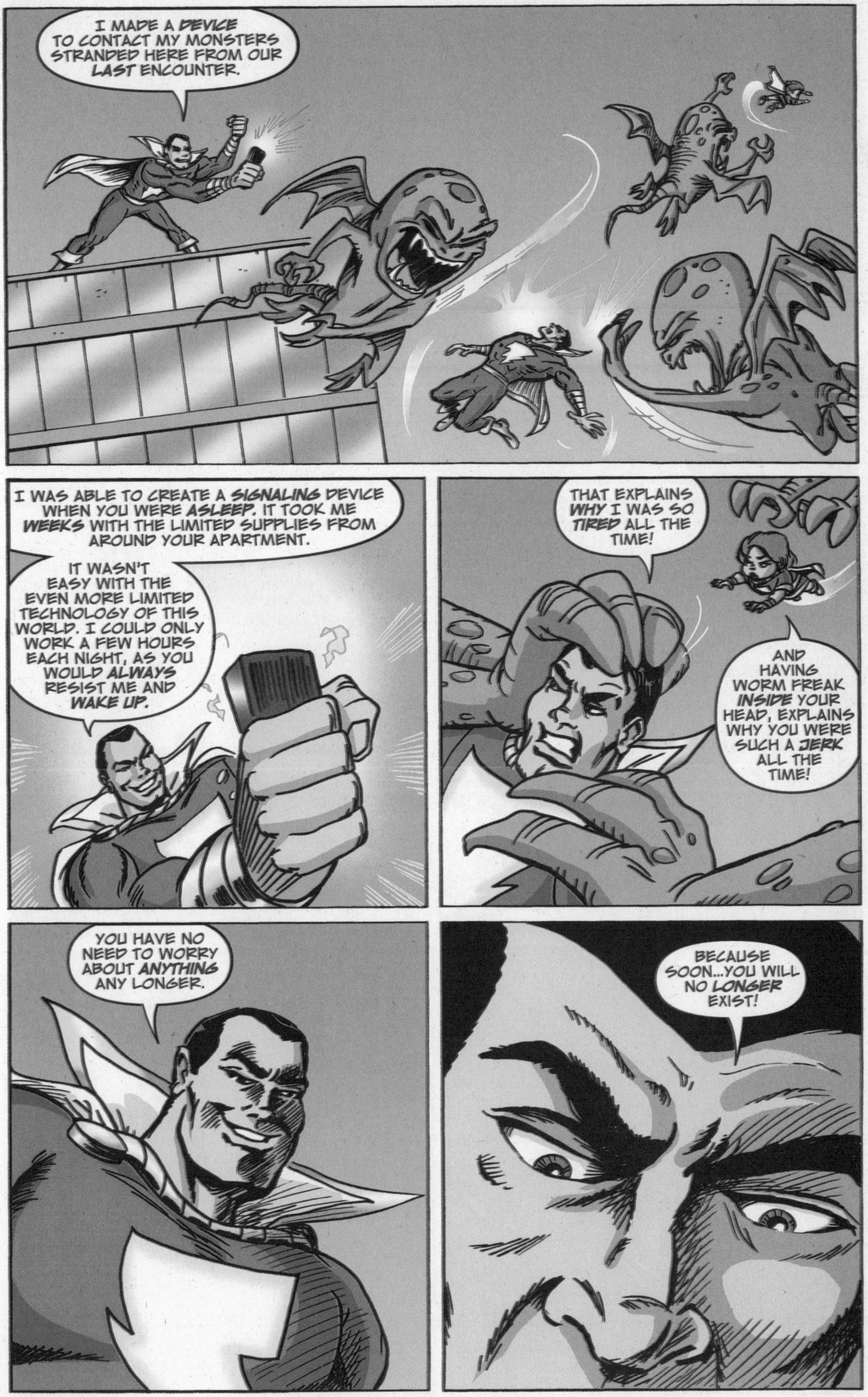
I MADE A DEVICE TO CONTACT MY MONSTERS STRANDED HERE FROM OUR LAST ENCOUNTER.
I WAS ABLE TO CREATE A SIGNALING DEVICE WHEN YOU WERE ASLEEP. IT TOOK ME WEEKS WITH THE LIMITED SUPPLIES FROM AROUND YOUR APARTMENT.
IT WASN'T EASY WITH THE EVEN MORE LIMITED TECHNOLOGY OF THIS WORLD. I COULD ONLY WORK A FEW HOURS EACH NIGHT, AS YOU WOULD ALWAYS RESIST ME AND WAKE UP.
THAT EXPLAINS WHY I WAS SO TIRED ALL THE TIME!
AND HAVING WORM FREAK INSIDE YOUR HEAD, EXPLAINS WHY YOU WERE SUCH A JERK ALL THE TIME!
YOU HAVE NO NEED TO WORRY ABOUT ANYTHING ANY LONGER.
BECAUSE SOON...YOU WILL NO LONGER EXIST!

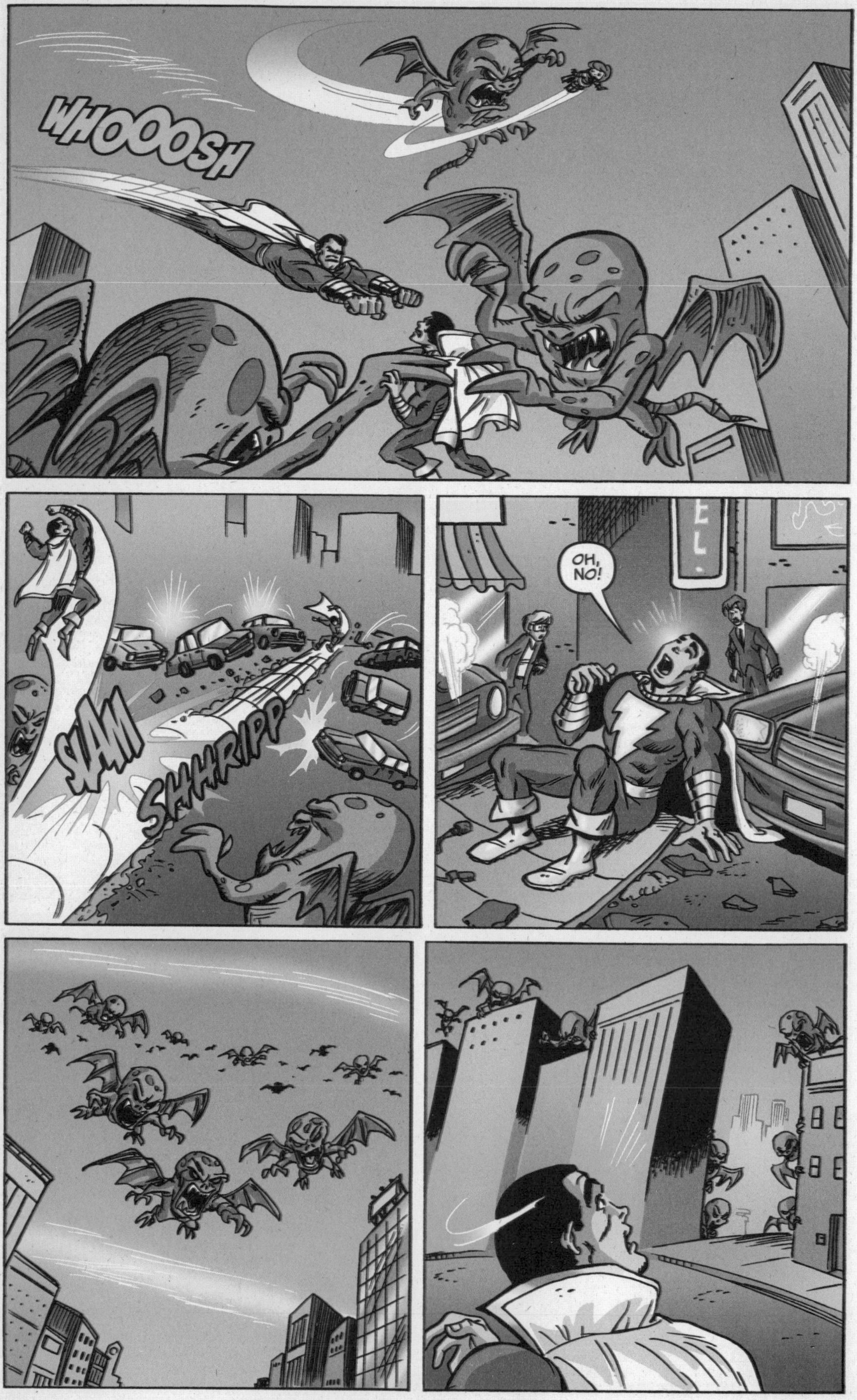
WHOOOSH
SLAM
SHHRIPP
OH, NO!

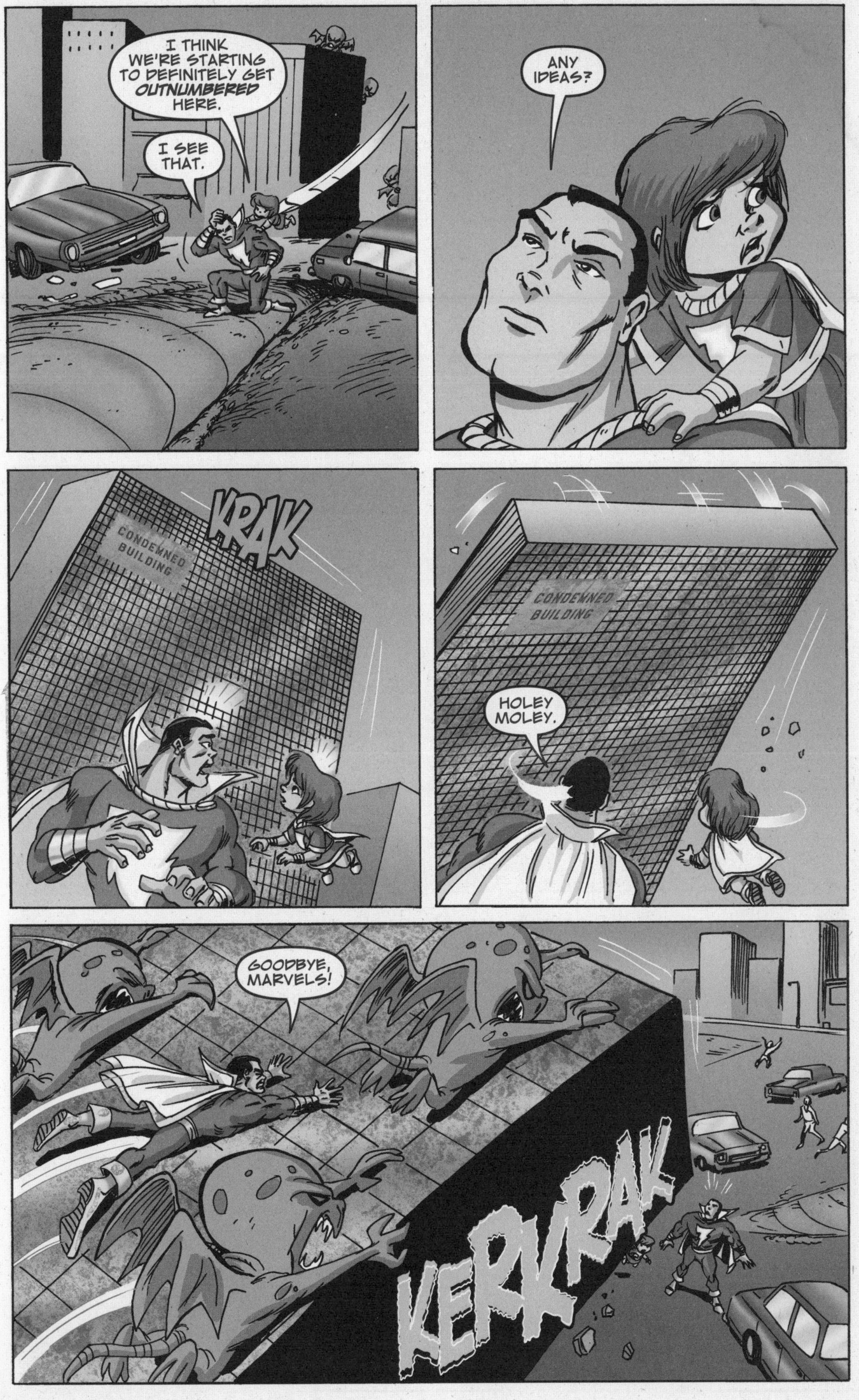
I THINK WE'RE STARTING TO DEFINITELY GET OUTNUMBERED HERE.
I SEE THAT.
ANY IDEAS?
KRAK
CONDEMNED BUILDING
CONDEMNED BUILDING
HOLEY MOLEY.
GOODBYE, MARVELS!
KERKRAK

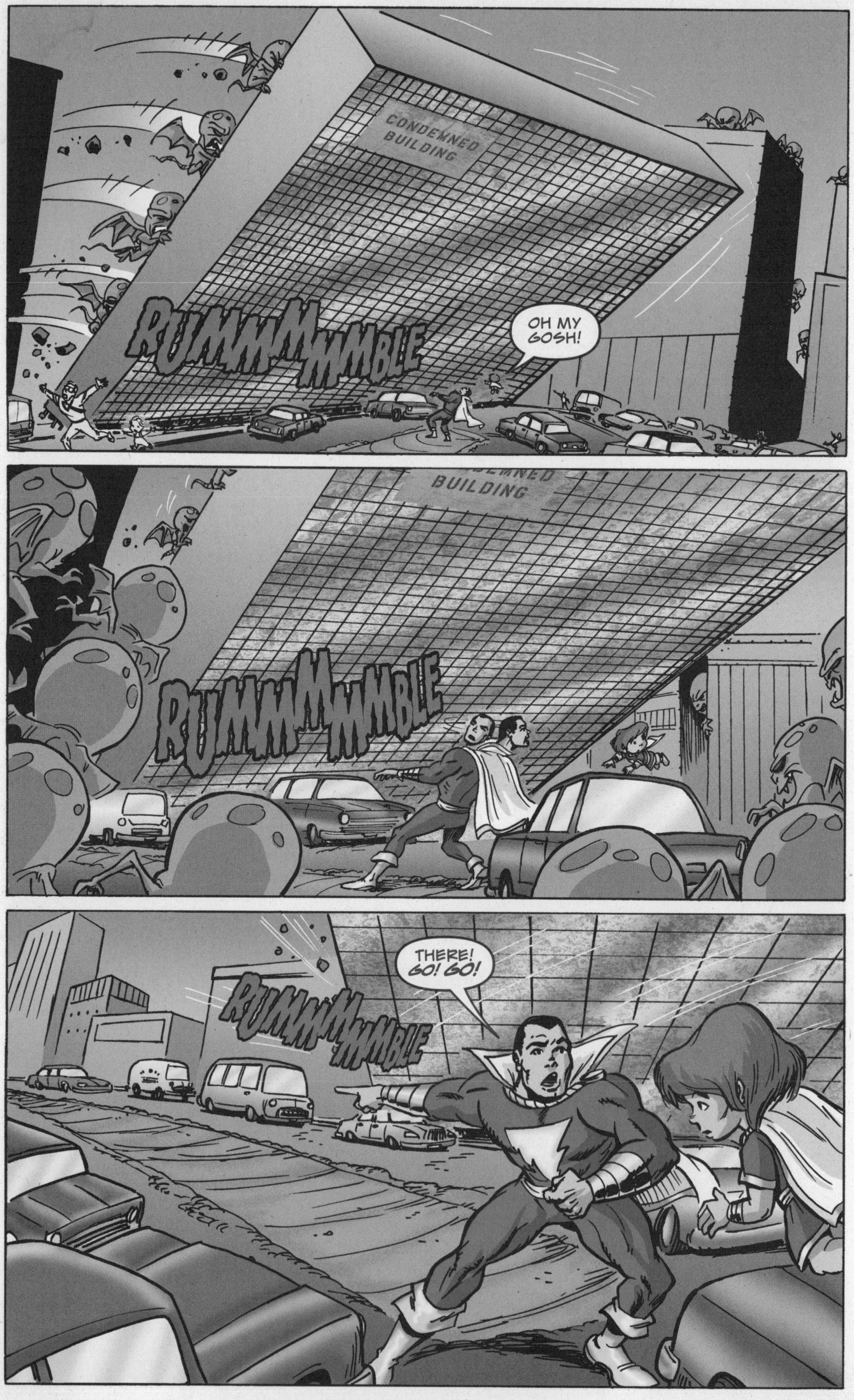
CONDEMNED BUILDING
RUMMMMMMBLE
OH MY GOSH!
BUILDING
RUMMMMMMBLE
RUMMMMMMBLE
THERE! GO! GO!

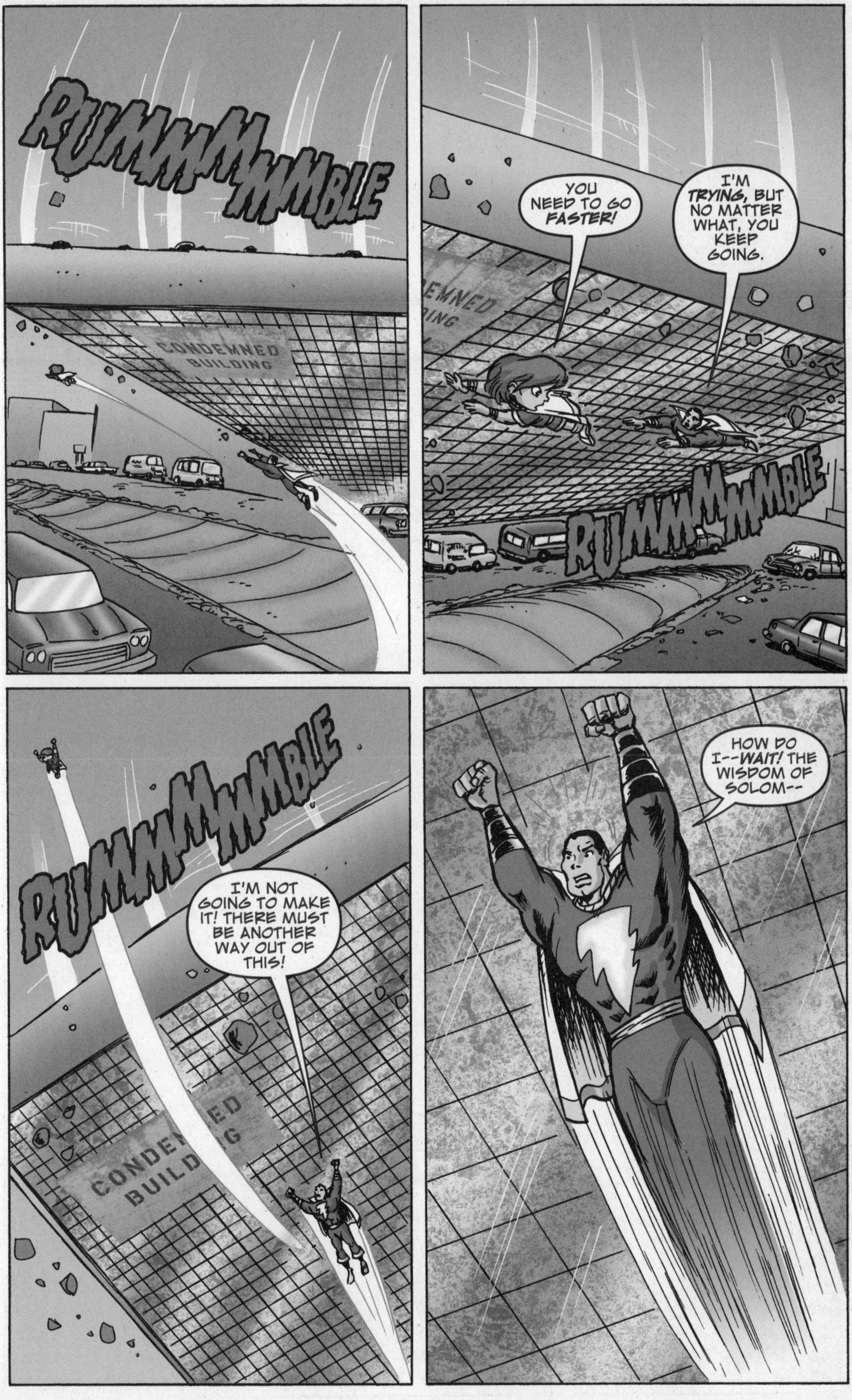
RUMMMMMMBLE
CONDEMNED BUILDING
YOU NEED TO GO FASTER!
I'M TRYING, BUT NO MATTER WHAT, YOU KEEP GOING.
RUMMMMMMBLE
RUMMMMMMBLE
I'M NOT GOING TO MAKE IT! THERE MUST BE ANOTHER WAY OUT OF THIS!
HOW DO I--WAIT! THE WISDOM OF SOLOM--

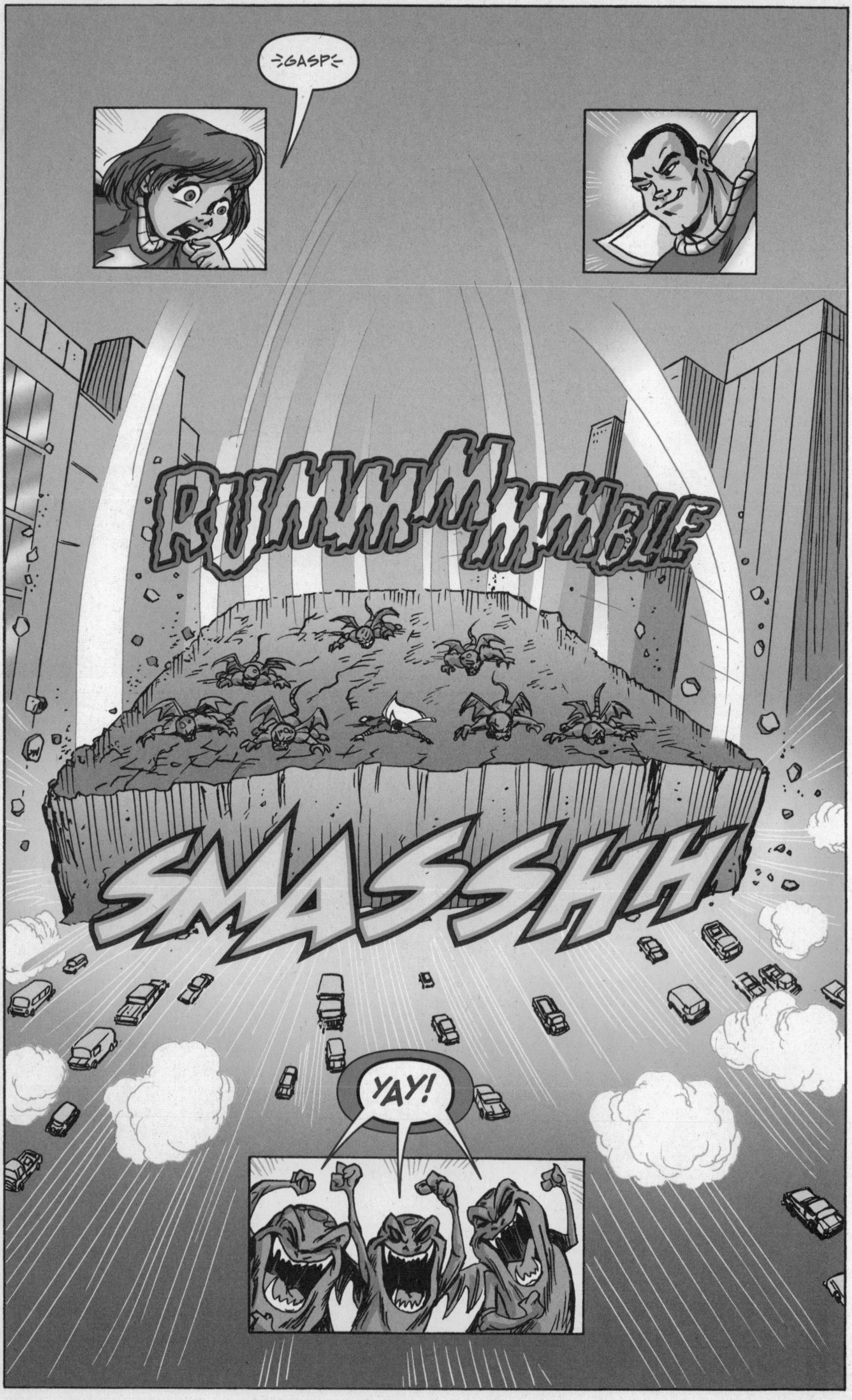
GASP
RUMMMMMMBLE
SMASSHH
YAY!

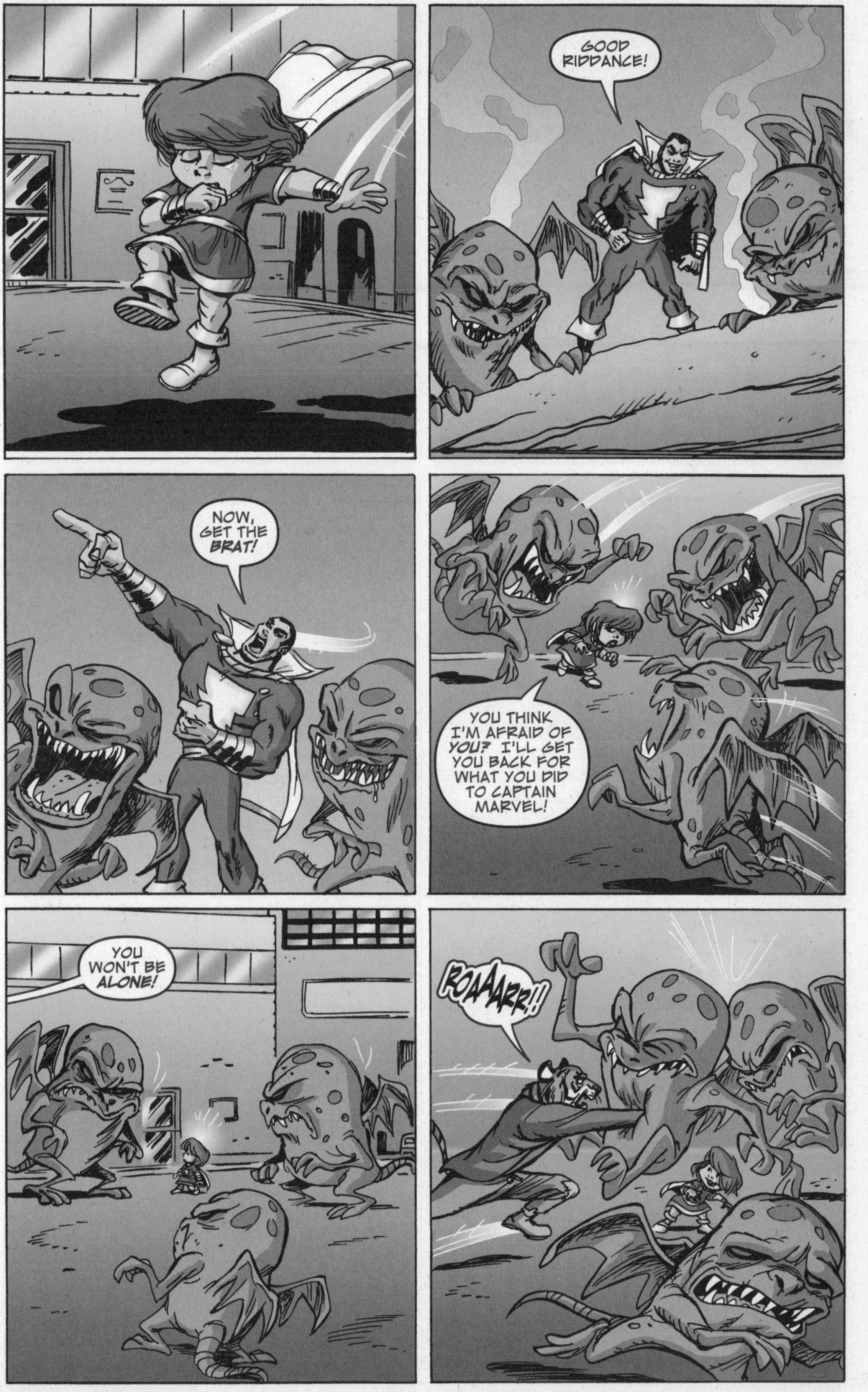
GOOD RIDDANCE!
NOW, GET THE BRAT!
YOU THINK I'M AFRAID OF YOU? I'LL GET YOU BACK FOR WHAT YOU DID TO CAPTAIN MARVEL!
YOU WON'T BE ALONE!
ROAAARR!!

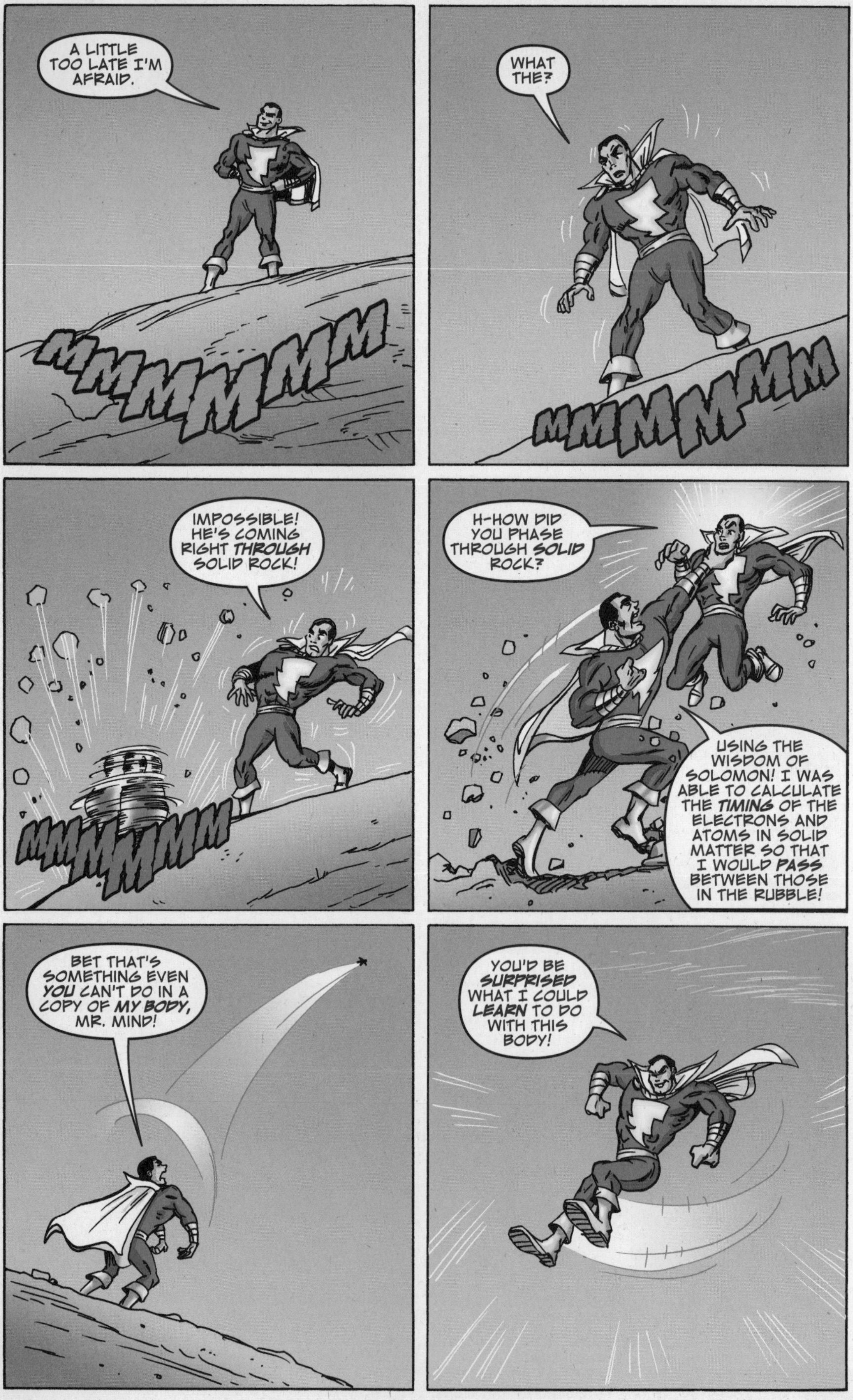
A LITTLE TOO LATE I'M AFRAID.
MMMMMMM
WHAT THE?
MMMMMMM
IMPOSSIBLE! HE'S COMING RIGHT THROUGH SOLID ROCK!
MMMMMMM
H-HOW DID YOU PHASE THROUGH SOLID ROCK?
USING THE WISDOM OF SOLOMON! I WAS ABLE TO CALCULATE THE TIMING OF THE ELECTRONS AND ATOMS IN SOLID MATTER SO THAT I WOULD PASS BETWEEN THOSE IN THE RUBBLE!
BET THAT'S SOMETHING EVEN YOU CAN'T DO IN A COPY OF MY BODY, MR. MIND!
YOU'D BE SURPRISED WHAT I COULD LEARN TO DO WITH THIS BODY!

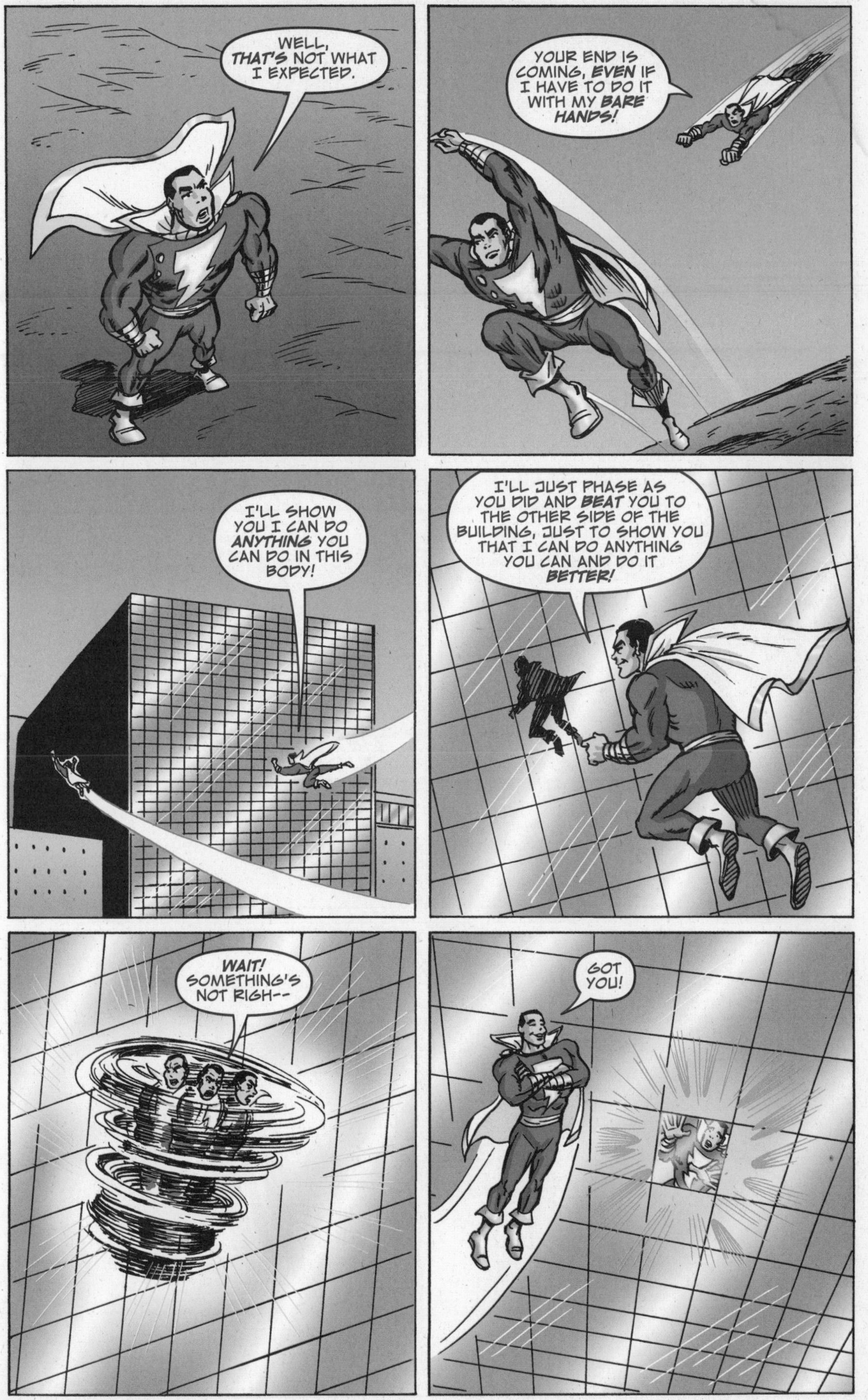
WELL, THAT'S NOT WHAT I EXPECTED.
YOUR END IS COMING, EVEN IF I HAVE TO DO IT WITH MY BARE HANDS!
I'LL SHOW YOU I CAN DO ANYTHING YOU CAN DO IN THIS BODY!
I'LL JUST PHASE AS YOU DID AND BEAT YOU TO THE OTHER SIDE OF THE BUILDING, JUST TO SHOW YOU THAT I CAN DO ANYTHING YOU CAN AND DO IT BETTER!
WAIT! SOMETHING'S NOT RIGH--
GOT YOU!

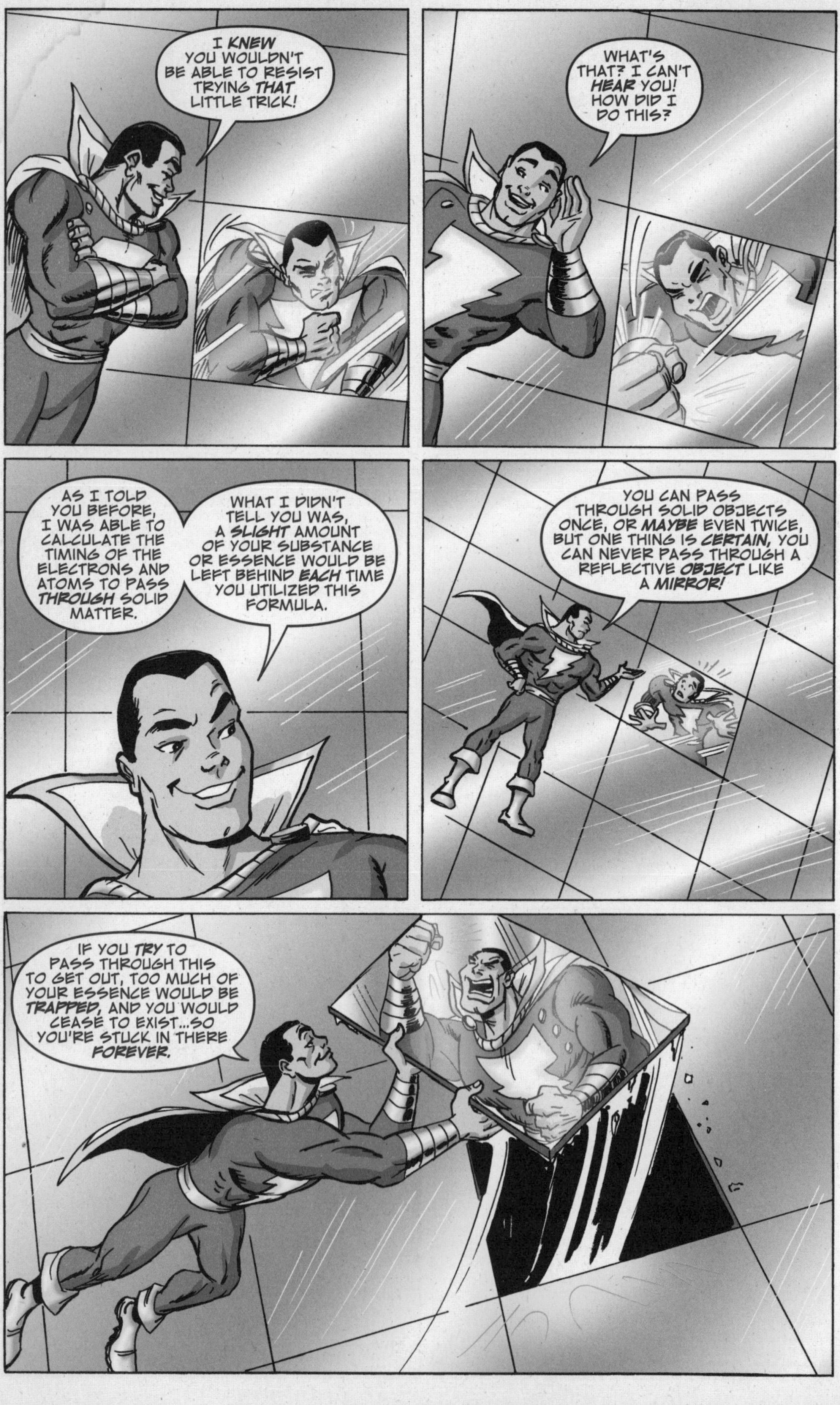
I KNEW YOU WOULDN'T BE ABLE TO RESIST TRYING THAT LITTLE TRICK!
WHAT'S THAT? I CAN'T HEAR YOU! HOW DID I DO THIS?
AS I TOLD YOU BEFORE, I WAS ABLE TO CALCULATE THE TIMING OF THE ELECTRONS AND ATOMS TO PASS THROUGH SOLID MATTER.
WHAT I DIDN'T TELL YOU WAS, A SLIGHT AMOUNT OF YOUR SUBSTANCE OR ESSENCE WOULD BE LEFT BEHIND EACH TIME YOU UTILIZED THIS FORMULA.
YOU CAN PASS THROUGH SOLID OBJECTS ONCE, OR MAYBE EVEN TWICE, BUT ONE THING IS CERTAIN, YOU CAN NEVER PASS THROUGH A REFLECTIVE OBJECT LIKE A MIRROR!
IF YOU TRY TO PASS THROUGH THIS TO GET OUT, TOO MUCH OF YOUR ESSENCE WOULD BE TRAPPED, AND YOU WOULD CEASE TO EXIST...SO YOU'RE STUCK IN THERE FOREVER.

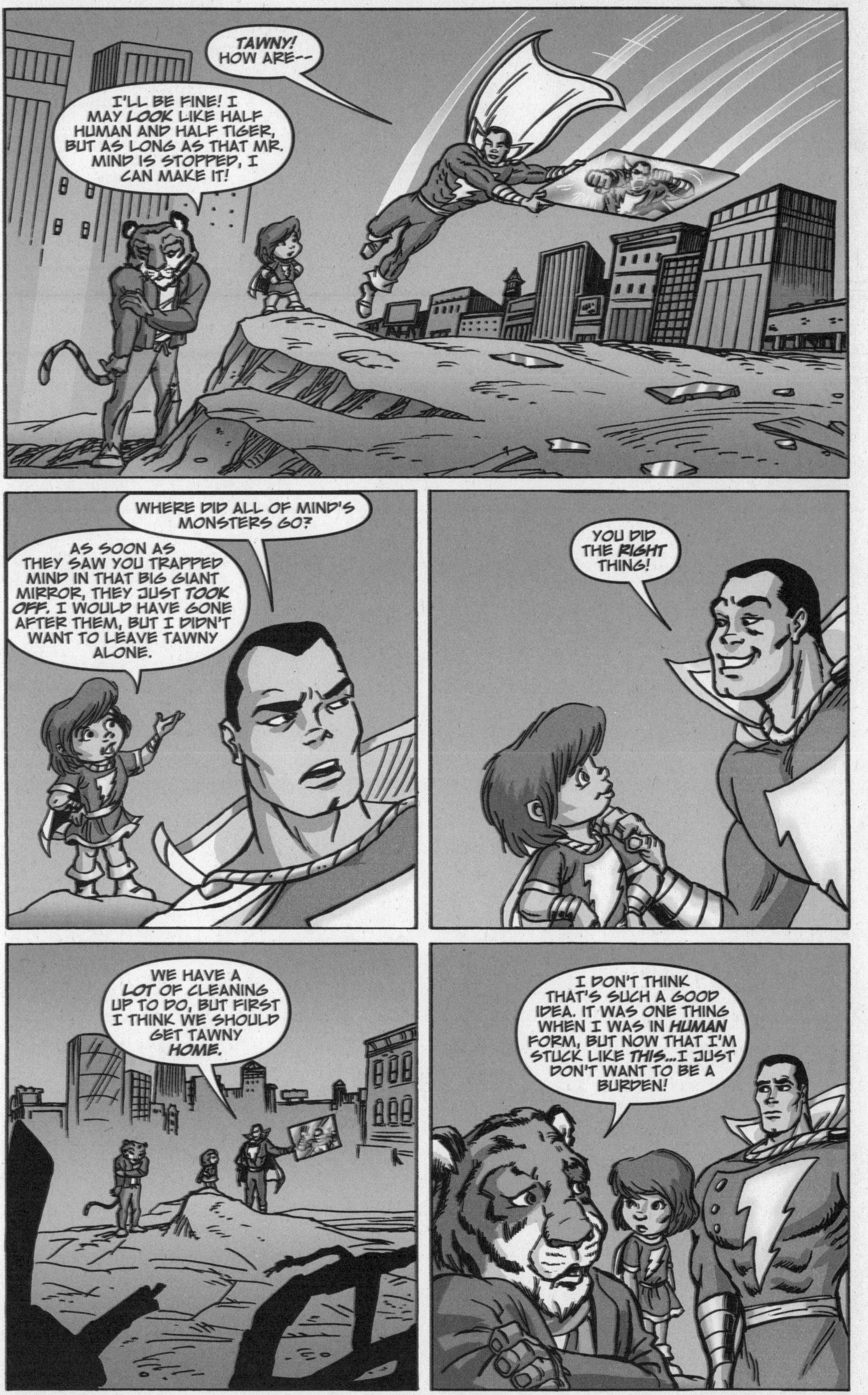
TAWNY! HOW ARE--
I'LL BE FINE! I MAY LOOK LIKE HALF HUMAN AND HALF TIGER, BUT AS LONG AS THAT MR. MIND IS STOPPED, I CAN MAKE IT!
WHERE DID ALL OF MIND'S MONSTERS GO?
AS SOON AS THEY SAW YOU TRAPPED MIND IN THAT BIG GIANT MIRROR, THEY JUST TOOK OFF. I WOULD HAVE GONE AFTER THEM, BUT I DIDN'T WANT TO LEAVE TAWNY ALONE.
YOU DID THE RIGHT THING!
WE HAVE A LOT OF CLEANING UP TO DO, BUT FIRST I THINK WE SHOULD GET TAWNY HOME.
I DON'T THINK THAT'S SUCH A GOOD IDEA. IT WAS ONE THING WHEN I WAS IN HUMAN FORM, BUT NOW THAT I'M STUCK LIKE THIS...I JUST DON'T WANT TO BE A BURDEN!

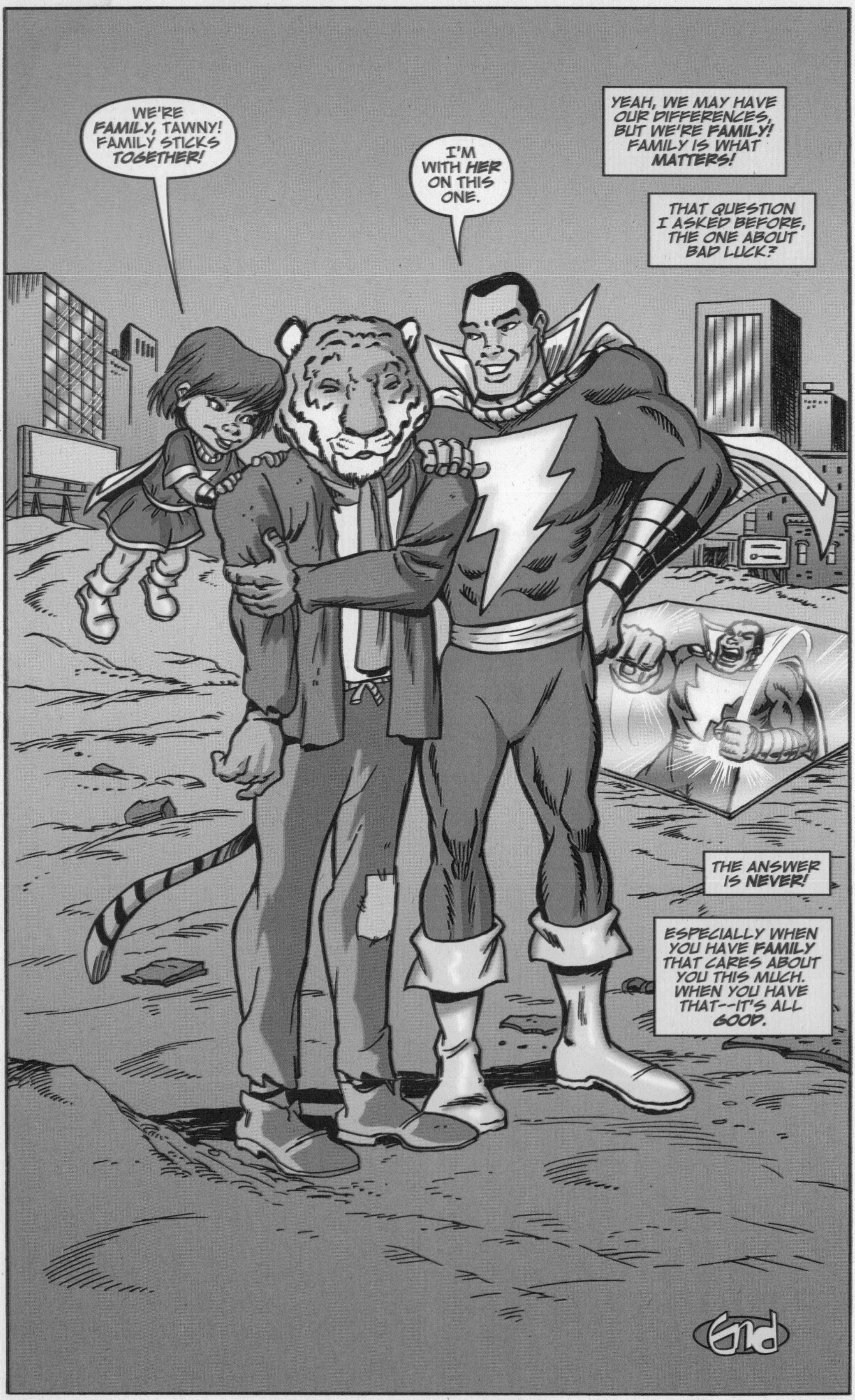
WE'RE FAMILY, TAWNY! FAMILY STICKS TOGETHER!
I'M WITH HER ON THIS ONE.
YEAH, WE MAY HAVE OUR DIFFERENCES, BUT WE'RE FAMILY! FAMILY IS WHAT MATTERS!
THAT QUESTION I ASKED BEFORE, THE ONE ABOUT BAD LUCK?
THE ANSWER IS NEVER!
ESPECIALLY WHEN YOU HAVE FAMILY THAT CARES ABOUT YOU THIS MUCH. WHEN YOU HAVE THAT--IT'S ALL GOOD.
End